THE SELF

DECODED

Get Off Autopilot

Experience True Freedom

Lawrence V. Fernandes

Book Title: The Self Decoded
Author: Lawrence V. Fernandes
Self-published by: Lawrence V. Fernandes
Address: Mapusa, Goa 403 507
Copyrights: ©Reserved with author 2023
Website: www.livingvithfreedom.com
Email: mail@livingvithfreedom.com
ISBN: 978-93-5737-571-9

ACKNOWLEDGMENTS

Everyone and everything is my Guru because it's they who give me an opportunity to learn. My sincere acknowledgment to all people and all events in my life.

This book wouldn't have happened in the absence of my clients. They are the ones who provided me with an opportunity to explore and lift the veil of certain paradoxes. I am grateful to every single client of mine.

Without the creators, a creation cannot exist. My deep gratitude to my mom and dad. It is only these two great souls who could have given birth to me.

My special gratitude goes to aunt Bernardine, late Ermeline, late Uncle Augustine, and late aunt Catharine. They stood by me in my difficult times. Thanks to my brother and sisters for being there as never-ending support. Thanks to all my friends and people around me, known and unknown.

When you know for sure that there is someone who has your back, it does not matter how difficult the situation is. You believe you can move on and face challenges. All these many years, THERESA has been that unconditional support on whom I could firmly lay my trust in completely.

My heartfelt gratitude to the creator for creating me, everybody, and everything that I could experience, directly and indirectly. I also thank the source for providing me with wisdom, insight and understanding into human nature. Without its blessing and providence, writing this book would never have happened.

I sincerely thank all the manuscript readers who took time out of their busy schedules to read the raw manuscript and gave their valuable feedback along with constructive insights

Karan Aswani

Venturing on a journey is one thing, but continuing it with the same passion is challenging. Karan Aswani, a Mumbai-based writer, has been my support from the inception of this journey of creating my books. Similarly, it is quite different having a concept and presenting it uniquely in the form of a book, so that readers who are laypeople may understand it. Making difficult and abstract ideas readable is an art that Karan has displayed well in his writing. Moreover, his passion for the subject matter was evident in our lively discussions and allowed him to express the ideas of the book lucidly and eloquently. I am privileged and grateful to have him as my writer. He can be contacted at - karan.aswani@gmail.com.

CONTENTS

INTRODUCTION

"The False Self must be abandoned before the Real Self can be found."

—Sri Nisargadatta Maharaj

A word of caution: The book reveals your behaviors, conduct and survival patterns of which you are unaware. For some of you, these revelations could be uncomfortable or even painful. I'm not implying that you do what you do consciously or intentionally. All of it is happening unconsciously, beyond your awareness, as a result of your survival mechanism and the Self. Importantly, it's worth bearing in mind that anything you discover about your behaviors from reading this book is a stepping stone to living a life of greater freedom. That's only possible when we unshackle our being from our survival patterns and the dominance of the SELF.

As humans, we are born so that we can live. It would be fair to say that most of us would like to not only live, but live life with ease and freedom. However, the vast majority of people rarely experience this, including those who are well-off or successful.

The reason for this is that our daily lives are driven by our survival mechanism, of which we are unaware. While we may believe we are adults living out of free will, making our own choices, deciding our goals, in reality, that is not true. We are compelled to exist in a certain way for security, acceptance, or approval, no matter who we are. There is an internal system that results in us feeling what we "must do," "have to do," or "should do."

If we are to live life with freedom, we need to first understand our survival mechanisms more deeply and patiently work through our traits with awareness. There are two systems within us that govern our lives, which we need to recognize and deal with. One of them is the Survival Mechanism, described in my previous book, *STOP SURVIVING START LIVING WITH FREEDOM: Understand and decode the inborn operating system that controls you.* Through this book, I will describe the other one, known as the Self.

As readers embark on their journeys of unraveling their survival systems, it would be important for them to remember the purpose underpinning it: to experience genuine freedom and ease in life.

*

This book is, in many respects, a continuation of *Stop Surviving Start Living with Freedom*. Every one of us is our parents' desire, but the chaos experienced by our parents at conception determines our survival mechanism. Our stories begin not at our birth or at conception but even before then. The unique circumstances and factors that led to our parents' union in partnership or marriage, along with their personalities, affect their emotions and decision-making around goals. There is no greater goal they have than to bring a new person into the world.

The couple's relationship dynamic affects the emotional state of the woman when she is pregnant, which communicates a message to her unborn child of him/her being wanted, partly wanted, or unwanted. I go on to explain how we receive an operating system for the body, known as the **Survival Mechanism** when each of us is in our mother's womb. It is responsible for our survival and preservation. This operating system becomes the de facto system of our body, making us adapt to the goal of survival, which overshadows any other goal we choose later in life. By way of making us adapt for survival, it affects and controls our identity, behaviors, communication, thinking process, decision-making, and the nature of our relationships. We operate out of a hypnotic trance due to our Survival Mechanism. The result is that survival becomes our primary goal throughout our lives, and we do not live. It limits us from living freely by compelling us only to survive. We are unaware of it because it was installed before we were born, so we are unconscious of how it governs every aspect of our life. The root emotion that fuels the Survival Mechanism is fear, an undercurrent in our lives.

The Survival Mechanism has three variants, each of which functions towards the same goal of making us survive. They are analogous to the different operating systems of mobile phones — iOS, Android, and Windows OS — each of which controls the functioning of the hardware of a mobile phone. The unborn child, who is wanted by both the parents, picks up the Survival Mechanism of a Wanted Child. The unborn child, who is not welcomed by one of the parents, picks up the Survival Mechanism of a Partly Wanted Child. If the unborn child is unwanted by both parents, especially the mother, but she is compelled to give birth, the child picks up the Survival Mechanism of the Unwanted Child. These three categories are different from one another because of their distinct **survival traits** — the personality traits and behaviors the children develop to survive, which are unique and diverse. The child carries these survival traits into their adult life. So, it is important to note that a Wanted Child is a personality type that one carries from infancy to adulthood, and I am not referring just to a child. The same holds true for a Partly Wanted Child and an Unwanted Child.

A **Wanted Child** is one who is much wanted by both parents, who have a shared goal of bringing a child into their family. The excitement, dreams, aspirations, and wishes of the parents get communicated to the unborn child through the pregnant mother's emotional state. Later, these are communicated to the child after s/he is born. Growing up, such a child understands well that s/he is the object of attention, much loved and cared for by his/her parents. S/he wants to prove worthy of the love and attention s/he receives. The way s/he does that is by fulfilling the expectations of the parents. To prove worthy becomes the overall goal and motivation in life for Wanted Children. Essentially, the child takes on the parents' dreams, wishes, and aspirations as their own goals. Take, for instance, the choice of a particular career or the pursuit of wealth and success. These goals may be explicitly communicated by the parent or done so subtly. Not being able to match up to parents' expectations becomes an unconscious threat to such a person's survival. That's because s/he is worried that will lead to non-acceptance. Think of a young prince or princess, groomed to perfection by the king and queen, petrified of losing their position (and the crown) in a royal family; if what they fear would happen, their survival is in danger. So, s/he develops survival traits that make them remain wanted, a few of which can be highly stifling.

The survival traits of the Wanted Child are living up to parents' expectations, performance orientation, fear of making mistakes, fear of judgment or being looked down on, impeccable integrity and loyalty to one's clan, risk aversion and shyness, and being demanding. An elaborate explanation of their survival traits has been included in *Chapter 17* of *Stop Surviving Start Living with Freedom*. Wanted Children live by constantly fitting into a self-image given to them by their parents. As they can see a self-image that guides them, it makes their visual faculties strong. They work untiringly for the sake of their parents, family members, and others who represent their clan. If they are unable to meet their parents' expectations, they grow frustrated and even depressed, preferring to withdraw from society. All that is described above is an unconscious process and the Wanted Child is not aware of or in control of any of it.

A **Partly Wanted Child** is one who is wanted by one parent but not welcomed by the other parent. It could be because the latter parent has different goals in life and doesn't want to be saddled with a child, or the birth is unplanned for which s/he is not ready. However, reluctantly, s/he goes on to play a supporting role in fulfilling his/her partner's or spouse's wish to have the child. This creates uncertainty or a pattern of doubt in the pregnant mother, which gets communicated to the fetus. The Partly Wanted Child feels rejected by the parent who hasn't welcomed them, so s/he doesn't feel fully accepted. S/he craves complete acceptance. The way s/he goes about getting it is by pleasing the parent who s/he feels has rejected her.

Pleasing others is the hallmark trait of the Partly Wanted Child. Some of the other survival traits are trying to be a "good girl" or "good boy," being highly conforming, non-assertive, being non-confronting and skirting issues, becoming a doormat for others, working hard for others, being a savior, being remarkably tolerant of injustices toward them, and showing excessive sympathy towards others. Their survival traits are explained in detail in *Chapter 18* of *Stop Surviving Start Living with Freedom*. As they have strong kinesthetic faculties, they have a capacity for physical work. They carry the above traits into relationships with all important people in their lives. Over time, they can get exploited and experience great fatigue or burn out, which can make them retaliate against others. However, they cannot stand to lose their tag of being "good boys" and "good girls." So they experience guilt and apologize or beg for forgiveness for their retaliation. Fear makes them stay this way. Their Survival Mechanism compels them to survive in the world by pleasing others.

An **Unwanted Child** is one who has unfortunately been rejected by both parents — especially the mother. This is mainly due to the mother not accepting the father on account of their unhealthy or unharmonious relationship, resulting in her rejecting the child borne through him. She doesn't want his child. Rejection of the father by the mother indirectly leads to the rejection of the child. Think of the unfortunate scenario of a woman being sexually abused. The unborn child is a constant reminder to her of that horrific act. This sends a message to the child of not being wanted. Of course, it does not have to be a scenario of abuse alone that can make a woman reject the man and his progeny. It has to do with the deep emotional state of the pregnant mother. The Unwanted Child who comes into the world experiences feelings of being rejected even before birth. His/her Survival Mechanism makes it appear that there is danger or a threat to their survival in their environment. This is not about actual physical danger that s/he experiences, but how the child perceives the situation. Not knowing who to trust, s/he develops unique survival traits.

Since they have been rejected, Unwanted Children direct most of their energies towards getting acceptance from the world. Some of their traits are avoiding another rejection at all costs, showing a lack of trust, loneliness, seeking sympathy from others, craving attention, having low self-worth, and seeking recognition and the limelight. Besides this, they develop personalities that can be highly manipulative and deceptive while wanting complete control over others in their relationships. Dividing and ruling over people is a skill they possess. Other notable traits include being extremely single-minded in the pursuit of their goals, molding themselves for it, and disregarding the means in favor of their ends. Their auditory faculties are dominant. A detailed explanation of their survival traits has been included in *Chapter 19* of *Stop Surviving Start Living with Freedom.* A number of the traits of Unwanted Children may appear negative. However, they do not do things intentionally but operate without awareness. There is an unconscious survival mechanism making them behave in a particular way.

All three types of personalities have their own Survival Mechanisms that govern their lives. No system is necessarily better than the other because each has its set of drawbacks. Each Survival Mechanism compels a person to behave in a certain way in order to be accepted and survive, making one believe that "that's the way life is." This is paradoxically even true when it appears that one is thriving. A Wanted Child who meets or even exceeds expectations is still only surviving, for s/he is acting out the need for acceptance. Whether one rebels against the pressure exerted by one's survival mechanism or submits to it (fight or flight), one experiences stress and a gamut of negative emotions. A person cannot defeat or control the operating system that is ensuring his/her survival. It's also important to note that one CANNOT opt-out of a Survival Mechanism. Everyone has received it from nature before birth.

*

The focus of this book moves to the topic of "**the Self**," which is another system within us that compels us to survive. As I explain, the Self is our parents and their beliefs, concepts, ideas, and rules of living that we absorb when we are young. As time progresses, there are more people we imbibe into the Self to form an expanded Self. They could be our spouse, boss, authority figures, peers, relatives, and friends. The goal of a person's Self is to protect their body against danger or harm.

A child's Self comes into existence between the age of three and eight. The main intention of every parent is to ensure a child is protected and safeguarded during his/her early growing years. The same positive intent is taken over by the child's Self and continues even when s/he grows up to be an adult. A person's Self performs its functions by repeating rules, beliefs, and ideas to him/her (sometimes through Self-talk) that were taught to him/her by parents when s/he was growing up. In that sense, the Self is always guiding us.

Parents start to place expectations on a child while s/he is growing up, which continues into adulthood. The child, using the survival traits of his/her Survival Mechanism, tries their best to cope with those expectations, which are the goals of the parents. Each of the three types of personalities has a different mechanism operating within them. The Wanted Child chases a Self-image — an image of what the parents would like them to be. S/he is anxiously comparing their own actual performance with the specifications of the Self-image. The underlying thought is, "Am I matching up to how others would like to see me?" The Partly Wanted Child is given no clear Self-image. Hence, s/he relies on direct instructions given by the parent, who is more significant to them, to fulfill the specific goals of that parent. The Unwanted Child is gifted with a unique mechanism, that of a dummy Self, which takes over the child's system whenever s/he faces the threat of rejection. This will be explained in Section III.

A child uses their Survival Mechanism to cope with the pressure exerted by the Self. This friction between two survival systems creates emotions and leads to Self-sabotage, where a person is overwhelmed by their Self.

The examples I use in the book are of people who have come to me for therapy or those who I know well. Their names have been changed to hide their identities.

Section I of the book is about how a child survives in the environment s/he grows up in. While parents may love a child, their own goals, wishes, and dreams for the child become the ones the latter unconsciously strives to achieve. The child does this to feel accepted. This is a natural and inevitable outcome, as the young one is wholly dependent on the parents for survival. Non-acceptance from them in any way equates to an existential threat at such a young age. The Self, which is the internalized parents, then takes over and becomes the internal compass that guides the child.

Section II elaborately covers the topic of the Self. It shows how a child's Self comes into existence. We look at its features and how it's different from the Survival Mechanism, which is the operating system of a person that tries to ensure their survival. Just like parents treat a child as their property, the child's Self does so too, with the core intention of protecting them against danger. You will learn that no matter where you go and how old you are, you carry your parents within you as the Self. It continues to play its role throughout the life of an individual.

In **Section III**, we look at the Self of each type of personality. You will understand how your decision-making and fate are governed by the Self, even though you may be an adult. It is the parents whose goals the child tries to fulfill. The Self of each personality type is different from the other in terms of which parent is given more significance by the child, thereby forming the core of the Self. The Wanted Child, being visual, is guided by a roadmap in the form of a Self-image — an ideal s/he strives to match up to. We will see how the Partly Wanted Child survives, as s/he is not given a clear image (hence no roadmap). The survival mechanism of the Unwanted Child, who is not a dream child of either parent, is peculiar. This category has a uniquely different Self and way of surviving, and we will look at that here. We will briefly touch upon the topic of the ego, which is a popular concept.

Section IV focuses on the solutions for gaining freedom from the Self. With the knowledge of one's Self, a person can redefine one's life and make conscious decisions in the present moment. As the three personalities have different survival traits and different Self, the same recommendations cannot be given to each of them. So, the path to living with freedom is explained individually for the three personality types. Alternative behaviors to one's survival traits are suggested, and a set of techniques are given on how to deal with a person's Survival Mechanism.

You might be unable to resolve certain emotions and patterns that you detect. In those situations, you need to seek the help of a professional to defuse the emotional charge and neutralize the pattern. Any person who is a Neuro-Linguistic Programmer can help you solve those issues. A book can provide information and instructions but cannot be a substitute for therapy. Individual sessions are targeted to a person's specific issues, and many things can get resolved that way.

Most of the time, the conflict is between your Survival Mechanism and your Self (others and their ideas you carry inside you). It feels like you are on one side and the whole world you need to adapt to is on the other. This is shown in the diagram below.

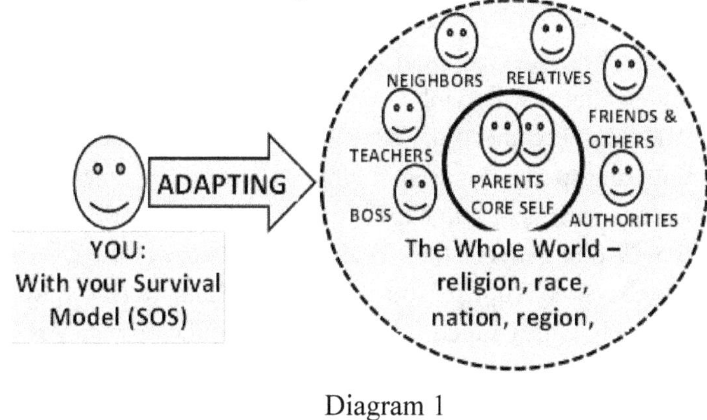

Diagram 1

We end up being sandwiched between our Survival Mechanism and Self. While our survival mechanism serves a useful purpose when one is a child or young adult, it becomes a shackle that prevents us from living freely, even when we become an adult. Over time, it causes us more stress and negative emotions that further affects our ability to experience ease and freedom. The Survival Mechanism needs to be discarded once our period in life for survival has finished — our adolescent or young adult years. We continue to live unconsciously and forget that we are here to live and not just to survive. More importantly, the Survival Mechanism makes us forget our BEING, our TRUE SELF that wants to express, expand, and grow. Through this book, I intend to make readers understand and become aware of their Self and survival mechanisms, the dynamic between the two, and how it constricts their true potential from being realized. This will allow you to exercise your free will in creating a life you consciously choose.

*

In Japan, during the Meiji Era (1869-1912), there lived a Zen master by the name of Nan-in. He was once visited by a university professor who was curious to learn about Zen. Nan-in, being polite, served the professor a cup of tea. As he poured the tea, the professor's cup became full, but Nan-in kept on pouring more. Watching the cup overflow, the professor could no longer stay quiet and said, "It is overfull. No more will go in!"

Nan-in smiled and said, "Like the teacup, you are too full of your opinions and speculations. How can I show you Zen unless you first empty the contents of your cup?" You have read a lot of about the Self, Inner Self, True Self, or Higher Self. As in the story of the Zen master Nan-in above, our cups are also full — full of limitations. Do we even know who has filled our cup and what these limitations are? Are these limitations of our own making?

The contents of the cup are the beliefs and ideas our Self has planted, of which we are unaware. The book is about exploring that Self, its formation, and how we relate to it. By understanding this Self, you will be able to decipher your True Inner Self or maybe explore the Higher Self.

Many spiritual masters and New Age gurus have referred to the Self as our Higher Self, something unique and extraordinary. In that respect, we shall not go into the Higher Self in this book. The Self we will discuss is the one we are familiar with in our everyday lives. It has been protecting and safeguarding your body. Only if your body survives can you thrive. This everyday Self controls your decision-making and also governs your fate. It's time to explore it in some detail. Let's begin!

PROLOGUE

The word "myself" is one I have heard my clients frequently use in sessions when they talk about their problems. It is also casually interchanged with words such as "I" or "me." I wonder if many people have given much thought to this word, or just think it belongs to the realms of philosophy, psychology, or simply to our everyday language. This can make it almost mystical sounding when it should be more easily understood, as it affects us all. However, given that many heavyweight thinkers in the past have been enquiring about the "Self," it is not surprising that common people feel it is an esoteric concept and has stayed away from exploring it.

"Know thyself," the Ancient Greek aphorism, has been attributed to different ancient Greek sages. According to the second-century Greek geographer Pausanias, it was one of the first maxims inscribed in the Temple of Apollo at Delphi, Greece. In ancient India, sages spent much of their lives contemplating the same subject, trying to describe what they discovered. This suggests that the exploration of the "Self" has been going on for millennia. In more recent times, philosophers have tried explaining their understanding of it to us. Since the advent of the nineteenth century, the "Self" has been an important topic of psychology, sociology, and, more recently, neurology. In the modern age, New Age gurus have been singing praises of it.

A whole lot has been written, discussed, and shared about the Self. I won't go into how others have defined or understood but will instead focus on it from the perspective of the therapy work I have done.

The Self That We Know is a Notion — It is Not Real

I've heard my clients say the below statements:

"I hate myself."

"I have no control over myself."

"I don't know what's wrong with myself."

"I don't understand myself."

"I don't trust myself."

Although grammatically correct, in the sense of referring to the same individual, there is something peculiar about the above statements. It almost seems like there are two individuals within the same person. One of them is "I," and the other is "myself." And they appear to be in conflict with each other.

You may also say similar things in everyday speech or hear others say them. If I take one of the above statements, "I hate myself," its subject is "I," and the predicate is "hate myself." It looks like someone who is "I" is hating someone who is "myself." To make this separation more apparent, one could practically express the statement as "Tom hates Tim." The verb "hate" expresses the relationship between the two proper nouns. But what happens when I substitute Tim with Tom in the statement? Then the statement would read as "Tom hates Tom." Let's look at it more closely. Whatever preference we may have, certain possibilities surface:

I am assuming that if someone has to be real, s/he must have a physical body.

1. One of the Toms in the statement "Tom hates Tom" is real and the other is unreal. But which of the two is unreal? The one having a tangible, physical body cannot be negated, so it cannot be unreal. Therefore, Tom with the physical body is real. The other one is unreal.

2. Both are real, which means both Toms have a physical body. Then it means that the body hates the body, which is not what Tom is alluding to above. Tom doesn't hate his body here. In the rarest of cases witnessed, a child has been born with two heads! But in most normal cases, it can be safely assumed that a person can have only one body.

3. Both are unreal. This statement cannot be true. As a person with a physical body is making this statement, s/he exists and cannot be unreal.

Among the three above possibilities, the first one is the most plausible. One Tom is real, and the other unreal. The second possibility is most unusual, where a person has two heads and cannot be considered the norm. The last statement is not possible.

There is only ONE being that is authentic and real between "I" and "myself." At times, I have asked my clients, "Who is this 'myself' that you hate? Which of these two are you, 'I' or 'myself?' Which one is authentic and real? Which one has a physical body?" These questions can make them feel rather perplexed for a while. But after discussion and giving it some thought, they say, "'I' is genuine," or "'I' has a body." Some of them go further by saying there is something imaginary they try to relate to, which they think of as "myself." My immediate question that follows is, "That means you hate something imaginary and unreal or is it the other way around?" This can go on to boggle their minds, putting them in a confused state.

The point to make here is that my clients concur that "I" is real. If that is so, then "myself" is an imagined concept. As it does not have a physical body, it can only exist as a notion or idea in their minds. "I" exists as a physical being, but "myself" is something subjective, based on beliefs, ideas, and concepts borrowed from others. So, now knowing them as different things, let's substitute "I" with Tom and "myself" with Tim.

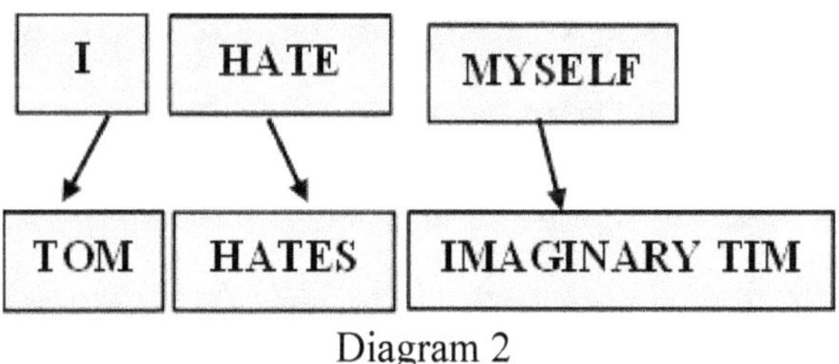

Diagram 2

Let's consider the statement, "I am fighting myself." As we know that "I" is Tom, and "myself" is something subjective, an imaginary Tim; we can say, "Tom is fighting an imaginary Tim." Place a sword in the hands of Tom and make him attack Tim. Let Tom swing and slash away for hours, days, or even longer if he wishes to. Who is going to win this fight? Is there any chance of Tom defeating an imaginary Tim? You can stand in the shoes of Tom, trying to resolve an issue by being in conflict with an imaginary person. Can you fathom how much of your energy and time will go wasted trying to fight with an imaginary self? Moreover, how much stress and negative emotions would this conflict generate in your system until you collapse from exhaustion? This will become clearer in the chapters ahead.

The Self we take to be true and tend to believe in is something imaginary. As we will see, it places expectations on us that we think we must meet. If we don't do that, we experience stress and anxiety, as if our very existence depends on how well we fit into a prescribed mold. An undercurrent of fear stems from our unconscious need to survive, which makes us conform and controls our behaviors. We feel compelled to follow the parameters set by the Self. The irony is that the Self that makes us do this is, in fact, not even real. It is an Illusionary Self with which we have an internal dialogue and fight. We have, all this while, related to it because we want acceptance from others. Through this book, we will see why this happens and how to get a measure of freedom from this way of living. Our Self is not the enemy — it is a system we need to understand and update. The more clearly we understand the Self, the better and more harmonious our life is.

SECTION I

SURVIVAL TRAP - FREEDOM LOST

1

TRYING TO FIT INTO AN IMAGE

Sumit was a young man who had reached a point in his life when he was confused about his career path. He took a year off in his muddled state to think over his choices and finally decided to pursue a master's degree in the USA. It seems that luck did not favor him while he was there. Sumit had developed a back injury earlier that was caused by a slipped disc condition. When the pain became excruciating, he opted to return to India for surgery, which meant he had to leave his courses unfinished. The long recovery period after his surgery made him forgo an entire year of graduate school studies.

Coming under increasing pressure to not lag further behind his peers, Sumit decided to pursue another degree. But the entrance exams for that course were less than a month away and looming large in his mind. The stress overwhelmed him, and he began to experience anxiety. It was in this condition that one day he came to see me for the first time.

"There will be a disappointment," Sumit said as he sagged into the reclining therapy chair. It had been established that his parents, relatives, and girlfriend would feel disappointed in Sumit, who they thought of as a capable individual. On further questioning, he soon changed his statement. "They won't be disappointed or put pressure on me. All this is self-inflicted pressure, I think," he said.

"Aha!" was my response. Sumit's choice of words was intriguing to me. "You have just said 'self-inflicted.' I wonder who this 'SELF' is which is inflicting pressure on you?" Putting it across to Sumit in another way, I asked, "Since you haven't done well this year, who is inflicting pressure on whom?"

"Me inflicting on myself," was his reply.

As I understood, every time Sumit failed and was not up to the mark for his parents, relatives, and girlfriend, he would have to inflict pain on himself. It was as if his right hand was smacking his left one. A pattern like this in Sumit's life would not have started only recently. The pressure he felt had gradually built up over the years, coming to a boiling point only now.

It turns out that while Sumit had taken a break to think over his career choices, he joined a gym to reduce his weight, which was at 116 kilos (256 pounds) at the time. In his quest to knock off his weight, he had lost twelve kilos (twenty-six pounds) in a short period. But he had to pay the price for it. Sumit pushed himself so hard during that time that he developed the slipped disc injury that went on to later afflict him in the USA. It was as if an invisible gun was pointing toward him, forcing him to push himself to a breaking point.

"I am punishing myself," he admitted.

As I showed him, in order to avoid displeasing his parents, relatives, and girlfriend, Sumit would beat himself up or penalize himself. Even though he had chosen to study for a new degree himself, he was pushing himself on in some way. It was as if he was being forced. On the days when his efforts to complete his study goals would fall short, he would feel discomfort. His self-harsh inner dialogue would become louder. Thoughts such as "I have to complete a portion of my assignments, and I have to be ready to take the exam in December" were no different from "I have to lose weight and become slim, come what may." I have to, I have to...

To make it clear to Sumit, I gave him the example of a child who would love to go outside to play, but his mother wants him to finish his schoolwork first. The child somehow drags his feet sullenly to do the schoolwork but finds it difficult to concentrate. Getting into more trouble with his mother, he revolts. But it is futile, for his mother shouts at and disciplines him and eventually, he must give in to her. Deep down, he knows he is dependent on her. He needs her for his survival and so has to listen to her. Buckling down, he forces himself to finish his studies.

Sumit's predicament seemed no different. To avoid displeasing his parents, he had been pushing himself hard. If he could not complete what he had set out to do for the day, psychological discomfort would kick-in, like that experienced by the young boy, making him force himself further. To avoid an unpleasant emotion that arose whenever he displeased his parents, Sumit would choose to push his mind and body. What's more, there was no room for failure in the goals he was pursuing. Even now, he had to push himself so forcefully that there should not remain an inch of uncertainty in the examination outcome.

A part of Sumit wants to take the exam and please his parents. But there is another part that does not support his decision to take the exam and is rebelling. Someone within him was revolting, not cooperating with him 100 percent. This "second part" of Sumit knew that he was doing what he was doing only to please others and not because he wanted to accomplish his goal. It was not supporting him. Sumit was stuck in a catch-twenty-two situation. If he went ahead to give the exam and failed, he would face disappointment. But if he chose not to do it, he would not feel good about himself. To avoid this uneasy feeling, he was pushing himself on. Whichever choice he made, he was experiencing negative feelings. But he needed to go on, for it gave him a sense of reassurance that he was "okay" by the standards of others.

Squeezing into a Hollow Statue

"What can I do? How can I come out of it?" Sumit queried me.

"Again," I asked him, "who is disappointed in whom?"

"I am disappointed in myself."

After a moment's pause, I went on to ask Sumit, "Who is this 'myself'? The 'I' is disappointed with someone having the name 'myself.' Do I understand it correctly?"

"Yes!" came Sumit's agitated reply, and he wanted to know whether he was bi-polar. Assuring him that he was not bi-polar or a split personality, I asked Sumit to close his eyes and imagine he was watching a movie screen. Whatever had been spoken about him, I asked him to see it out there on the screen.

I then went on to ask Sumit, "You notice this person repeatedly saying, 'I am disappointed with myself.' Who is this 'I' and who is 'myself?' Which of these two is real?"

"Both seem real," responded Sumit.

"Which of these two has a physical body? I or myself?" I asked.

"'I' seems to be real and has a physical body," said Sumit.

"What about 'myself'? Is it real and does it have a physical body?"

"It looks real too, but it's not real," came Sumit's reply.

"Then what is it? Does it physically move, communicate, or do other activities?" I asked.

Sumit replied, "It does not move or perform any activities. It looks like a statue or an image."

Sumit's use of the words "statue" and "image" was very apt for what was to follow in the session. He revealed that "myself" was like a statue or image that resembled him. I asked him to imagine some of the times he had performed badly in college or school, which disappointed his parents and others, and to now look at the image. How did he feel? Immediately, Sumit felt uncomfortable, stating, "I don't like this feeling. It makes me uneasy."

Then I told him, "Think of a time you have achieved and performed well. Everyone is proud of you and applauds you. Now, look at the image. How do you feel?" Blushing, Sumit said, "that's comforting."

Next, I wanted Sumit to check how he felt when he imagined being unprepared for his exams and failing them. I asked him to take a look at the image. Sumit felt uneasy once again. The image was no longer shining or sparkling. It seemed like an automatic process was going on inside Sumit beyond his control. The moment he began to think that he would fail and others would be disappointed; he would start to feel uneasy and anxious. What's more, the image also changed.

When asked to look back and reflect on his life, Sumit shared that the image went through modifications over a five-to-ten-year period, to his knowledge, but he wasn't the one changing it. So then, who was? How did the image know that it had to change as Sumit grew older?

One aspect came out very clearly for Sumit during the session: he had been pleasing his parents for a long time. It was his parents who were modifying the image — what's expected of him — not Sumit. What was even more significant was that it was his parents who created the image in the first place. Sumit, the "physical being" believed he had to try to fit into that hollow image or its physical counterpart, an imaginary statue, to the best of his abilities. As long as he fit into that image or statue, he felt a sense of assurance. He felt safe and secure. Was Sumit really living his life or living it to fit into the perceptions and specifications of his parents? The important people had changed in his life, of course. But what he was doing earlier for his parents, he was now doing for his girlfriend. His parents and girlfriend were essentially driving Sumit's life, and he had never really lived life for himself or his own authentic aspirations.

Is it even possible for someone like Sumit to align himself to the shape of a hollow statue so that he fits into it? As ludicrous as this notion may sound, Sumit was unconsciously driven by his survival mechanism. All his decision-making was being routed through it. He wasn't doing it intentionally; he was not even aware of the unconscious process. Sumit was in his twenties, and he had been stretching himself beyond his limits to please others. Initially, the others were his parents. Now in his twenties, he had swapped the "others" for his girlfriend, but the repeating patterns went on for him.

Sumit had some of the classic traits of a Wanted Child. A Wanted Child's survival traits create a lot of internal pressure in that person to live up to the expectations of his near and dear ones. Their expectations, whether real or imagined by the Wanted Child, become his/her goals. The very thought of not being able to live up to what's being asked of him creates discomfort, stress, or even anxiety. Sumit experienced the same emotions when he wasn't able to prepare for his exams. The prospect of unfulfilled dreams, for the sake of others, was unbearable to him. He was pushing himself on, just as he had done in the past with his weight loss goals, his master's degree, and even as a sportsperson when he was a child. He always wanted to prove himself worthy and capable to his parents.

Wanted Children also tend to be visual. So the idea of an image or statue as something external to be seen could take shape easily in Sumit's mind. It was easier for me to guide him visually. A Partly Wanted Child is kinesthetic and an Unwanted Child is auditory, so they need to be guided differently.

We can see how a self-image, one that has no connection whatsoever with one's physical being, can be the driving force in a person's life. S/he can expend enormous amounts of energy throughout life to accomplish whatever is necessary to fit into an image being given by others. What's even more disconcerting is that this image is a projection by the "Self."

2

LIVING UP TO OTHERS' EXPECTATIONS

Goals are the desires that bring meaning, purpose, and direction to our lives. They are the reason we get out of bed. Some minor goals in our everyday lives revolve around our routines, such as cooking dinner and shopping for groceries. But deep within, we harbor bigger dreams of marrying someone special or of maybe owning a business someday. While many of us have goals and dreams in life, rarely do we, as human beings, see *ourselves* as the goals of others. After all, we were once only a wish or a thought in the minds of our parents.

All Goals Begin in the Mind

At the most basic level, a goal is about fulfilling a desire. If one is thirsty, one may reach out for a glass of water, lemonade, or juice. We cook, pick up a snack, or order takeaway when it comes to satisfying our hunger, as we are unconsciously programmed to eat when hungry. A baby's unconscious program makes it cry, which is his/her way of asking for the mother's milk.

One may even say that all our actions are essentially about fulfilling goals. As adults, from the beginning of our day to the end, our minds are filled with goals that take the form of our daily tasks. We wake up to the sound of our preset alarm clocks, workout or do yoga, and think about what to have for breakfast. If we have children, we get them ready for school, reach work on time, and remember to fill up the gas in our car. A day at work is spent trying to achieve multiple work-related goals. Sometimes even our lunch is a working lunch with a colleague. On our way back home, we pick up groceries. Once home, we cook dinner and help the children with their homework, maybe watch some TV, before finally turning into bed (not before we have set our alarms for the next morning). Even relaxation and sleep have become goals today, aided by wearable devices. Once, they required no effort and not much planning.

Every goal connected to our dreams or aspirations begins first in our minds. When it comes to bigger goals, we imagine buying our dream house, marrying someone special, owning a car we would love to have, becoming wealthy and successful, or traveling to exotic destinations. We plant a few seeds many years in advance, unconsciously, and using a combination of planning and effort, make a number of our dreams grow into reality.

Diagram 3

The Goal of Marriage — a Venture for Procreation

Marriage is perhaps the most cherished goal people have in their lives. However, it sends a signal to one's partner and society that a couple has come together with the intention to procreate. Of course, some who marry do so only for the sake of companionship. Motivations to find a partner have changed over time. But in most cultures, especially those with a family orientation, the primary goal of marriage is to start a family. Couples may remain unmarried and have children outside of wedlock, so I'm also including civil partnerships here.

Each parent's goal for having a child may be different. Often both partners explicitly state their desire for children or a child. But sometimes, the intensity of one person's desire could be much greater or lower than that of his/her spouse. Maybe one of them doesn't want a child or is not ready for one for various emotional, career, or financial reasons. S/he may or may not have clearly expressed this wish. Sex within a marriage is a desire, which makes it a goal too. While sex is a natural activity shared by couples, it is not always consensual and can lead to the birth of a child. Such life events and personal circumstances are no small matter. The different scenarios send a message to an unborn child (the fetus), whether s/he is wanted, partly wanted, or

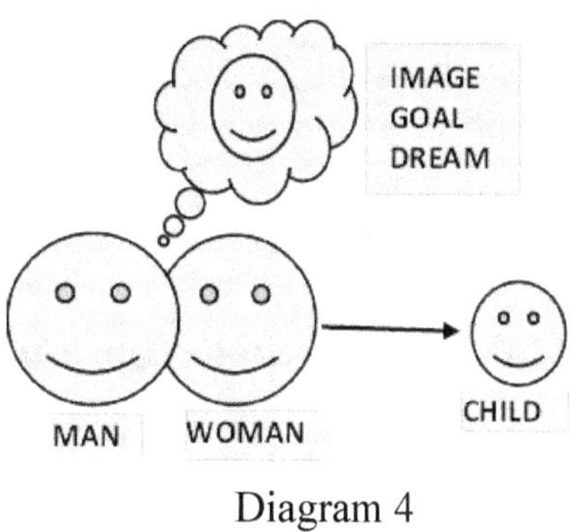

Diagram 4

unwanted by their parents. This is communicated through the predominant emotional state of the pregnant mother. If she feels excitement and anticipation, and her partner shares such emotions, their child is likely to be a Wanted Child. I have explained the different scenarios relating to types of children in Chapters 4 and 5 of my book *Stop Surviving Start Living with Freedom.*

Objects of Desire Need to Meet Expectations

If we drink water, it means we are doing so to satisfy our thirst and to stay hydrated. Water must meet our end of thirst-quenching and hydration; else, we would drink something else. An artist may be looking for a specific kind of ink pen, so that she can create her own unique drawings and paintings. A person who has a passion for photography may invest in a state-of-the-art camera to shoot pictures of a desirable high quality. To beat the sweltering summer heat, someone may choose to install an air-conditioner. Each of these items has to meet the expectations of the person using it.

If the artist above was handed pieces of chalk to sketch or paint, she would reject the ludicrous offer as they wouldn't meet her artistic needs in any way. If you are a regular coffee drinker but can only find tea being served in a cafe because the coffee machine isn't working, you may settle for drinking tea. Unfortunately, tea won't give you the same satisfaction as your preferred cup of coffee. You have made a compromise. So, you feel a measure of internal dissatisfaction, but you *try* to settle down with your disappointment. You could not avoid experiencing a degree of disappointment if the coffee was what you wanted. The level of disappointment varies depending on the intensity of your desire, what's been offered, and its price. If a product does not meet one's expectations, there certainly will be some disappointment.

Children are No Exception to the Rule

Now imagine the same principle being applied to our wish to have children. We don't just want children; we have specific dreams and desires we want to fulfill by having them. A child is a product born out of the parents' sexual activity to fulfill a desire (including children born from surrogacy or through assisted reproduction). It's not unusual to say that parents start having expectations from children even before they are born. "What gender will my child be?" or "I hope s/he is born a healthy baby," could be some of the basic ones. But there can also be tiny visions of what they would want their child to grow up to be, even while the mother is pregnant. A parent may wish to have a child who could grow up to be a good human being or citizen of this planet, well-behaved, educated, secure, and healthy. At times, parents may project their own unfulfilled desires onto their children, such as to become an artist, professional athlete, filmmaker, or someone financially successful. Such thoughts can send ripples of delight through the bodies and minds of expecting parents.

It is important to notice that all the above are the desires of the parents. They are embedded in their minds. Not all of them have clearly taken shape before a child is born. Parents' expectations of their children and the need to see them fulfilled keep evolving in the different stages of a child's life. Multiple expectations keep getting placed on the child. Ones for an infant are different from those for a school-aged child. The expectations for a school-aged child are different from someone who has gone to college or is a young adult. The child keeps conforming to their wishes and thinking. It's because the child's survival mechanism makes him/her adjust and adapt in order to survive. Only if a child conforms to expectations are parents satisfied with their product. Of course, many parents also accept a child's nature or wishes.

They are willing to accommodate the child's behavior and choices as being different from what they would want them to be. But it is not true that even such parents have no expectations from their children. Children unconsciously pick these subtle messages about the expectations of their parents, just like they pick up the beliefs, we will go on to describe. They sense and know when a parent is happy or is disappointed with them.

Just as a product has to prove its usefulness to a person, every child must live up to the expectations of the parents. Sorry to compare a child who is a human being to a product. It will become more apparent to you in the chapters that lie ahead how we operate, function, and perceive our close relatives, making it seem like we treat each other as commodities. The closer a product is to a consumer's satisfaction, the more complete the fulfillment. Such happiness may have a time duration, just like a bottle of water quenches thirst for some time only. Then other desires and expectations may crop up, which a different product could fulfill. But a child alone may have to attain all the different benchmarks set by his/her creators, which can become tiring. The difference between a product we buy and a child we have is that we can return a product or reject it if it fails to meet our expectations, whereas a child is constantly compelled or molded to match our expectations. Parents are not happy to settle for their children's apparent shortcomings.

Expectations are Another's Goals/ Desires/ Dreams

Expectations are somebody else's goals fulfilled by us. Others directly or indirectly demand that we achieve certain targets. Parents want their children to get good grades at school. At the office, the boss demands that you deliver to expectations by a certain deadline. Expectations are most certainly not our own goals, but we fulfill them for our survival.

Many of the desires of parents may appear well-intentioned, and they indeed are. However, the point to note is that those desires or goals come from the parents, so they are their aspirations or wishes. They are not desires or goals that lie in the heart of the child, freely chosen by them.

The subject of how we pick up goals will become clearer. We live on autopilot mode throughout our lives, achieving the goals of others, not understanding the deeper structures that control our beings. This book aims to get you off autopilot mode so that you can become more aware of yourself and take ownership of your behavior and actions.

The Impact of Parents' Desires on a Child

What could be the possible impact of parents' desires and expectations on a child? Let's go back to the previous chapter, where we read about Sumit's dilemma. You will notice that Sumit is a goal-oriented person. Since childhood, he has been fulfilling his goals. He was an accomplished athlete and a good student when he was young. None of these were his own goals, but they emanated from his parents. He took it upon himself to meet those expectations because he unconsciously believed his survival was at stake. By survival here, we are referring to what Sumit was experiencing psychologically, not about any actual physical danger he was facing. It is the pressure exerted on him by his survival mechanism. Sumit, a Wanted Child, needs to prove himself worthy in the eyes of his parents. He does it by meeting expectations, a pattern he has had for a long while.

As the goals he has been fulfilling are not his own, Sumit later becomes unsure about his future path. He decides to take time off to sort out his confusion. In the process, he loses a year and sees his peers move ahead of him academically. Not one who enjoys being left behind, he experiences pressure as well as the guilt of not living up to a standard that has been set for him. Losing weight and losing it quickly is another goal he sets for himself. Eventually, he decided to pursue an MBA degree in the USA. By making himself capable, he wants to prove he is a worthy son to his parents. Even his relatives and girlfriend think he is capable, and he wants to avoid disappointing them. It's necessary to point out that Sumit is not conscious of his behavior or decision-making. With expectations mounting on him to deliver, his system starts collapsing, but he believes his issue is a physical problem of a slipped disc. Despondent, he returns to India for surgery, which means his MBA ambitions remain unfulfilled.

His latest goal is to take an entrance exam to another course to resurrect his professional life, but his system is tense because he is unable to meet his daily study goals. The exam is less than a month away and he wants to crack it. This creates tension and unease in his system, making him restless. Sumit's inability to complete his minor goal — his daily study targets — has raised internal alarm bells. Things are not going the way he planned, and the outcome could be disastrous in his mind. Facing anxiety, he has been referred to me. He wants a therapist to fix his issues, given that his exam is so soon. You can observe how his chaos and pressure have spiraled out of control. They are being pushed from one person to another. His expectations have been transferred to the therapist, who must deliver a favorable result. In fact, he wants to get over his self-sabotage and demands that I perform a miracle through hypnosis. Thereby, he has added a new goal to his list because the goal of doing well in the entrance exam seems to be unattainable by his standards. It has become all too much for him to deal with. Thus, he could be procrastinating, and the issue spirals out of his control.

Sumit isn't even aware that the goals he wants to achieve are not his own but what is expected of him. Throughout his life, he has not experienced what it means to have his own goals but has strived to fulfill the outcomes expected from him by his parents, thinking they were his own goals. There is an unconscious mechanism in Sumit that makes him behave this way. Whether it was about getting high school grades or winning sports medals, they were goals set by others. Therefore, these were not Sumit's own freely chosen outcomes. His survival mechanism was compelling him to attain certain standards.

We may not all feel the same magnitude of emotional pressure as Sumit, but how many of us are truly pursuing our own goals? We may not be behaving exactly as Sumit, but what are the underlying drivers making us pursue goals? As stated earlier, Sumit is a Wanted Child. For Wanted Children to be left behind the pack or to be sidelined is unbearable because it affects their self-image. Their quest is to prove themselves worthy. Partly Wanted Children and Unwanted Children also chase goals, but their deep motivations for doing that are different from those of a Wanted Child. This is discussed in the chapters ahead.

It is not by accident that we accumulate goals that don't belong to us in reality. Goals get picked up along with vast amounts of information that we absorb from our environments after birth as a part of our survival process. Over time it becomes very difficult for us to differentiate between what truly belongs to us and what is gathered from our external environment.

3

NO CHOICE - COMPELLED TO ADAPT

Parents may have fulfilled their dream by giving birth to a child. However, the story of the child's survival has just begun. S/he has to learn to survive in the surroundings into which s/he is born. As a creation of his/her parents, s/he has no say but to adapt to them, the environment, and others around. The child's body has to acclimatize to the natural environment in which s/he is born, whether it is a hot desert, mountainous, icy arctic, or humid tropical climate. This happens right after birth. Equally significant, if not more, is that the child has to adapt to his/her family conditions. This is true regardless of whether the parents are rich or poor, young or old, or have experience in parenting or not. Without choice, a child's system learns to cope with the world they find themself in.

Every child has an internal survival mechanism that absorbs everything s/he is exposed to, quite like a sponge absorbs fluids and dirt. S/he does not differentiate between what is healthy and what is not. Absorption is a way in which a child's survival mechanism makes the child adapt to his/her environment. Let's look at how this happens.

A few years ago, I was doing voluntary service teaching soft skills to Grade Nine students at a school. I posed a question to the class of fifty children, "How many of you know bad words?" A "bad" word was another name for a swear word. There was a hushed silence around the classroom, with students looking at each other. None of them raised their hand. After some persuasion, two boys put up their hands and I asked them to come forward. While I praised them for being brave and honest, I gave them instructions in private to come up with a swear word they knew, along with a gibberish word and a neutral word (such as tomato, tarantula, or superhero). The boys were asked to say each of the three words aloud in front of their classmates. The remaining students in the class were asked to identify the swear words among the pair of three words. Even the most innocent-looking children could easily identify the swear words (those were the days before smartphones became ubiquitous).

All the students had absorbed useless words within their minds. Some may have picked up these swear words from peers, who in turn would have picked them up from parents or elders in their environment. No one had necessarily taught them such language. On asking how they knew them, something was preventing the students from being fully honest with me, which could have been their fears. Because they also knew the words were unacceptable in society or at school.

Children Learn to Adapt and Survive

Every seed planted in the soil must adapt to its environment. The seed has no choice in choosing the environment it wants to grow. It has to make the most of what exists in it in order to survive and grow. We may plant a coconut seed in soil that is suitable for its growth, with enough space to allow it to grow and expand. Sunlight and moisture may also be sufficient. In all cases, it might not be true that these criteria are met. Soil combinations could differ, and water supply or sunlight may be inadequate. But the seed still adapts to whatever it is exposed to, whether supportive, harmful, or neutral, and continues to grow, making the best use of resources and constraints. It does not choose its surroundings but tries to survive within it.

Likewise, children also learn to adapt to the family and the climatic conditions they are born into for the sake of their survival. This is even true for children who are most loved or pampered. Children must conform to the environment they grow up in, as they depend entirely on their parents or elders for survival.

As humans, we can live as long as our bodies are alive. It is the body that has to be protected and kept safe against harm. In the earliest years after birth, that responsibility is in the hands of parents and the guidance the child lives with. In those formative years, we tend to absorb whatever we come across. To do so, nature has equipped us with five senses to gather the information that we will use as we grow older. The five senses act as input modes. We also have output modes in the form of sounds, language, and our bodies. Using words, we communicate our needs and requirements with each other. We perform many functions using our bodies, such as walking, playing, and reading. All modes work in a synchronized way for the overall well-being of a person at any given point. All these tools help us to survive.

Absorbing and Filtering

Young children have not developed conscious thinking or reasoning. So they interpret life by absorbing and filtering information received by the senses. The sources of external stimuli which matter the most to the child are the parents, who depend on those two people for care, protection, and survival. Hence, they pick up not only what their parents say or do, but numerous other aspects from them over time. Their survival mechanism keeps them absorbing, adjusting, and adapting to different aspects of family life. This could be language, thinking, experiences, food choices, ways of dressing, cultural celebrations, routines, and norms of their families. Religion, in many places, decides what we eat, the way we dress, our names, and other rituals. Children's bodies continue to adjust to torrid heat, extreme cold, or muggy climates that they may live in. All the factors, strengths, or limitations of their environment become a part of the systems of children. In addition to parents, children are influenced by other family members, such as siblings, uncles, aunts, and grandparents. These people shape children's overall beliefs and perceptions, which the latter carry with them when they grow up to become adults.

Before information can reach a child's senses, the parents scan some of it. Children's parents are primary filters on what they can do, eat, or watch. Not everything is within the control of parents, however. Everything that children see their parents do or hear from them (very often through eavesdropping) goes on to influence them unconsciously. Children can begin to unconsciously role-model or imitate their fathers or mothers. A child who is eight, nine, or ten may begin to ask questions about things that don't make sense to them, but by then, s/he has already absorbed vast quantities of inputs that shape his/ her beliefs and perceptions about life. In effect, the program about life has already been installed in them. They believe in all that is offered to them — they take it in and think of it as "reality."

GIGO - Garbage In, Garbage Out

A child keeps on accumulating all that s/he is exposed to. S/he cannot distinguish between what is good or bad, healthy or unhealthy, relevant or irrelevant. Thus, over time s/he collects and stores vast quantities of beliefs, ideas, and impressions that eventually become irrelevant to the child's life once s/he grows up or becomes outdated with time. Much of this could be termed as "garbage." They are like the items stored inside a house in its attic or basement, antiquated and unused, but are kept there, often for sentimental value.

Adults carry a great deal of "garbage" from their formative years that has never been looked at or closely evaluated. That's because we internalize many perceptions at such an early age that we may not be aware that we carry them. These could be beliefs about life, achievement, money, relationships, one's culture, and life goals. It could be about what it means to be a man or woman in a certain culture. Many religious and cultural ideas are forced on us when we are children before we can even think about or evaluate them. In India, the concept of caste is introduced to a child. We tend to protect the sanctity of many of our beliefs because they come from our families or culture. As we grow up, we continue using those beliefs or ideas that are no longer relevant to us, serve us, or truly resonate with us.

There is an acronym that suitably describes this phenomenon - GIGO (Garbage In, Garbage Out). Beliefs accumulated from our early life heavily bog us down, preventing us from living a less burdensome, happy life to our full authentic potential. I don't mean to denigrate our parents or cultures. Not everything we have absorbed during our childhood is garbage. There is a lot that is valuable and was well-intentioned at its time. But there is so much that has outlived its usefulness or validity.

The primary objective of any organism is to survive. Only then can it try to thrive and express itself fully. Our survival mechanism is a gift that has been bestowed on us for our survival. But it has already served its purpose, which was to protect us when we were young and dependent. I meet adults in my practice today who are in their forties, fifties, or sixties, behaving no different from children who are trying to survive. A lady in her forties, who is a Wanted Child, was trying to please her in-laws by trying to fit into their perception of what she should be so that she gets acceptance. A man in his seventies, a Partly Wanted Child, had difficulty saying "NO," and kept complying with his wife's demands. A man in his seventies, an Unwanted Child, was still building buffers of financial security when he has enough wealth.

We were compelled to accept certain beliefs and perceptions as children. Unknowingly, we accepted them because we needed to survive. Rather than aiming to dislodge these unwanted beliefs, habits, and thinking when we grow into adults so that we can live our lives freely, we get more entrenched in them. On the other hand, if one possesses awareness, a person can look beyond his/her survival mechanism and live a life of freedom. Before we can do that, it's important to know what else we have picked up from our family environment.

4

OUR IDENTITY IS A CONCOCTION

Everyone would like to think of themselves as individuals with separate identities. However, no human can have an independent identity that is absolutely pure. Instead, one's identity is a concoction of multiple ingredients taken from others.

Through a process of adaptation, a child unconsciously absorbs everything from his/ her environment. S/he doesn't have a choice in what's being offered; s/he absorbs it all. No questions asked. In order to survive, a child picks up an identity too. No child has an identity of his/her own making. Slowly and gradually, one gets created for him/her, or sometimes, it is enforced. Nature gives us a core identity and the rest we acquire from parents and others in our surroundings. Together they compel us as children to fit into the requirements of many predetermined parameters.

Formation of an Identity

The parent who has a child as a goal also has an image of what s/he would want the child to be like. This may take a rough form in the earliest years of the child's life but it keeps evolving and even changing as the child grows up.

A child receives a name and identity from the parents. Some aspects of it can be regarded as permanent and the rest is non-permanent identity, as its subject to change. Our core identity comprises the genetic traits we inherit from our biological parents. One's facial features, gender, height, and skin color remain permanent features of his/her core identity. This is shown in the inner circle in the diagram below. They remain mostly unchanged throughout a person's adult life, some of it only affected by the aging process. There are cases of people changing their genders, but for a majority of people it remains constant throughout life. Initially, a child may not be bothered by these core physical factors until s/he is made aware of them as strengths or shortcomings. In this way, nature, via our parents, plays a primary role in determining our physical identity.

Finally, but not insignificantly, every child also receives a Survival Operating Mechanism (SOM) from his/her parents, which could be that of a Wanted Child, a Partly Wanted Child, or an Unwanted Child. Although our genes do not determine it, our parents greatly influence which one we inherit. Our SOM goes on to shape many of our core personality traits, as I have explained in *Stop Surviving Start Living with Freedom*.

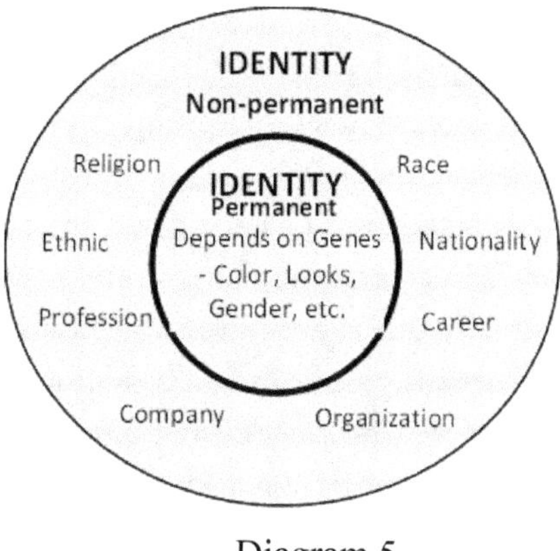

Diagram 5

Environment Molds Who We Are

Other than a core, permanent identity that is inherited at birth, a child doesn't have any other identity. The rest is gathered from the environment s/he lives in. Again, parents play the most important role in shaping a child's identity after birth. New layers are gradually added by relatives, friends, neighbors, teachers, a peer group, and religious leaders, who can play a role in its development. The child's identity keeps changing as s/he grows up to be an adult.

Through a natural process of indoctrination, parents pass on to us ideas of a community, culture, religion, nationality, and family values. Once again, as young children who are dependents, we have no say in this matter. We take on all that comes with our conditioning. Parents themselves have inherited these ideas from their own parents. While they may not pass on all of what they have received to us, often they are unable to do much differently. Customs are passed on from one generation to another, with a few having existed even for centuries, as in the case of the Indian caste system. Some enjoy their caste identity, some dislike it, while others just carry on without choice. The country of our birth and where we grow up also affect who we see ourselves as — British, American, French, or Indian. National identities that may have formed over centuries get dumped on us. We may also get classified in an ethnic group, those that share common traditions, language, ancestry, history, or culture.

As the child grows older, s/he starts to believe that "this is who I am." However, as humans, we are never a pure identity but a concoction of many others around us, including their thinking and experiences. Besides the groups listed above, those who inspire us, our heroes and people we wish to emulate become a part of our personality. At some stage, our professional identity becomes an important aspect of us. Depending on the career we have chosen, we take on identities such as teacher, engineer, soldier, banker, plumber, doctor, or scientist. We exhibit behaviors and thinking that are expected from those professionals.

There will arrive a time when most people will conform to a specific identity that will bring rigidity to their thinking. When anyone unconsciously follows a particular way of thinking, it's like the person is living in a hypnotic trance.

Depending on the individual, the attachment level to any one influencing factor may be greater. Someone may gain more of one's identity from religion, while another from one's profession. Others may identify themselves predominantly by their nationality. Today, it has become popular to define yourself through your profession. But professions are temporary and changeable. They are something one acquires through learning, specialized training, and experience.

In the above diagram, the outer circle consists of different influences, such as family, religion, region, caste, career, profession, organization, nationality, etc. It's important to note that while genetic factors, represented by the inner circle, are mostly permanent, that which is in the outer circle can be changed through choice and conscious effort. Our name and religion may seem an indelible part of who we are, but one has the choice to change them if one wishes during one's life. The same is true for language and nationality, which can be modified or supplemented. As we can change what's in it, the outer ring becomes our non-permanent identity.

A way of looking at our identity is through the analogy of computers. All computers have a manufacturer and come with their initial configuration – a motherboard, processor, graphic card, RAM, monitor, and other input and output modes. In some cases, some apps are pre-installed. Similarly, humans are also born with their permanent inner core, such as facial features, skin color, and gender, that represent their initial configuration. We then install different applications (apps) from the digital ecosystem to our devices that do various functions to serve our needs, such as photo or video editing, playing music, word processing, etc. The apps that get added later are analogous to the ingredients in the outer circle, where parents and others have transferred their identities to a child. In one case, it is done consciously, while in the case of children, it is picked up without choice. Newly installed apps must be compatible with a computer's operating system. We have core genetic features which create a platform for the installation of an operating system for our survival. Gradually new apps such as religion, culture, and language get added to the operating system. However, as these are not part of your core configuration, they can be changed by you. For instance, living in a new country will introduce a new culture to your identity and sometimes a new language too.

The result of all that has been described above is an individual who is an amalgamation of various identities in addition to his/her core identity. An English-speaking American Jewish banker living in London may cross paths with a Portuguese-speaking Brazilian Catholic teacher from São Paulo, each having a very different identity from the other. They may think of themselves as unique and original. But neither of them holds a pure identity that they have chosen freely from birth. While it's almost impossible to change our core identity, what's essential is to accept the gifts given to us and live to the fullest.

5

FREEDOM LOST - YOU ARE A PROPERTY

As fragile little children are totally dependent on their parents during their formative years, they rely on them and their guidance as core protectors. Parents lay down rules for the safety and well-being of the child. Those well-intentioned restrictions and compulsions become internal guidance for protection, which continue to be operative in later years in the form of a Self. Many messages get planted into the child, which becomes the child's core beliefs. On such foundations, other ideas get shaped. One of the fundamental ones is that every child is the property of his/her parents, who exert their ownership rights over the child. Let's explore this core foundation in this chapter.

There is a core assumption planted in us by nature that we are someone else's property and that we belong to someone. From the day we are born, there is a deep unconscious craving in us to belong to someone. Every child wants to belong to his/ her parents. To put it another way, every child from birth wants to feel safe on planet Earth. And this can happen only if the child's parents accept and protect him/her in every possible way until such a time when the child can be on his/her own. The consequence of this is that parents, who are co-creators, executing the responsibility of protecting and raising a child, end up having ownership rights over their children.

Feeling accepted and safe are the intrinsic needs of every child. S/he can only feel assured through the parents' behaviors and actions that show s/he is accepted. There is a deeper understanding within the child: "You are my creator, protector, and provider. I depend on you fully. Thus, I belong to you, and you have every right over me. I will oblige you with my compliance." There is a subtle exchange taking place in this manner.

The Prince - Fighting Whose War?

In the mythical kingdom of Surviva, there lived a king and queen in the olden days. The king faced a border dispute with the ruler of the neighboring kingdom, which the two couldn't solve through peaceful negotiations. Instead of coming to a consensual understanding, the neighboring king declared war on the kingdom of Surviva. The bordering king and queen were well prepared for the battle; much to their elation, their army won the war. As compensation, they ransacked the property and treasury of the kingdom of Surviva. The losing king had to part with his precious stones and metals but could save the lives of his kinsmen and retain most of his kingdom. He felt disappointed and helpless, while the victorious king's ego swelled with pride.

However, the fortunes of the king who had lost the war were to change. His wife, the queen, had given birth to a son who would be the heir to their throne. The king and queen named him Wan. While he was still only a boy, Wan was told the story of his family's defeat at the hands of the vainglorious neighboring king. The young boy became totally immersed in his family's history and wholeheartedly believed in the story told to him by his parents. Indirectly and without conscious awareness, they planted a message in him that, when he grows up, he would need to avenge their losses and regain their plundered wealth. As prince and future king, he saw this as his duty. When he reached his twenties, having mastered the art of war and the use of weaponry, the prince announced war on the neighboring king. The young man wanted to prove that he was a worthy heir — a direct result of his survival mechanism.

Before we proceed further, let us pause to ask a few questions. In the story you have read above, what would happen if the young prince wins the war? What happens if the young prince loses the war? And what would happen if the young prince dies in the war?

If the young prince, Wan, wins the war, there will be a joyous celebration in the kingdom. He has proven his worth as a prince and as the future ruler of Surviva. As a result, he feels proud and his self-esteem gets a huge boost in the eyes of his parents. Winning the war also makes his kingdom's people feel proud of him and themselves. The king, courtiers, other dignitaries, and people of Surviva start to perceive him with respect, honor him, and believe in him.

But what happens if Prince Wan loses the war? Just the opposite of what's described above. The defeat would inflict a crushing blow on his self-esteem. He would feel embarrassed and lose face in the eyes of his people. The soldiers on the other side may even imprison Prince Wan. His parents, the king, the queen, and the kingdom's people may feel worried about his safe return. But they would also look down on him contemptuously for the humiliating defeat. Faith in their future king would be lost, as he was not competent in the art of war.

Now, the next one is critical. What if the prince dies on the battlefield? If Wan dies while his army has won the battle, then unquestionably, he will be honored by his people. The dead prince will be martyred. If he loses the battle and dies, then there will be remorse and disappointment for the king, queen, and their people, who would have lost a son and future king. They will have to, once again, compensate the neighboring king. But, with time, the dead prince may not be remembered fondly for his exploits in death and maybe, he would be forgotten someday.

On reflection, here are some crucial questions we could ask. *Whose war was it? Whose war was the prince indeed fighting? Was it his or someone else's?*

The king and the queen had presented a script to Prince Wan when he was a child. His survival mechanism simply absorbed it. That's how they influenced him as a young boy, and it became his overwhelming life goal to avenge his kingdom's loss and restore its former glory for the sake of his parents. It's obvious to anyone that the war he grows up to fight is that of his father and mother. It wasn't his war. He did not truly have any enmity with the neighboring king. Secondly, he may not have even been born.

Since his childhood, has Prince Wan really lived his life? Indeed, he had been preparing for the war ever since he was a young boy and was ready to sacrifice his life for a great cause. *But who is Prince Wan living his life for?* Has he lived his life, or has he only sacrificed it for the king, queen, and his kingdom? It seems like he was an asset of the king and the queen to be deployed at the opportune time. To be milked, like an investment. The prince behaved as if he was owned by them and had to prove to them and the kingdom that he was worthy enough to fulfill their expectations. If he died, did he sacrifice himself for a noble cause, one that was his? Was he conscious of what he was doing when he declared war against the neighboring king? In other words, did he act out of true awareness?

If the prince is a Wanted Child, he is a slave to the monarchy system. As he gains his status and position from the king, queen, and kingdom, he is their property while he remains a prince. He has no choice but to adhere to their set of behaviors, performance, and etiquette, which befits his position as heir to the throne.

The son goes to war — his parents' war — thinking it's his responsibility as the crown prince. He feels obligated to his parents and acts for the sake of his family's pride, settling old scores. The king and queen unconsciously assume that their son is their property. While the young prince validates this belief through his actions, he hasn't realized it's his Survival Mechanism that has trapped him, making him sacrifice his life for a cause that was not really his, to begin with.

The Deeper the Belonging, the Stronger the Ownership

The tale of the young prince may sound outlandish to us, but it isn't so when we reflect deeper on how we develop notions of belonging to others and of owning them. Let's explore this further here.

Ownership is established when someone has property rights over something such as real estate, a business, or even over items as simple as a pen or watch. Generally, it is understood to arise when someone has created something (gaining intellectual property), purchased something, or inherited something (like wealth from parents).

"This is my laptop" is a statement that implies ownership. A more emphatic way of putting it across is, "This laptop belongs to me." On the one hand, it states that "I own the item," and so it belongs to me. But, from the perspective of the laptop (if it could have one), it just belongs to you. If it could speak, it may say, "I belong to him/ her. This is my owner." From one direction, it is about belonging to someone, while from the other, what it really means is there exists a claim of ownership. We also use the word "my" every day, either to lay a claim of ownership over our possessions (my iPhone, my car, my apartment, my book collection, and my wine cellar) or to signify belonging (my college, my bank, my employer, or my religion).

What's significant to notice here is that someone may own an item, but the item cannot own its owner. Even if smartphones today have come to own the attention of their owners, they can be switched off or traded for a new one. There can be no claims of ownership from something that belongs to someone.

Degrees of ownership and belonging vary. Usually, the stronger the sense of belonging one feels for something or someone, the stronger will be the sense of ownership. A doctor who is conscientious about the Hippocratic oath he has taken will take ownership of his patients and their health. Similarly, a teacher may take ownership of her students and of their learning. One may take great care to preserve the possessions one has accumulated that are a true reflection of one's personality, such as a book collection. An artist who has poured her soul into creating a painting feels it's a unique expression of her art. The feeling that the painting has literally been born out of her imagination and talents makes her feel she completely owns it. This feeling may persist even if the actual owner has changed when she has sold "her baby" to a buyer who now owns the painting. She will continue to refer to the painting as "mine."

What appears to be true from the above is that we feel the strongest feelings of ownership towards something we have created and worked hard for.

Every Child is the Property of a Family System

Parents who have brought a child into this world have painstakingly nurtured the child and made multiple sacrifices. The mother has carried the child inside her womb for nine months. It is inevitable that parents will start to think of themselves as owners of the child. Moreover, the child's survival needs make it dependent on and hence belong completely to the parents, reinforcing this sense of ownership.

We have become the property of others at birth, whether we are aware of it or not. This is an unconscious belief that has been transferred to us by nature. A subtle message has been communicated to us that if we wish to survive, we must comply and obey the wishes of our parents. We do not have a choice in this regard when it comes to our earliest years. We have to surrender to figures of authority who care for us, but also think of us as our owners. Our survival mechanism compels us to accept this.

"My teenage son loves to cycle."
"My mom will pick me up from school."
"My eight-year-old has started to learn tennis."
"Yes, that's my sister."
"This is my dog, Buster."

Statements such as those above reveal something about the nature of relationships in a family. While all of them broadcast who belongs to whom, a mother referring to her son as "my teenage son" and her daughter as her "eight-year-old," carries a sense of possession that only comes from ownership. When her son knows his mother will pick him up from school, he knows he can always depend on her. That means there is acceptance from his mother based on a dependable relationship. It also implies he belongs to a specific woman only.

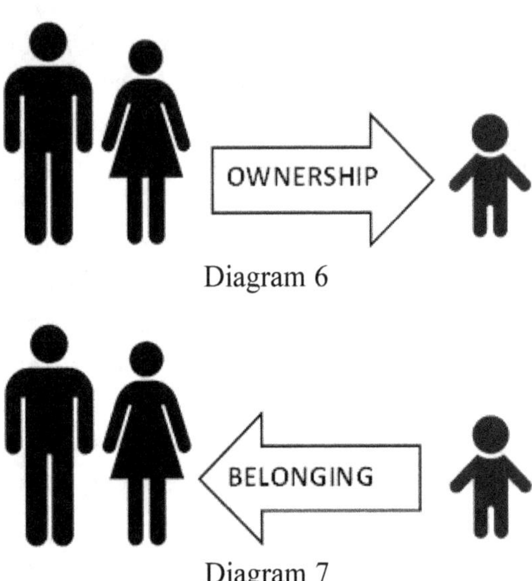

Diagram 6

Diagram 7

Parents have ownership rights over their children, but the reverse is just not possible. For it is only creators that can own their creations, not the other way around.

Ownership rights convey authority over a thing or person. It also says something belongs to the creator or buyer, and the owner has full rights over the child (in this instance) or the thing. For belongingness to exist, the owner has to accept that the item or child belongs to him/her. It implies the person could reject and therefore forfeit his/her ownership right. Acceptance and rejection play a major role in the child's life. And so, feeling a sense of belongingness is one of the primary intents of the child, especially when infantile or very young.

Parents are a form of a system — the family system — that creates the child. A child cannot have dominance or control over a system, something it depends on for survival. If it appears that some children can get anything they want if they throw a tantrum, the family system has allowed them to be this way through pampering. Eventually, the expanded system (teachers, relatives, or a boss) will clamp down on the child's absolute freedoms. Therefore, the child always feels vulnerable to the power of authority figures in the system because s/he unconsciously knows s/he is weaker and depends on them. In fact, parents have an overwhelming say in whether the child is born in the first place. A child understands and knows this truth unconsciously.

In the story of Prince Wan above, the prince is treated like the property of the king and the queen. There exists in him an unconscious dependency on them for his survival ever since he was a little boy. *The belongingness is an undercurrent that compels the prince to oblige his parents*, the king and the queen, eventually by going to war for their sake when he grows into an adult. He tries hard to prove he is worthy in their eyes by fulfilling a destiny they have charted for him. How many of us have unconsciously chosen our life goals in this way? You can peep into your own life and see whether you have been living your life or have been unconsciously living in a way defined by others, whoever they may be.

Every child who is born also feels indebted to his/her parents. This is especially true for the mother, who has brought the child into the world and lovingly raised him/her. The same sense of indebtedness continues even when a child becomes an adult. Either this is a well-understood emotion in the adult or a subtle undercurrent. Unconsciously, a person knows that someone has created him/her. Even a child who has been neglected and possibly hates his/her parents does not deny this truth. A child's sense of belonging doesn't change if s/he hasn't been treated well. Maybe such children don't like their parent or parents, but they can't escape the fact that they owe their existence to them.

It has been embedded in our systems that we belong to someone from birth. As we grow into teenagers and then young adults, we continue to want to belong to someone else who is special. Our unconscious search for someone who will accept us has already been established in us as a pattern. Until such time, we feel incomplete; only a specific person can make us feel whole. Even people who choose to be solitary are seeking completion in some other way, to fill up their emptiness.

Levels of ownership vary depending on the relationship. The ownership between parent and child will be stronger than, say between a grandparent and a grandchild or between an aunt and a nephew.

Likewise, the degree of belongingness will also be different. A person may have a deep connection with another person or animal. It depends on the length of the relationship, the quality of intimacy, or the emotional connection the two share, which leads to a strong bond.

Husband or Wife - You are a Property

Property rights are, of course, not restricted just to our parents or blood relatives. The statements below strongly express feelings of possessiveness, belonging, and even ownership.

"That is my wife!"
"My husband is a vice president at an investment bank."

Two individuals who are different in their upbringing and thinking come together to create a new system known as "a family." But what's peculiar is that both parents have their different Survival Operating Mechanism, which they operate from — that of a Wanted Child, Partly Wanted Child, or an Unwanted Child. Since all three categories have a different styles of operating and surviving, their core beliefs, thinking, and behaviors are different from each other. This makes the functioning, needs, and decision-making of parents very different. Things can get complicated when one wants to enforce ownership rights over the other. The resulting dynamics are like two different governance systems coming together — one could have the values of a monarchy and the other of democracy — to start a family. Usually, one of the two can be the more dominant one. If there is consensual leadership, the family can survive for a prolonged period, as the two enjoy a mutual understanding.

In a union such as marriage, the understanding is very different from that of a child born to a mother and father. In parenthood, the mother and father exert ownership rights towards the child, whereas the reverse isn't possible. In marriage, both people seek to fulfill their inborn inadequacies. They come together to form a new system, the family, but they begin to have an ownership right over each other. For both people in a marriage, the same deep undercurrent of wanting to belong to someone from childhood plays out. There is a vacuum that only the other person can fill. Without belongingness, one experiences a sense of emptiness or incompletion in life. So, when one eventually gets it by being with someone, one demands a pact of security that has a sense of permanence to it. The need for belonging is sanctified through a religious marriage ceremony, leading to a legal agreement. This creates new property rights. The culture and system prevailing in their country bind them together as if they belong to each other as permanent properties.

An example of a property right from marriage could be that a person will now share one's body only with one's spouse. This agreement of fidelity creates an ownership right over each other's body. While this is no guarantee that a sexual relationship will exist between the couple, it generally precludes them from seeking sexual partners outside their marriage. The message is quite clear: "Only I have a right over your body." A person can adamantly uphold this right even if there is no mutual affection between a couple. It implies that "I am the actual owner of your body. If I can't enjoy the use of it, no one else can either." In some cultures, it gives men strange notions that they can force themselves upon their spouse or partner for sex, as a way of demanding it. A dominant person can abuse his/her powers. Thankfully, this mindset is changing, but it illustrates how property rights get entrenched in the minds of married people.

Thinking of others as "mine," maybe not with the same intensity, may exist towards brothers, sisters, grandparents, uncles, aunts, friends, teachers, and even for plants and pets. The mindset of belonging and ownership in relationships becomes solidified and we behave with this preset conditioning. We also pick up messages of authority and subordination from this.

If one cannot find belonging within one's relationships or friendships, one may want to seek it more strongly in marriage. The patterns we experience with our parents continue when we are with a spouse or partner — a husband looks for belonging and thinks of his wife as his property, and vice versa.

In the process, we begin to treat each other as our personal assets. We expect or demand that our "other halves" conform and fit into our perceptions. If s/he doesn't squeeze into our preconditioned thinking, then we can even develop a dislike for him/her. It could be the source of conflict and, eventually, we may come to "disown" our relationship. As long as the other person toes the line, we can accept him/her. If not, the relationship may come to a swift end. Ownership thinking is at the root of this phenomenon. It is not limited to our personal relationships only, but manifests in organizations, religions, and countries as well.

In the chapters ahead, we will explore the concept of the Self. You will understand the implication of goals, our survival mechanism, identity and conduct as others' property.

SECTION II

TIME TO "KNOW THY SELF"

SUBSECTION - A

THE SELF

6

RISE OF THE SELF

After birth, a child's connection with the mother continues until a certain age, as the child is totally dependent on her for survival. Although there is now a physical separation from the mother — the newborn baby has left the womb — there is no real disconnect between the two from an identity perspective. The child fully identifies with the mother. It is only at some later point when the child realizes s/he has to face the world on his/her own, that the child's own Self emerges.

When a baby comes into the world, s/he is totally dependent on the parents for his/ her every need. This continues for a few years, especially when the mother nurtures and protects the baby, keeping him/ her away from all harm. If the mother does what she does well, it is unusual for the baby to experience any significant trauma during these years.

Once the child has grown to the age of a toddler, s/he is taught ways to act and is imparted a set of do's and don'ts. This is often done to keep the child away from harm. Ironically, it is here when a dormant survival mechanism of the child gets activated. In whatever primitive way, the child realizes that s/he has a separate identity from the mother. This feeling is particularly heightened when the child leaves for school and is separated from the mother for a prolonged period. The child begins to learn how to cope in a novel environment, away from the protective cushioning of home.

The Emergence of the Self

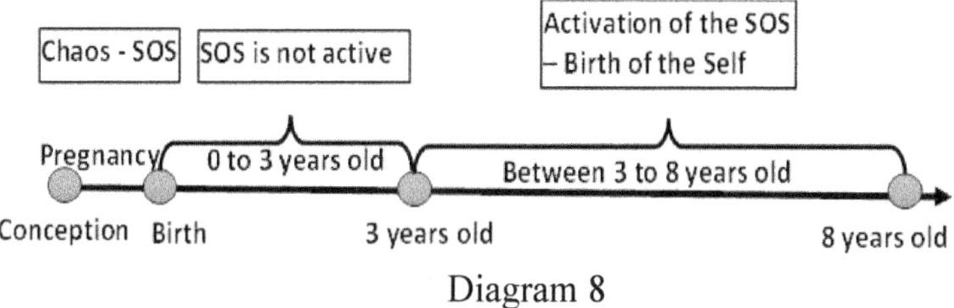

Diagram 8

The diagram above shows the birth of a person's Self. As I have explained in *Stop Surviving Start Living with Freedom*, a degree of chaos in the parents' life has an impact on the conception of every child. Chaos has to do with the limitations a parent experiences while dealing with life situations during pregnancy or when a child is conceived. It can be positive or negative in nature, and ultimately, it affects the emotions of the pregnant mother, which sends a message to the child. Chaos also results in the installation of the Survival Mechanism in the child.

But this survival mechanism, the child's own Survival Mechanism, lies dormant for the first few years. In the first twelve months after birth, the parents administer every need of the child, from being fed, cleaned, changed, bathed, and burped to being placed into bed snugly. In the second and third years, the child slowly learns to crawl or walk, talk, eat, and do some actions independently. S/he still relies on others to fulfill his/ her basic needs and for protection. Since the child is totally under the care of the parents, feeling safe and protected, the Survival Mechanism remains dormant. In fact, there is no need for it to be functional. Even if it is active, the child doesn't take its assistance because the child is helplessly and fully dependent on others.

We notice similar instincts in animals when they are very young. Their mother usually protects them against predators and feeds them to the extent they require, so they don't learn survival skills at that time. Later, when the mother puts them through some drills, young animals pick up new skills that they will hone and use in the wild for their survival.

In a child, the protective sheath usually erodes between the ages of three and eight. "You are now three years old. You need to learn to eat with your own hands," is a common message a child could hear at such an age. The child may be eating playfully but, eventually, s/he has to master a skill, or else it may invite a look of disapproval from the mother. An element of fear causes the child to believe that this time s/he is on her own. S/he is in unfamiliar territory and must learn to deal with this unusual problem. A distinct identity starts to form and take shape. Along with it, the child's survival mechanism gets activated.

Other events down the line, such as going to school, playing with neighborhood kids, and traveling on a school bus, further awakens the child's survival mechanism. The implicit message the child receives is, "You are on your own. You must learn to survive." Children are exposed to the schooling system at two and a half or three years of age, where they meet strangers in the form of other children or teachers. Their whole being is in the hands of others, which makes them go through fear. This is also the period that makes him/her experience some mild traumas that are beyond his/her comprehension. Traumas could be bullying, teasing, physical abuse, or being made fun of, which makes the child feel defenseless and vulnerable. S/he does not know how to deal with the situation and is helpless. But the child is unconsciously aware of the need to survive. S/he knows she is vulnerable in a new environment and seeks the support of other elders, such as a schoolteacher, older sibling, or caretaker. When they experience fear, their survival mechanism gets aroused, and this is where the child's Self also gets activated. In every situation where s/he experiences danger and a defensive cover is missing, his/her survival mechanism gets triggered.

The day a child's Survival Mechanism becomes active, the Self comes into existence. There was no need for it while the child felt wholly protected in the safe hands of his/ her mother, father, grandparent, or nanny. Once the Self starts to form, different people gain more prominence in it. The one whose identity will be more readily absorbed into a child's Self depends on whether the child is Wanted, Partly Wanted, or Unwanted.

7

SELF-IN-FORMATION - AN ILLUSION

The identity we have taken on since birth may seem real to us, but in reality, it is not. It is imaginary and a conditioned one. As dependents, we were given an identity by our parents, relatives, and culture and took it on as we couldn't create one on our own. Moreover, we had to take it as a part of our survival process on Earth.

The idea of an identity that is derived from multiple people and sources is one people may be able to relate to intuitively. However, one of the purposes of this book is to make readers understand what the Self is. One's Self is something that goes beyond just one's identity. It includes all the core and impermanent ingredients of identity listed in the previous section. But it also contains the rules, limiting ideas, beliefs, and concepts we take in from those sources. Let's look at this through the eyes of Mary.

Mary Relies on the Self for Protection

Mary, a newborn infant, comes into the world. A fragile body in need of care enters a family home. Mary's mother and father take all the care in the world to protect her body from harm.

Even while Mary is still an infant, certain rules are introduced to her in the form of sleeping hours. She is placed in her crib, and the lights are switched off. Crying aloud may change her situation, but over time she learns that this is a rule with which she must fall in line. When Mary is a toddler or slightly older, she is able to comprehend more. Family norms and values start being taught to her for her own protection. She may be taught how she ought to obey, not throw food on the floor, respect elders, keep away from sharp objects, or just general conduct. Mary has no identity of her own. She needs to feel secure and is fully dependent on her parents for survival. As such verbal instructions come from her protectors in her home environment, Mary begins to follow them.

Every child seeks acceptance and approval from their parents. Deep within, there is a craving to belong. The more the child feels accepted and receives approval, the more secure the child feels, and the belongingness strengthens. On the other hand, disapproval or non-acceptance can lead to insecurity for the child. Mary also senses that her caretakers will look after her well-being and protect her from possible danger. Eventually, whether she likes it or not, she ends up complying with what her parents expect from her. Mary has to adjust and adapt to their wishes. Through role modelling, she may also take on characteristics, mannerisms, and behaviors of parents. Her Self starts to get more defined with time.

More people enter Mary's life. Grandparents, aunts, uncles, siblings, the nanny, or house help shower affection, but they also introduce to her their own standards of proper behavior. Mary feels she must take heed of them so that she is accepted. Rules could be about how to share things, behave with guests, or follow certain family customs, such as praying in the church. Religion and a set of associated beliefs could be imposed on Mary by a parent or family elder before she is capable of apprehending them. Mary's Self begins to expand to take in more people and their instructions regarding safety. For instance, she may be taught to pray before a meal and thank the food on her plate. It sends a message to her that her survival is being taken care of, at least for today.

As Mary moves out of the home environment, say to visit a neighbor, it must be with the clear consent of her mother, often under her mother's vigilance. Unconsciously, there is fear instilled into the child for her own good. This makes the child cautious not to cause any damage to her body. When Mary is a bit older, she starts to go to school. In this new environment, away from the cozy protection of her parents, she learns how to gain the approval of teachers and classmates. She may need to deal with an older child who is a bully on the school bus. Survival means the preservation of the body. Only if the body survives can one continue to exist. Mary's Survival Mechanism is responsible for her safety and relies on Mary's Self to protect her against harm. Mary's Self remembers the rules about staying safe that have been imparted to her in such moments. Parents also want her to look after herself in different situations and may rebuke her for not following their advice. Mary is well aware of this.

At such an age, it is possible that Mary starts to ask her own questions about different things she experiences. She may or may not be encouraged to ask questions by her elders or get satisfactory answers from them. While she can ask questions, express herself, or even throw tantrums, in many matters, the final decision lies with the parent. This is especially true for situations when it comes to her safety and Mary learns she has to conform. Mary's Self goes on absorbing more rules, norms, and concepts about staying safe.

As she grows, Mary continues to take in more stimuli from a variety of sources. In addition to people such as relatives, teachers and neighbors, books, culture, religion, and the nation also influence her. What it means to be Indian, or a good Christian, becomes more defined in her mind. The story of her community is told to her. Mary's Self continues to absorb, expand, and form through these ideas. History books telling her country's narrative create an idea of nationality in her. Only when she is much older, can she begin to question the idea of nationality or whether her community has to define her identity. But by the time she is a teenager or young adult, she already carries a well-formed identity that is an amalgamation of a host of people and borrowed ideas.

As an older teenager, Mary is allowed to go out with friends. Her mother may teach her what's appropriate behavior with boys or how to dress. When it comes to money, she may be given certain lessons about its value or none at all. All such concepts and ideas come from the parents' own conditioning that they received when they were young and their life experiences. Those ideas, imparted as advice, instructions, or warnings to Mary, will shape her attitudes in the same way toward men or money.

When a child is growing up, s/he experiences dominance from several people who impose their thinking on the child. Often s/he is compelled to follow instructions directly or they are indirectly enforced on them. A child feels vulnerable at such moments. As a dependent, s/he remains under the control of others until s/he is a grown-up. Rebellion may occur, but it only happens when a child is a bit older. Until such time, s/he learns to adapt to different situations, rules, and compulsions. The child has no choice but to adhere to what's being imposed and adjusts to protect his/ her body from the punishment that, at worst, can cause physical harm.

The child's Self encompasses all these rules, norms, and behavior s/he needs to abide by to keep his/ her body away from harm. Over time, Mary understands the consequences of non-compliance with certain rules on her own. The Self is a survival mechanism that keeps on expanding as the child grows up. It is the body that we have to protect from danger. As children, we learn to maneuver our way on planet Earth, and we fall back on our Self to guide us to safety. The core protectors of the body are the parents. So they become the foundation of our Self. This survival mechanism continues to operate in us even as adults.

How Does the Self Come into Existence?

As mentioned earlier, every child is a goal or dream of the parents. The diagram shows how that goal gets fulfilled.

There was a time when the child was a dream imagined by the parents, and it became a reality after some time. In the diagram, the arrow goes from the parents to the child (left to right), which symbolizes the fulfillment of the goal.

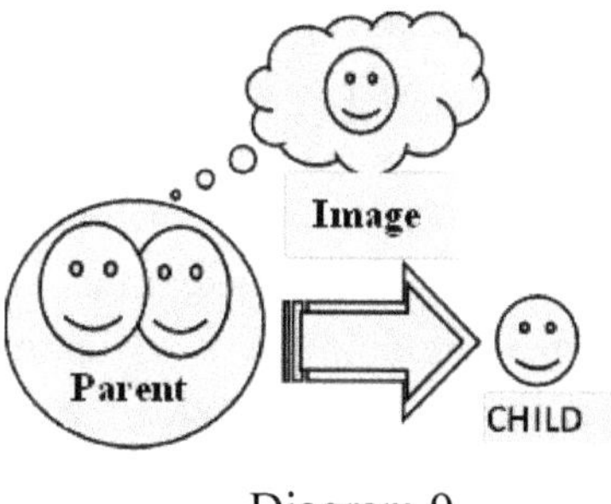

Diagram 9

As mentioned above, the parents are the core of a child's Self. Let's look at the diagram below.

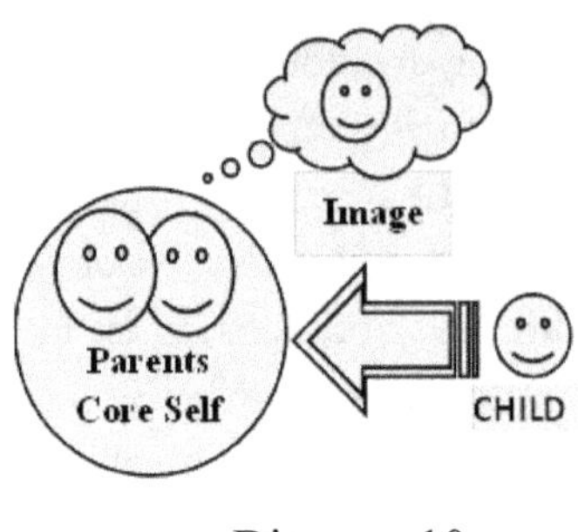

Diagram 10

In the diagram, the arrow goes from the child to the Self, where the child has internalized the parents. The child on his/ her own doesn't have an identity. A core identity comes from the parents. As a child is totally dependent on parents after birth, they make up the whole world for the child.

In the beginning, the child requires the support of parents to fulfill most of his/her physical needs, such as feeding, movement, washing, burping, and comforting. As the child grows older, unconsciously, this external support system gets internalized by the child. Parents become an inner guidance system. They become the child's internal map, providing necessary direction. A child has not developed conscious thinking and simply takes in everything from his/her environment. Parents are the ones who select what information reaches the child, or they unconsciously pass it on to him/her through their behavior and speech. In a short time, the parents become an imaginary representation in the child's mind in the form of memory.

As the child grows up, this inner guidance system keeps developing, which we refer to as the Self. A person's Self functions as an internal navigator, a sort of Global Positioning System (GPS), showing him/her possible ways to avoid harm and injury to the body and how to survive on planet Earth. Though that system is not perfect, it is the primary system the child has to rely on. And the child has no choice. Whatever rules and limits the parents enforce on the child continue to operate at the foundational level. The child's Self keeps expanding and growing as s/he gets older and new people keep getting added to it, which is what happened to Mary too.

However, as the primary ingredients of the child's Self come from the parents, it is inevitable that s/he also inherits their baggage. Baggage may consist of their limitations, beliefs, or even strengths, which were transferred to them by their own parents (the child's grandparents) and society. For example, a father who didn't receive a good education when he was young may want his son to be highly educated and could emphasize it while raising the boy. This is the direct result of what the father felt deprived of in his life and a reason why he feels inadequate. The boy goes on to achieve his father's unfulfilled dreams, not realizing it has to do with the father's past.

What is the Self and what is it made of?

Offering, as a definition of the Self, we can say that the *Self is the internalization of the parents and later on others by the child, along with all the rules of living they have taught him/her. Together this acts like a system that guides and imposes limits on the child, for his/her own safety and well-being.*

A simple way of looking at the Self would be to think of it as an identity plus rules of living. By rules of living, we mean all the rules, beliefs, concepts, or ideas the parents have imparted to the child to keep the child safe, protected, and doing well in life. They are limiting in nature because others have predefined them from the perspective of safeguarding us. They limit one's freedom by imposing restrictions in the way one ought to live. This is even true for those children who are born into an educated or affluent family and must pursue certain notions of "success" that conform to their family's values. It could be wealth creation or picking a high-profile career rather than doing what makes the child feel happy.

Parents, who are outside the child, get internalized by him/her over a period. An example of this is how a child's relationship with time changes. In the beginning, a child doesn't have a concept of time until the mother instills it into the child's mind. So, if the child comes home late from playing outdoors, the mother may be stern with the child. At a later time, she may also reprimand or punish the child for repeating the "error." The moment punishment comes into play; the mother starts to exist within the child's mind. Now the child is always mindful of the time and the possible consequences of returning home late. Similarly, children internalize their parents through the other things they have imbibed.

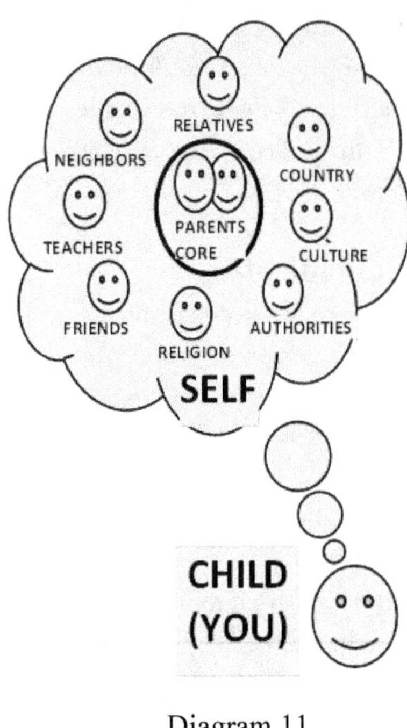

Diagram 11

A person's Self is like an imaginary container that holds their conditioning — all the limiting rules and ideas that have been picked up since childhood and internalized by the child. Parents, who are the source of this conditioning, start to exist inside the child in the form of these rules. Such norms could be for the child's everyday survival, or they could also be doctrines acquired from the lineage, which a child is taught to follow. Family values, cultural traditions, religion, and the Indian caste system are examples of the latter. That a person must pick an educational program and learn to be independent of parents after the age of eighteen could be considered a cultural norm in some countries. A person's Self reminds them of all such necessary requirements regarding different aspects of life.

In this way, a collection of personalities and influences get absorbed and accumulate inside a child, from which the child takes his/her identity in the world. As s/he grows older, s/he begins to think, "This is MY SELF." And that Self is made up of different people and influences. The child has built up an identity through the eyes of others. The Self helps the child fit into his/her environment.

Parents and Elders Shape the Self

Zeena's parents separated when she was seven years old. Her mother and aunt raised her. Over a while, Zeena's mother poisoned her mind against her father by describing his many negative qualities and the reasons for their separation. Her mother prevented Zeena from meeting her father, even though he had come twice to see Zeena soon after the separation. Zeena believed her mother's story and her aunt upheld it too. On regressing back to when she was not yet seven years old, Zeena recalled many happy and healthy encounters with her father. This changed her perception of him. Certain misconceptions got corrected, which neutralized the hatred she carried for him. In this case, her mother had played the dominant role as a Self in Zeena, influencing her thinking. Her information came from a credible source, or sources when including her aunt, which was difficult to challenge.

As the child grows, s/he takes the support of the knowledge pool s/he acquires from parents and others in the formative years, which acts as a protective shield. A child has no way to verify the validity of this knowledge but has to take it as the ultimate truth because it comes from a credible source — the creators — and the child has no discerning capabilities. Examples of these rules could be to look on both sides of the road before crossing it, brush your teeth in the mornings, respect elders and others, bow your head before a deity, and so on. Few rules are valid and necessary; some valid in certain situations and others may no longer be valid as one grows up to be an adult. "Do not talk to strangers" is an example of a rule that was valid in some situations during childhood but would be impractical for adults. A lot of knowledge from parents becomes the main resource for a child; for its credibility, it is difficult to challenge when young.

Rules are Enforced

Rules get emphasized more when a child goes to school. All children have to obey a school's regulations, even if they are very young. They may be different for playschool, kindergarten, primary, and secondary school. Some rules may be for a child's safety, while others may inculcate discipline and conformed behaviors. If a child does not follow the rules, at some point, a reward and punishment system is bound to impose those behaviors and habits on the child. The child with a survival mechanism will most often learn behaviors expected of him/her. While teachers have become increasingly flexible, a child still has to learn to adapt to a particular teacher's personality and teaching style. The child has to modify his/her behaviors to adapt to a system. Rarely will it be the other way around where a system will fully adjust to and understand a child. Likewise, the Self also operates as a system and to survive the child has to adjust to all the system's rules.

A family becomes a system for a child that makes and implements various rules for the child's safety. Some of these could be valid concerns. But they can also be dogmas or doctrines from the past, unquestioned cultural assumptions, or at times personal agendas, like in the case of Zeena's mother. Zeena's aunt authenticated what her mother said and even added more to her mother's stories. In Sumit's Self, mentioned earlier in the book, his mother played the dominant role. His father, sister, and girlfriend subsequently became part of his Self, applying subtle pressure on him to attain benchmarks and prove himself worthy to them. A child cannot survive independently without parents or family. Unconsciously, all rules and beliefs that come from them become part of a child's psyche, which continues to govern the child in the name of protection, even when the child grows into an adult.

Sometimes these rules are applied without discretion. When Jaydeep was five years old, he usually returned home with his older cousins, who stayed a few blocks away. One day, his cousins forced him to come to their home, which meant he returned to his home a few hours late. His angry mother mercilessly punished him without even listening to his excuse. Jaydeep said, "I was a kid and did refuse to go to my cousin's place, but they dragged me there. It wasn't my fault." Here, Jaydeep had broken an important rule of his mother, which was to return home on time or to inform her.

Illusionary Self

A child's Self is an identity through which s/he experiences life, always keeping security as the foremost objective. It also makes him/her believe what s/he should be or do when s/he grows up. However, whether one realizes it or not, it is always an imaginary identity that appears to be real. As mentioned earlier, "Tom is fighting imaginary Tim." That is why it is an Illusionary Self.

The Self that has been described in this chapter is in fact, an outdated Self. Beliefs that have been picked up by us when we were children came from people's collective imagination, may they be our parents, grandparents, society, or culture. They may have been someone's legitimate experiences, but they became notions of "that's the way life is," passed on from one generation to the next. A child who is young needs to be taught principles and ideas about life. But as the child grows into an adult, s/he needs to follow his/ her own thinking instead of living as per the definitions given by others. But this rarely happens because of our conditioning. What was true, real, and necessary when a child was young unconsciously affects the way s/he ought to live as an adult. A person's Self solidifies past experiences into definitions regarding living.

Within every person there is a powerful system known as the Self without which it would have been impossible for us to survive as children. This whole system is now within every person's mind. As it is based on mental concepts and memories, it is imaginary, an illusion we unconsciously follow. Some of the notions in our Self do get updated as we grow up, but many hardly undergo change. Since they come from reliable sources, at times, it is difficult to challenge those deep-rooted beliefs. An individual's Self is so potent that it can completely overwhelm a child or an adult, irrespective of which Survival Mechanism we have.

An Alternative Experience

Not all experiences a child has during childhood have to do with his/her survival. The experience of love leads to a different feeling within the child. Take the example of some special moments Mary spends with her grandmother who makes her feel loved and protected. Mary waits for the days when she can sleep in her grandmother's room so that she can listen to all the bedtime stories her grandmother narrates to her. Blissfully sleepy in a short while, Mary falls into a deep slumber in the warm embrace of her grandmother.

Here, Mary experiences a feeling of oneness with her grandmother. It's unlike what she feels when she complies with the conditions imposed on her by her parents or elders, however well-intentioned they may be. There is no agreement she shares with her grandmother to give or take anything, no reward for good behavior or punishment for poor conduct. Her grandmother's love is unconditional. Such a union is not based on fear. An alignment takes place between the child and another person that is different. Surely, there are similar experiences Mary shares of love with her parents or certain teachers. The child is allowed to simply 'be.' Here, hardly any rules and regulations are enforced on the child, so the child experiences a different sort of bonding. Therefore, this does not become part of a person's Self, although such experiences may vary for everyone.

8

FUSION OF THE PRIMARY SELVES

In the introduction, I have described three types of operating systems humans carry that are responsible for their safety — The Wanted Child, The Partly Wanted Child, and The Unwanted Child. All three survival systems function in different ways from each other. Children carrying one of these operating systems will have a unique way of surviving on this planet compared to the other two. Their primary sensory modes of learning, decision-making styles, behaviors, communication, and deep-rooted beliefs are as different as different programming languages. However, all three systems arrive at the same outcome — to protect and preserve the child, who is later the adult.

Fusion of Two Systems

This means there are two systems within every person — one that has created us (the Self, representing parents) and a survival mechanism that got installed at or before birth (the Survival Mechanism). The Survival Mechanism gets activated when the child experiences insecurity or uncertainty during childhood. A child's Self comes about at the same time s/he can take some action to protect his/ her body against harm. The process of setting rules is the job of a person's Self, and to cope with them, we use our Survival Mechanism. Rules are imposed on human beings so that we can stay together and do things together. Even when a child's Self comes into existence, s/he is still dependent on their parents. Later, as adults, the dependence remains on what one has been taught during the formative years. Parents are no longer sitting next to the child (now adult) but reminding the person through the Self on what's right or wrong, acceptable or unacceptable, commendable or unworthy.

Different Combinations of the Primary Self

There are three types of operating systems (Survival Mechanisms) in human beings and each of us will fall into one of these categories, having its traits. When two people come together to create another human, there is an interplay between their Survival Mechanisms. So far, in my observation, I haven't come across couples where both people have the same operating system. Both can't be Wanted Children, or Partly Wanted Children, or Unwanted Children. If both had the same Survival Mechanism, it would appear to violate a principle of nature, such as, "like poles repel and unlike poles attract." The same observations hold true in same-sex couples.

I have categorized, below, the different combinations a couple comes together in a union to give birth to a child. They become a Self to a child that continues to operate as an invisible entity within the child, even when the child grows to be an adult. There are six combinations that can give birth to a child (boy or girl), where one of the partners falls into a survival category - Wanted Child, Partly Wanted Child, or Unwanted Child — while the other falls into a different one.

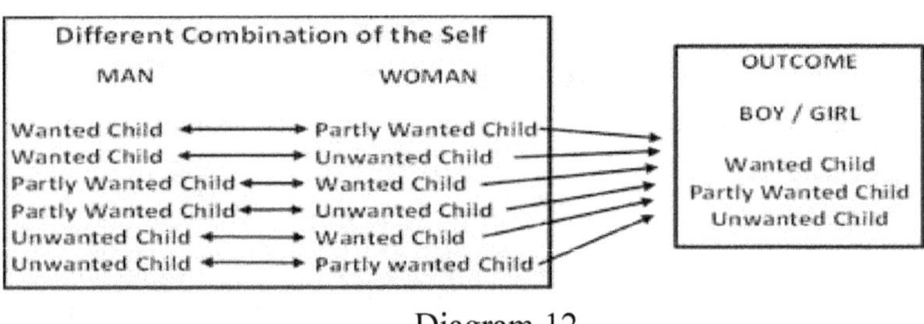

Diagram 12

While the above diagram shows a merger between two SOMs, two SOMs cannot truly merge. Remember, an SOM is one of a Survival Mechanism's three variants. A new Self of the child becomes a container, which imbibes the rules and perceptions of the parents with distinct SOMs. SOMs by themselves do not integrate. People need a common meeting ground. Certain norms are created so that humans can learn to live together harmoniously. This is a way in which we learn to co-exist. The child adapts and represents a coming together of two different SOMs.

Regarding the child's own SOM, the parents' emotions decide the child's fate, whether s/he is wanted, partly wanted, or unwanted. If the couple wants the child, s/he is born as a Wanted Child. If one of the partners is disinterested in having a child, that parent will play a major role in the life of the child, who will be a Partly Wanted Child. In the third case, a woman rejects her male partner and thus child, resulting in the birth of an Unwanted Child.

The mindsets of the parents influence the child's Self. Many cultures are male-dominated and so also are religions that influence a cultural mindset. Other than the above, education, social status, wealth, beauty, ethnicity, nationality, etc. also play a role. These subsets are part of the psyche of the parents, who will transfer at least some of their thinking to the child. In this way, they will become part of the child's Self.

A dominant parent may have a greater say in what gets incorporated into the child's Self. The push and pull between the parents' differing operating systems will also become a factor here. The parent who is the decision-maker or has a stronger will can enforce family rules that get adopted by the other partner and the child. In certain scenarios, there is only a single parent raising a child, as in the case of Zeena above. So that person's mindset will influence the child's Self most. The more decisions the couple makes through consensus, the better the environment for a child's healthy development and growth.

All the above factors will impact a child differently, but whatever the combination, it becomes the core of the Self that stays with the person for life and what we relate to in our everyday life.

Caretakers in the Core Self

It is not just parents who can become part of the core Self. Environments may be different for children when they are growing up. There can be various factors affecting the family and hence the child. The structures of families may differ. Some are what is known in India as a "nuclear family," comprising just parents and children. Others are joint or extended families, with grandparents, uncles, aunts, and cousins of the child living under the same roof. All these members will impact the child while growing up and become part of the child's Self.

Working parents will have a nanny, caretaker, or grandparent looking after the child while they are away at work. Each of these personalities will influence the child differently, based on their own upbringing. There never will be uniformity in raising two children in the same family.

In the absence of parents, people caring for the child can also become the core of the child's Self. I have had a few clients who were adopted soon after birth. Some were told they were adopted, knew their biological parents, and were also in contact with them. Others were denied the knowledge of their adoption. Finally, some knew they were adopted but didn't know who their original parents were. The parents who adopted children provided resources for their growth and development. As the adopting parents laid down the rules for their protection, they became the core of the Self of those children. For some of my clients, their grandparents or other relatives occupied their core.

Whoever plays the role of caretaker during the formative years can essentially become a part of the core Self.

9

PURPOSE OF THE SELF

To put it simply, if we don't have a body, then there is no existence. Only when we have a body we are who we are. It is our body that gives us our physical appearance. Without it, our survival traits and personality do not hold any ground. The primary job of any parent or caretaker is to safeguard the body of the child. In turn, the child's Self, too, becomes the child's bodyguard in the absence of the parent's physical presence in later years. It plays the same role as that of the parents, even in adulthood.

If a child has grown up and survived his/her formative years, we can conclude that s/he had a protector who safeguarded his/her body. The parents' groundwork of giving rules and instructions allows the child's Self to get trained as an invisible bodyguard. It relies on the information fed by parents and others during the child's early years, which becomes the guide for protecting the individual in the future.

The difference between a real bodyguard and an invisible one is that the former follows the instructions given by the person s/he is protecting. The Self follows guidelines from parents and others, not from the child who it is protecting. In a way, even real bodyguards also receive training from their organization or boss and apply best practices in guarding their clients. If a person's Self senses danger or harm to his/her body, it will overrule the best intentions of the person. It does not accept orders from the one it is protecting, which creates internal conflict in the person.

10

DISTINCTION BETWEEN SELF AND SURVIVAL MECHANISM

Both the Self and the Survival Mechanism work towards a common outcome, but they are very different from each other. All this while, as these two have never been segregated, we have been perplexed about their individual functioning and outcomes. This chapter aims to make the reader understand these systems broadly so that you can notice how they operate within us clearly. The chapters ahead will describe the features of the Self in more detail so that the distinctions become more apparent.

The role of a parent is to protect and nurture a child until the child can sustain on his/her own. The child's Self also performs the same function by providing inner guidance. On the other hand, the Survival Mechanism does the job of helping the child survive within his/her environment. The Survival Mechanism ensures no harm is done to the child and s/he grows up safely. Parents impose restrictions on the child for their safety, which is taken over later by the child's Self. The role of the Survival Mechanism is to help a person cope with these restrictions, which come from the parents and then later from the child's own Self (inner guidance). However, the objective of both the Survival Mechanism and the Self is the same — to preserve the child.

While both ensure the preservation of the child, what are some of the significant differences between the two? The Survival Mechanism helps us survive in any environment or system, be it the family, school, or workplace. Any time laws are imposed externally by those who a child comes in contact with, it is a system. A person's Self acts like a system by imposing rules and restrictions on them. But the Survival Mechanism does not operate on human laws. It is a natural survival mechanism inside a human being, protecting the individual. This is a key difference between a person's Self and Survival Mechanism. One is a survival mechanism; the other is an internal guidance system imposing limits. The differences have been elaborated on below.

1. Structure: The Survival Mechanism has three varieties, known as Survival Operating Mechanism (SOM's), each of which has its survival traits, which remain the same for the rest of our lives. Survival traits are personality traits a person uses in order to survive (e.g. avoiding risks, pleasing others, seeking the limelight). The core structure of a child's Self is made up of parents and their rules of living. However, the Self keeps expanding and changing as the child grows older, as new rules or laws get added.

2. Time of origination: The Survival Mechanism comes into existence at a child's conception or during pregnancy, though it's not active in the first three years of a child's life. A child's Self comes into existence only a few years after s/he is born.

3. Purpose: The Self expects you to follow the rules and regulations for your safety. The Survival Mechanism does what needs to be done at the moment, and it need not be right or wrong but protects one's body from harm and danger, even from the Self.

4. Position: Survival Mechanism is within us, functioning as an operating system. A person's Self contains rules and regulations made by others, which are initially external and later get internalized to become part of our system.

5. Changeability: The Survival Mechanism is an inbuilt mechanism for preserving a child with the help of its tools (survival traits), which mostly remains unchanged throughout the person's lifetime, even when the child grows into an adult. It helps the person survive against possible harm and dangers.

The Self designs and implements rules or regulations for the child's safety, which s/he must obey. These rules do get modified and updated from time to time depending on the people who inhabit the child's Self and the child's progressing age. Parents may make it compulsory for a young child to hold the parent's hand while crossing a street, but once the child is a little older, s/he is allowed to cross the street without the parent's physical support. A child is not allowed near the stove or a hot vessel. S/he does not know that it could burn the hands. Later on, this sort of rule is dropped. Some rules we update as we grow older. Certain rules belonging to a system, like a person's religion or the Indian caste system, are taken by the individual to the grave.

Rules contained in a person's Self need to be updated regularly. If not, they will create conflict and disharmony within the person over time. The Survival Mechanism's toolkit of survival traits does not get updated and remains unchanged with time. It finds ways to safeguard the person's body throughout his/her life.

6. Dependence: The Self depends on two or more people for its existence. These two people have their individual Survival Mechanisms. The Survival Mechanism, on the other hand, operates independently. Two or more people in the person's Self will implement rules and s/he has to rely on the Survival Mechanism's tools (survival traits) to adapt to those rules.

7. Power: The Self (comprising parents and others) is powerful. It can trash and discipline the child. The Survival Mechanism is no match for it and has to find a way to comply with the Self. Even though an internal (psychological) split between the child and mother has happened before the age of eight years, the child is still dependent on the parents.

8. Ownership: The Self (parents) treats the child as its property and will do whatever it can to protect it. The Survival Mechanism is chiefly compelled to follow the rules imposed on the child.

9. Sub-parts: Systems can exist within systems — wheels within wheels — and interact with other systems. For example, a nuclear family can exist within a joint family. A family system needs to adjust to a schooling system. A person's Self takes on the same characteristics as rules imposed on an individual by different systems, which can lead to conflict or confusion. The Survival Mechanism operates on its own with its tools (survival traits) within the child's body.

10. Rewards system: A person's Self enforces itself through a system of rewards and punishment. The Survival Mechanism and its tools try to avoid punishment and pain by moving toward rewards and pleasure.

11. Alterable by effort: It is possible for a person to change and update rules made by the Self, but survival traits in a Survival Mechanism are unalterable through effort. Only a tiny minority of people can defuse them.

12. Effect on each other: An individual's Self, too, cannot change the traits found in his/ her Survival Mechanism. However, in later years, a person with certain survival traits may revolt against the Self, creating an imbalance within the person.

In the chapters ahead, you will get to know the features of the Self and understand how it functions more clearly.

11

LIVING IN AN ILLUSION
- A DISTORTED REALITY

As we have seen through the example of Tom and Tim given in the prologue, the Self is an imaginary identity we hold on to. It is different from the physical body of a person, which is real.

The Self comes about at a time when a child, who is dependent, experiences trauma. Till then, s/he is part of the system of parents, especially the mother. Trauma could arise from mild forms of punishment, such as scolding or admonishing a child, or more severe forms, such as hitting or beating. Such events become future reminders for the child to avoid those mistakes and seek approval. In the absence of the parents, the Self is the one the child seeks approval from and continues to do its job even as we grow into an adult.

Although the Self is an entity within a person, it is imaginary and invisible. The Survival Mechanism is invisible as well. Almost all issues in therapy sessions sprout from these two invisible entities. A person's Self is the parents s/he carries around everywhere, reminding the person of a violation of a norm or principle given by them.

Sunder, who is a vegetarian, accepts the invitation of his friend, Victor, for dinner. Sunder's family follows a particular religion that practices eating only vegetarian food. Since his childhood, Sunder has been made to eat only vegetarian dishes, as his family's religion is against the killing of animals. Victor, who eats meat, puts in a great deal of effort to convince Sunder about the benefits of meat, as a source of proteins, iron, and minerals. He is led by well-meaning intentions towards his friend, whether his views are agreeable with Sunder or not. Sunder is confused if he should try meat on this occasion or follow his family's practice. He could eat meat to please his friend and may even enjoy it, but he will feel guilt internally. Sunder's Self will remind him that he has violated his family's code.

Another source of conflict for Sunder is within his Self itself. His parents occupy the core of his Self, with friends on the outer ring. Sunder may continue to eat meat behind the back of his family, but somewhere inside him, there will be guilt or shame of doing something wrong. Or Sunder may desist from eating meat and avoid meeting Victor over a meal in the future. Wholesome food is something that nourishes the body and doesn't generate such inner conflict on its own. The invisible Self applies direct pressure on Sunder.

Yet another reason for internal conflict within a person is the clash between the two invisible forces of the Self and the Survival Mechanism. Although, because of trauma, there is a psychological split between the child and parents at an early age, it is not visible as the child tries to cope with the situation through a new tool that was dormant since birth — the Survival Mechanism. It is the survival mechanism of the child, which helps him/ her deal with the pressure exerted by the Self. Each Survival Mechanism (an SOM) uses different survival tools.

Sunder's Survival Mechanism knows that food is required for the sustenance of the body. According to it, it's alright to eat meat if it provides you with good quality nutrition. But his Self has introduced concepts of what's good or bad for the body or what's allowed or not from the religious viewpoint. Sunder's family may have chosen their diet based on tradition rather than out of independent choices, and the same values are being passed on to Sunder. The question here is not which diet is superior or ethical but how people are compelled to make choices based on certain beliefs. These beliefs become part of the child's Self, who cannot question them at a young age and hence carries them into adulthood.

Where there is a clash between a child's Survival Mechanism and his/her Self, in almost all cases, the Self will overrule the former, which gives rise to Self-sabotage. The Self functions on laws imposed from the outside and the Survival Mechanism relies on its survival tools. If laws are obeyed or broken, then a reward and punishment dynamic come into play. Breaking the law will inevitably cause internal discomfort to a person as the person's Self, an imaginary entity, will remind him/her of the transgression.

12

EVERYWHERE MARY WENT...

Abhijeet had returned to India from abroad because his marriage of twelve years had fallen apart. He did not understand what was going on in his life and wanted to know himself better. So he started visiting different spiritual gurus and their ashrams to find answers to his quest. Abhijeet would devote his time and energy to serving those organizations.

He went from one guru to another till he finally chose one he would fully dedicate himself to, giving all his time and knowledge to his teacher's school. But after spending a few years as a seeker, his doubts and questions yet remained unanswered.

Mary had a little lamb,
Its fleece was white as snow;
And everywhere that Mary went
The lamb was sure to go.

The popular nursery rhyme above could be poetically rephrased as "Everywhere that Mary went, the Self is sure to go." Little had Abhijeet realized that there is a Self within him that goes everywhere he does, and stirs up the same problems he has experienced before in his life. When he came to see me, he was dejected and angry with his own Self for having been a failure.

But many of us are like Abhijeet. When faced with a crisis, we seek refuge in a spiritual guru, a new religious organization, a cult, or a commune. I know of many who have joined gurus and stayed at their ashrams to find inner peace and freedom. They want answers for their restlessness, which has been tormenting them. However, it's beyond their awareness that the restlessness they experience indicates a Self throwing out of the garbage they have collected along the way. People may go anywhere on this planet (or even out of it), but they still carry their Self. No person can escape this inner mechanism by going away to a place, be it a secluded cave, mountain, or island. The Self will surely follow and resurface when a person once again interacts with people who will trigger it. So, one cannot hide from one's Self or simply drop it.

Some will attain temporary peace as long as they are in an ashram, spiritual camp, or retreat, doing meditation and other practices. However, the moment they are back in their regular environment, they have to deal with the people who usually inhabit it or new people they meet. Exchanges with some people will make the same old Self show its face. Others can't distinguish between you and your Self. To them, the Self is you, and you are the Self. It may have been suppressed for a while, but it is a part of your system.

When we are mentally disturbed, we often try to escape from the clutches of our Self. Or we want to control and tame it, just like humans do with horses. An overweight person wants to follow a strict diet to reduce weight and tries to compel the Self to do as instructed. But s/he is able to follow through with the diet only for a few days before flipping.

People carry their parents along with them everywhere. This means invisible entities (and voices) inside them create disharmony in their minds. Parents exist in the form of a memory, which goes everywhere with a person. One may change one's residence or migrate to another country. By meditating or going away to the mountains, we try to eliminate our non-stop internal chatter. But a person's Self remains an integral part of the person and continues to reside within him/her till the last breath.

We may experience peace when we move away from the core Self (parents and others). But that sort of peace is short-lived, and a trigger can activate the same Self to resurface. Later in life, it may not be parents who bring out our uncomfortable emotions or take away our peace and harmony. It could be a spouse, boss, or other people who do it. It's an unconscious process that happens so swiftly that it becomes difficult to detect the culprit. On the other hand, if we slow down and understand the core Self and how it functions, it's possible for us to attain peace and harmony.

13

SELF WILL DEFEND ITS PROPERTY

Whether we like it or not, our parents have had an ownership right over us ever since we came into this world. Just like the mobile phone, you own is your exclusive property. No one can even access it because it is password protected or needs your fingerprint to give someone else access. You may have even installed an anti-theft tracker so that you can locate your phone when it's lost. If you can go through all these measures to protect your property, you can imagine parents will do everything they can to preserve their precious possessions.

The very fact that you are alive and reading this book means they have done something well enough to protect you. For children who were unfortunately aborted in their mother's womb, it was an indication that parents were not willing to take on ownership. For those who took birth, your Self took over from your parents once you started to grow older.

Vishal, an Unwanted Child, is the only child in the family who has been rebelling against his mother. He has no clue about the real issue making him hate his mother. His perception of his mother changed after he learned about the facts surrounding his birth and what may have made his mother not want to have him. When he regressed to his childhood years, I asked Vishal to review his upbringing and understand who had taken care of him and protected him as a child. Despite harboring animosity towards his mother, Vishal understood how she had played an instrumental role in his development during his growing-up years.

Some children may be unwanted, but if they have survived, it means that there were those who were kind enough to protect and nurture them, however well or poorly they fared. The caretakers of such children have treated them as their own, no matter what difficulties they had to face. Even an abusive parent may have managed to do enough to ensure a child also grows up.

Not Always About Obvious Physical Danger

The child's Self plays the role of protector when s/he grows up, but safety does not always have to do with obvious physical danger. Sometimes it has to do with cultural or social beliefs. Ryan, now in his sixties, married his first wife simply because he had consensual sex with her before marriage. I inquired whether there was any commitment to getting married. "No," said Ryan, but added that he felt guilty. If the sex was consensual, where was the guilt coming from? He said it was unacceptable according to society. My obvious question was, "Who told you that?" Ryan said it was his parents. Certain norms were passed on to him by his parents for his safety. Many of them were about being accepted by society. In the eyes of society, the perceived shame from doing something wrong made Ryan feel so guilty he chose to marry the woman with whom he had sex. Being marginalized by society was unthinkable and the fear of it made him do what he did.

Our Self continues to hold its grip on us even when we are grown-up adults, making us fulfill certain expectations. At such times, one tends to lose the ability to question the validity of things through reasoning. One can feel the weight of one's Self and their best defenses against it are ineffective.

In the section on Systems, we will see how macro-systems also protect their property in the same way.

14

─────────────

THE TRAP - SELF HOLDS BOTH THE ENDS

A relative of mine would look at her daughter with wide eyes every time she would do something that she disapproved of. Her daughter would take it as a sign that she ought to stop doing whatever she was doing. Parents set rules and prescribe behaviors that their children must obey if they are to get approval and acceptance or other benefits of being their child. The intent of the parent is the safety and well-being of their child.

There are many potentially dangerous situations and items in a child's environment, and the parent tries to insulate the child from possible harm. The child is unaware that some of these could be life-threatening for him/her or can cause serious injury. Danger could come from sharp or pointed objects, inedible things, crawling to places from where s/he could fall, or other harmful situations. As the child grows to two years of age, verbal instructions are uttered by the parent, hoping the former will follow them. Or else the parent or elder could even reprimand the child. It may come in the form of mild scolding or, sometimes punishment, such as being sent away to the bedroom. Somewhere, at an unconscious level, the message gets embedded that we have got to obey our elders.

But a child also learns that instructions are given for his/her own good and protection, that parents mean well, and the child must imbibe what they teach. While learning to walk, we fall many times and it hurts. At times, children make other mistakes and experience pain. When this happens, instructions get reinforced to avoid repeating the act that caused that pain. Sometimes despite a parent's utmost precautions, we, as children, are careless and get bruised, cut ourselves, or cause a serious injury. We are then taken to the doctor or hospital. All such events teach us that parents know what's best for us, and we should listen to their advice. Unconsciously, beliefs start to take shape in us. Accumulation of similar experiences strengthens the belief that to avoid pain; we must obey our creators and their guidelines. As such guidance becomes a part of our Self, we unconsciously conclude it is well-intentioned and there to safeguard us.

Rules Keep Changing Based on Different Factors

When Myra is a young infant and starts to consume food, her mother feeds her until Myra learns to put food in her mouth. As she learns more about food, she starts to feed herself. However, her mother supervises Myra in segregating what food she can eat with her own hands and what she cannot. In the latter category, it could be fish with bones or the like. The same process of guided supervision is there when Myra learns to walk. In the beginning, her parents hold her hand. But when she knows how to walk, she is given the freedom to do so within safe surroundings. Even when Myra becomes competent, her parent may still hold her hand while crossing a busy street. When Myra is eight or nine years of age, she is allowed to walk independently.

The Self sets boundaries for a child's safety, which keep getting modified as the child grows older and progresses. In certain situations, rules are dismantled because they don't hold validity anymore.

On the other hand, certain specific restrictions may be imposed. While Myra is allowed to eat on her own, if she comes from a vegetarian family, her family members will make sure she isn't served meat, eggs, or fish at home. Families following a certain faith maybe even more specific about the prohibition of some foods or practices. The child's Self makes sure that these rules are learned and obeyed by the child, else it reminds the person of a transgression that can make them feel guilty.

Certain rules around discipline may be individualistic and depend on the parent's preferences. Myra's mother may demand that she finish eating the food on her plate, while her father may want her to go to sleep by 9 pm. Her mother may allow her to play on an iPad or tablet, but her father disapproves of the habit. At all times, the child has to adapt to each parent's style of functioning and obey. Some requirements can be more demanding and have lifelong implications for the child. One parent may want Myra to specifically follow a religion and its rituals, while the other parent may want her to develop a liberal outlook. It is the child who has to make the adjustment as per the parents' requirements and personalities.

However, Myra's parents not only make the rules, but they also ensure that they are complied with by her, at least to a large extent. The child experiences a compulsion to follow, else there could be consequences. Rules set by her parents become laws of living or beliefs that unconsciously govern Myra even as an adult. If she violates a rule, then some emotions are bound to surface, creating discomfort within Myra at some point.

Makes Laws and Also Enforces Them

Enforcement is another way in which parents make us learn rules. Punishment is a tool they use for that. The type of punishment will vary based on the parents and their personality traits. Each parent has his/her own survival traits and Self. The harshness of the penalty will therefore differ from one to another.

As a child, Lavina was punished by her father because she threw potato chips on the floor and enjoyed the cracking sounds while stamping on them. Her father told Lavina to stop doing it in front of a guest, but she ignored him and went on. When the guest had left, Lavina's father made her stand naked on the balcony on a cold winter night. In another instance, I know of a mother who locked up her two-year-old son in a dark bathroom for playing with the oven dials when no one was watching him, which led to dinner getting burned. She had warned him earlier not to do so. While parents may have committed the above acts out of rage, the message has been communicated to the child that s/he did something terribly wrong. A child may want to play and explore as a part of learning. The parent was unwilling to consider whether the child was getting a sense of joy by stomping on chips or experiencing curiosity while changing the oven dials.

If the child is over-pampered, then the repercussions of it will be different in the future. When the child grows up, s/he will wrap the parents and others around his/ her finger. In this case, the person takes the bodyguard for a ride which means s/he becomes a law unto themselves. If the parent doesn't discipline the child, then those in the expanded Self will discipline him/her (e.g. relatives, teachers, boss). Such children might take the parents for granted, but the expanded Self will not tolerate their nonsense. They will eventually learn the hard way from the external world, which will be more painful for the person who is forced to realize his/her mistakes.

At home, boundaries are set by parents and other elders. At school, the dean (or principal) and teachers will set rules — students must adhere to them. Children have to adapt to different rules in the different set-ups in which they find themselves. Not only do the groups mentioned above set and enforce rules, but they also control the interpretation of what is right or wrong.

Teachers or school principals can not only determine what is wrong, they can also decide the quantum of punishment. Vishnu, a second-grade boy, was standing in a queue to get his arithmetic sums corrected by his math teacher. A boy standing immediately behind him loudly mouthed off some foul words. When the teacher inquired, who had said those words, the boy who had said them pointed the finger at Vishnu. Without delay, the teacher called Vishnu forward and punished him mercilessly without listening to him or checking if he had indeed spoken those words. Children are often not heard or given the opportunity to fully express themselves before people in authority make decisions on what's right and wrong. In these times, how the child will be dealt with is in the hands of authority figures.

When authority figures establish rules, sometimes those rules become absolute orders to be followed without discretion. After the COVID-19 outbreak, wearing a mask in some places in my city became mandatory as per law legislated by municipal authorities. The intention was a good one — the protection of your fellow residents. This rule was enforced strictly in some public places, where officers fined offenders for not wearing masks. However, quite soon after the law was passed, fines began to be levied without discretion in any scenario. People who were walking on an empty street, where the next person was fifty meters away, were stopped and fined. Families sitting inside air-conditioned cars and individuals traveling on motorbikes were also caught and penalized. Any logical reasoning offered by the rule-breaker was not considered valid when such an important law was broken.

If adults cannot question laws, children have a much harder time doing it. When they are young, they cannot use logic or reasoning. Children cannot debate whether a rule is arbitrary or not needed. As a result, if they break a norm, they are usually at the receiving end from their elders, unable to defend their actions verbally. The consequences for the child can be more unfortunate when a parent is rigid, impatient, or intolerant. In those cases, the parent may react severely with little empathy, much like a human robot, as Lavina's father did. Even though rules are made for the safety and well-being of the child, punishment ensures that children comply with them mechanically rather than determine whether what they have done is right or wrong.

What this ultimately means is that a child's Self helplessly absorbs many rules and notions of what's right or wrong. When a person is older, the same Self inflicts psychological punishment on a person, in the form of negative emotions or self-criticism, when s/he apparently breaches a norm.

15

EMOTIONS AND SELF-SABOTAGE

Sue's mother repeatedly told her to finish the food on her plate as a child. She instilled the idea that she must eat well and it is wrong to waste food. Her mother's intentions were to make Sue grow up strong and healthy. However, Sue grows up to become an overweight adult and wants to lose some unwanted weight. She is able to stick to her diet only for a few days, after which something snaps within her, compelling her to eat as usual. Her regimen quickly falls apart and Sue gains a few extra kilos. Unconsciously, Sue is fighting with her Self (which contains her mother). Although Sue's messages to her Self were positive commands and had good intentions, she is unable to cope with the Self.

Sue is battling guilt, which is one of the powerful emotions that gets triggered when we do something wrong. Sue gained her mother's approval only if she ate well as a child. But as she tries to do the opposite today, she is affected by guilt without understanding why. Every time we break a norm, there is an unconscious reminder that there will be repercussions. The fallout could be disapproval from our parents, and, as adults, our Self plays the role of the parents. Sue's Self, in this case, gave rise to the guilt she was experiencing. Sue does not understand where the real issue lies but wants to control her eating. In reality, she wants to control her Self. Some of these triggers may be neutralized by using an NLP reframing technique.

A child's Self and a dormant Survival Mechanism come into existence simultaneously whenever the child experiences some trauma or abuse. This is also what gives birth to negative emotions. The core unconscious issue for the child is that of survival. When a child experiences any uncertainty around this, s/he begins to feel a primary emotion — fear.

Parents and elders set boundaries for a child. Every time the child fails to obey those measures, as a dependent, s/he unconsciously experiences insecurity regarding existence. A sword keeps hanging over a child's head, causing him/her fear. It's not that the child intentionally feels such negative emotions, but s/he has no control over them.

Even as adults, we have no control over our emotions. It could be silly mistakes that petrify us, such as an error on a work presentation. Although it doesn't truly threaten our existence, the fear we experience makes it seem so. At the most, we may try to move away from negative feelings in the best possible way. But it is not always possible to do so. On the other hand, the more positive emotions we experience, the safer and more secure we feel, knowing that our survival on the planet is going well. It gives us some temporary respite.

Fear is the base of all emotions. Whenever negative emotions surface within you, it is a sign that you are at war with the Self. Your Self is entrusted by nature to keep you safe, and it disregards what may be logical other than what is required to protect you. When emotions surface, the Self will unconsciously brush aside the best of logic or reasoning. One's ability to, therefore, objectively reason may get eclipsed in such times, as all thinking will be concerned about protection against harm.

Self-Sabotages Your Goals and Dreams

Another aspect related to emotions is self-sabotage. The meaning of sabotage is "the act of destroying or damaging something deliberately so that it does not work correctly." If one substitutes a person for a thing, then someone is deliberately being destroyed or damaged. Another meaning of sabotage is "to intentionally prevent the success of a plan or action."

When Self-sabotage occurs within a person, the person's Self deliberately obstructs him/her from going ahead and has a well-meaning intention behind it. Through sabotage, a person's Self tries to protect him/ her from causing possible harm to the body by thwarting the person's plans. The Self is safeguarding the body in some ways the person may not be aware of.

Parents are our primary protectors when we are young, who later become internalized in us. They continue to hold a dominant position within our minds. There are many things we would like to have or want to do or be, but if it doesn't align with the intention of the Self, it will prevent the goal from being achieved. You may choose a goal that is in your best interests today, but according to the Self, it will cause you harm and endanger your well-being. It will then prevent you from achieving that goal. It's like when you want to quit your current job to pursue your dream career, the Self doesn't allow you to do it. It places security above everything else.

Neel visited my clinic because he had been coughing excessively while making his business presentations. He was diagnosed with MDR Tuberculosis (TB) five months ago and was currently on two months' sick leave. In the first two months after the diagnosis of TB, medicines did not make any improvements to his health. Doctors and his family were concerned about the deterioration of Neel's health, as he was continuously losing weight and had a poor appetite.

He revealed that there were compatibility issues with his wife and that they were always fighting. She would argue and abuse him even when he was unwell with TB. In one of these arguments, he fainted, collapsed, and had to be rushed to the hospital to be put on oxygen support. Since then, the two have started living separately and his health has significantly improved.

Neel was a Wanted Child, living with his parents, and had to live up to their expectations. The responsibilities of the family were on his shoulders. His wife and mother were of the unwanted personality type, always at loggerheads with each other. There was always a tug-of-war between the two ladies, with Neel as the rope being pulled on either side. Their conflict had been going on for many years. He said, "He felt suffocated every time he came home. They would sometimes disturb him even while he was at work."

He had to do a weekly presentation to their customers about the progress made on various projects. A year ago, in one of these meetings, a member of the senior management of the client's firm blamed him and his team for misrepresentation of facts. The manager humiliated and embarrassed him in front of his team. Neel was not at fault, but tactfully, tables were turned against him. Since then, he started coughing before giving a presentation.

All this while he enjoyed going to work, but since that event, Neel felt trapped at the workplace. Besides, he was already feeling suffocated at home. He was feeling choked on all sides and didn't know how to resolve his issues.

While growing up, Neel was influenced and controlled by his mother. Since marriage, his wife also started pressuring him. He was trying to do a balancing act but was sandwiched between the personalities of the two women in his life. It was a Self-sabotage situation where his system had no answers and was stuck in an endless loop of negativity. Something similar was also happening in the workplace. He was in a catch-twenty-two situation on all sides. Neel was helpless, having no resolution to his problems which also affected his health. His mother is the core ingredient of his Self. Later it was his wife and, subsequently, his manager who also became part of the Self — the Self that sabotaged his progress in his personal relationships, his job, and also his health.

In another case of Self-sabotage, Ravina, a lady in her late twenties, made a distress call to me early one morning from her building terrace. Her six-month-old relationship had fallen apart. She said she felt like committing suicide.

Ravina was an Unwanted Child. To seek sympathy from her boyfriend, she revealed to him some of the family's dark secrets. To impress and seek approval from him, she also sent some nude pictures of herself. Now her boyfriend had rejected her. He also sent her an abusive and nasty text message in connection with her family's secrets and her character. One of the inborn limitations of Unwanted Children is that they cannot take rejection. Ravina has been rejected, and he was throwing filth back at her. She is feeling trapped because she cannot even express what she did to her parents. This is a catch-twenty-two because she can't see any hope of solving it. Thus, she wants to end her life. Her boyfriend plays the role of the Self and corners her, Self-sabotaging the relationship.

Both Neel and Ravina were overwhelmed by the pressure of their respective Self. Self-sabotage can occur in any area of your life. It can happen in your relationships, business, health, sports pursuits, etc.

16

THE SELF "TALKS"

We have all heard words such as "self-talk," "positive self-talk," "negative self-talk," or the like. Now the question we could ask is "who is talking to whom?" If you consider the word "self-talk," it implies that the Self is talking. But it is not clear to who it is communicating. One aspect is, however, quite clear: "self-talk" is our internal dialogue, and it emanates from the Self. Positivity and negativity will depend on our core Self.

Tushar complained that he has a critical voice within him that drives him nuts. He told me he wanted to get rid of this irritating inner dialogue. I asked him to close his eyes and remember a time when this dialogue was at its peak. Then I told him to focus on and listen to it. What is this critical voice saying that he doesn't like hearing? Tushar said the voice was telling him how he has been a good-for-nothing man, not up to the mark, not doing anything right, etc. I suggested he close his eyes and listen more intently to the voice. How does it sound? What is its tone, tempo, pitch, and volume? On paying attention to it, Tushar replied that the volume was too high, the tempo fast, and that he didn't like listening to either the tone or the pitch at all.

Asking him to remain focused on this voice, I took Tushar back into his life when he was young. "Could you remember whose voice it resembled?" I asked him. His instant reply was that it was his mother's voice. She was always critical of him when he was a young child and still is even today. He feels like running away from her, but she is old with no one to look after her.

Tushar was in his forties and a Wanted Child. He was married but had separated from his wife and started to live with his mother. When Tushar regressed to earlier times, he recalled more about the critical voice inside him. He remembered just how his mother would scream at and belittle him for not getting good grades or on his performance in other activities. All of us have such voices within us that we carry for the rest of our lives.

For any dialogue to occur, there must be two or more people. Without this prerequisite, a dialogue is just not possible. The same is true for the one that is going on inside our heads. There is an invisible person or several imaginary people with whom we are communicating internally. The interactions happen so swiftly and frequently that we get entangled in the dialogue, making it challenging to identify just who we are talking to. When it happens in our minds, it looks as if everything is real, going on back and forth in an endless loop. But this can end up making us feel fatigued or restlessly keep us awake at night. When we are busy, maybe the voice subsides, but it keeps running in the background, exhausting us, like a mobile app that's running depletes a phone's battery. Often, certain triggers, which could be a stored memory or an external event, can activate this inner voice.

In Tushar's case, it was mainly his mother's voice that he was constantly interacting with inside his head. Even though she was not at the clinic with Tushar, she exists in the form of Tushar's Self and follows him everywhere. Some triggers in Tushar's life may affect him from time to time. When he hears someone speak in the same way as his mother or with a similar pitch, tempo, or tone, it will involuntarily start his internal dialogue and arouse the same emotions. He may develop an aversion towards the person speaking at that moment and not know why. It could be his spouse, boss, or another person who triggers this voice. In a fraction of a second, he may cease to be a grown-up adult and regress to a little child who is being criticized by his mother. Tushar may become reactive in the current situation, only realizing later that it was not required.

The internal dialogue inside your head is your verbal communication with the Self, which represents your parents or the guidance you have received. The Self "talks" to us and what we respond to are our memories. Communication is a way in which our Self (inner parents) keep us safe in their own way. The voice of the Self gets activated mainly on certain issues you are having difficulty resolving. It can remind you that you need to take action for your safety, but at times you feel lost or helpless because you are confused. In the present time, you know you don't have to do what your Self demands. So, an internal tug of war goes on within you. People of all three Survival Mechanism categories have internal dialogues and they try to cope with them differently.

Conflict Within the Self

Other than the core of a person's Self — the parents — there exist many different people in the expanded circle. Those people could have diametrically opposed views on matters. Initially, it may be one's parents who have opposing views which may leave a person perplexed in life. At times, a small child may have seen his/ her parents quarrel or get abusive with each other, even physically. The child feels vulnerable in such a situation and may end up aligning with one parent. Such memories could still haunt the child once s/he grows up to be an adult.

If a child sees the father hit the mother, it makes him/her have a soft corner for the mother. The child's mother may have presented a story to him/her, and the latter absorbed it as the whole and complete truth, as it came from a credible source. In this case, the child starts to look at the father as an abuser. All such memories become part of the child's Self. As s/he doesn't have awareness at a young age about issues between the parents, the child starts to fight the mother's battle, and the father becomes the opponent. But it is not an easy position for the child to be in.

Zeena, whose example was given earlier in the book, was influenced by both her mother and her aunt. She did not arrive at her own independent conclusions that made her hate her father but did so under her mother's influence. As children, we can't comprehend the disputes and misunderstandings of our parents. But we draw certain conclusions, and they remain with us as unfinished business. When I hear my clients tell me their fathers are shouting and beating their mothers, I recognize the issue is at the level of their Self, where the person feels very insecure. Even if such a child faces physical abuse, s/he may refrain from sharing it with her mother, knowing that the mother is weak and doesn't want to burden her any further.

All such experiences add up to the child's inner voice and continue to affect him/her even in adulthood. Most issues when we were children were beyond our comprehension and we lacked an idea of the whole picture. So, as we grow up, memories never get updated, and issues remain unresolved. What makes it more difficult is that those memories keep showing up in our minds at a swift pace. One of the valuable tips in such times is to SLOW DOWN. One of the ways in which a hypnotherapist can help a client is to help him/her SLOW DOWN. This allows the individual to get fresh insights and solutions to unresolved issues.

17

GOVERNING OUR DECISIONS AND DESTINY

Mina once told me, "I am tired of living in this marriage. I've waited for sixteen years and, finally, my daughter is completing her education. I want to separate from my husband. I've made up my mind." Although Mina had had a love marriage (marriages can also be arranged in India), she later came to realize that she had been living with a narcissistic husband. With all the explanations she gave me, it looked like she should have separated a long time ago. She also said, "I hate myself for being such a stupid, dumb fool, having prolonged my relationship for so long."

From how Mina had described her marriage, anyone might agree that she was right in making her decision to separate from her husband. Also, it seems like she is the one making the decision. But the question we can ask is, was Mina making her decision? The answer is an emphatic NO.

Mina has become tired and exhausted from pleasing her husband. In all these years of marriage, no amount of pleasing him has given her joy. Instead, it has gradually taken her frustration level to its maximum. At last, she is willing to take a bold decision to separate. But is she really making a choice here? Again, the answer is no. There is no choice when there are only two choices to choose from. It's either this or that, yes or no, etc. Mina is arriving at this decision out of many years of frustration and helplessness. The decision does not have any direction, and it's an emotional decision. Let's look at this point further.

Yes and No is NOT a Choice

Say you would like to have chocolate ice cream and your friend offered you the vanilla flavor. You can accept the offer by saying "yes" or reject it by saying "no." There could be a variety of ice cream flavors, but your friend is not giving you a choice. You feel compelled to eat what is offered or you simply decline it.

When one makes a decision that is made from choice, there is a direction. YES or NO means someone else has made a choice, and you have to approve and give your consent. It also implies a conclusion is arrived at by another person, and you are giving permission to go ahead or not.

Preeti once told me, "I have dedicated twelve years of my life to my organization and last week, my boss got unreasonably angry with me for no fault of mine." Preeti became emotionally charged and wanted to quit a well-paying job because of a misunderstanding with her boss. According to Preeti, her boss was quite understanding, but his wife sometimes provoked him. This decision comes under a YES or NO category. Preeti is making an emotional decision; secondly, there is no direction because there is no second job offer that she has in her hand. It was not even her decision, as it was her boss's wife who had indirectly compelled her into making that decision. When Preeti understood what she was doing, she said she would like to make her own decision instead of being influenced by others.

Our Self often does not offer a choice but an elusive option of YES or NO. We assume it's a choice, and accordingly, we give our consent. Mina was in the same dilemma.

Further in the session, Mina learned that her husband resembles her mother, who has the same survival traits. Mina also learned that she had all the characteristics of a Partly Wanted Child. All this while, she experienced rejection from her husband in the same way that she did from her mother, both at the time of her birth and while growing up.

While we grow up, our parents make all the decisions that affect us; they know what's best for us and our well-being. If we are safe and alive, it's because of their efforts and intentions to protect us. The fact that they are our protectors becomes an embedded belief in us. In other words, we perceive them as our bodyguards. Even when we grow older, this decision-making process continues in our personal life. In our need to survive, our Self, which takes over from our parents, becomes the one we unconsciously pay more heed to. We try to go with the flow of things, even if we are uncomfortable in the process.

It's difficult for us to do things differently because we have a Survival Mechanism operating in us, making us programmed to survive. It compels us to comply with the Self for the sake of our own safety and protection. As these patterns have conditioned us over the years, we feel imprisoned by them and live our lives through them, believing that's the way life is. Both the systems — the Survival Mechanism and the Self — have the same aim of protecting us. But in the process of protecting us, they inhibit our decision-making. We cannot detect this as it has been this way since our birth. Many of our personal decisions need the approval of our core Self and, at times, the expanded Self as well. It is crucial for our survival, even though we may be grown-up adults. Mina's Survival Mechanism had compelled her to please her husband, who unconsciously represents her mother. Mina's mother makes up the core of her Self.

Self also Controls the Direction of Our Life — Our Destiny

A client who is an Unwanted Child told me, "While growing up, I was never heard. But when I grew older, I realized I also had a voice. The voice guides me."

I asked her, "Who is making decisions — you or the voice?"

She replied that the voice helped her to make decisions.

My following question was, "If your voice is helping you make decisions, then who is governing your life? Who is controlling your destiny?"

The answer she gave was, "The voice."

The fate of every child — whether allowed to be born or aborted — depends on his/ her parents. For a child who is born, safety and survival are in the hands of parents until such time when a child is competent enough to look after his/her body. As you have read above, parents make decisions for us, and our internal system gets tuned to that process. As we grow older, we rebel and want to make our own decisions. However, our Self is still operating in us and will try to compel us to follow its dictates.

All three SOMes have their different internal programs and so decision-making through them will be unique and distinct. And so, the direction of a person's life will also be different. But certainly, the Self will play out its role and influence our destiny without our awareness. We call that process self-sabotage.

The survival process is intriguing and complex, quite like a maze. You will understand how our Self governs our decision-making and destiny better when we come to Section III, where every Survival Mechanism category is explained individually.

18

AN INVISIBLE GUN POINTING AT YOU

There comes a time when we want to take charge of our life in every way, whether it is to make new choices or to live differently. However, because we don't understand how the Self operates within us, we experience a major hurdle. We want our Self to adhere to our demands, new ways of thinking, or aspirations. But it will continue to perform its primary function of protecting us against perceived harm.

When we are growing up, we take instructions from our parents that become almost like commands inside our heads. The Self becomes like our proxy parent. Now, as adults, we want to reverse the roles and control the Self. That's like the creation controlling its creator, which is not feasible as it goes against the laws of nature.

We often revolt against our creators (our parents) during our teenage years when we want to express ourselves and break free from their shackles. Not visible to us, our Self has a hold over us. As parents have ownership rights over us, the grip of the Self is an unconscious undercurrent that exerts those rights. We can't tell when it will take over our system, so willpower is ineffective against it.

Willpower is the ability to control yourself with strong determination, which allows you to do something difficult. It could be quitting smoking, losing weight, giving up the urge to watch porn, being free from addiction, or other challenging things. According to my understanding of willpower, as a person using your body and thinking, you would like to challenge the Self. The body itself is someone else's creation (refer back to the chapter on ownership rights) and under the control of the Self. It will do everything within its means to protect its property.

What you are trying to control is invisible and imaginary. The Self does not get subordinated through your willpower and is too powerful to be bulldozed. It has its own independent mechanism by which it controls you. For some time, it may seem that you are winning against the Self by using your willpower. But after a while, things will boomerang to where you were in the beginning or to possibly a worse position. Self-sabotage can reverse all the work you have done to get you somewhere. Logic and reason are also not capable of subduing the Self. If one's intended goal is in alignment with the goal of your Self — to keep you safe — then one is allowed to accomplish it. But if it may endanger you, then the Self will prohibit it and one can't just ignore or fight it off. This is not to discourage a person but to point out where not to waste effort.

Vani, a lady in her twenties, found the love of her life and wanted to settle down with him. She had been pursuing this new man for the past six months. She had had her share of broken relationships and flings in the past. When the current courtship was going on, she met her old boyfriend at a party and had sex with him. Vani disclosed to her current boyfriend that she had met her ex but never told him the whole truth. She was too scared that their future would fall apart. Although she may have gotten away with it, the memory of her actions was haunting her. What if her current boyfriend got to know the truth? This is a catch-twenty-two or a Self-sabotage. Whether she speaks the truth or conceals it, she feels trapped. The current boyfriend replaces the core Self and reminds her of her wrongdoing. She couldn't ignore her feelings of guilt and fear. Controlling the Self was too difficult.

You Can NOT Defeat the Self

When the child's Self gets created, it is the parents who occupy the core of it and, therefore, indirectly govern it. As the child depends on them for protection, the domain of the child's Self belongs to the co-creators.

The dominance of one's Self continues even into adulthood. There are cases where people have killed their parents out of rage. One may destroy their parents' physical bodies, but the Self continues within the person. It is a powerful and invincible entity to try to challenge or conquer. Defeating one's Self will be like trying to defeat an army battalion of 1000 soldiers single-handedly and, still, the Self will prevail. To make matters more difficult, the Self is invisible. As mentioned earlier, it would be impossible for Tom to fight an imaginary Tim. In that sense, as long as a person is alive, his/her Self is indestructible and continues to rule over the person. If one persists in fighting against the Self, one can feel totally overwhelmed.

The core intention of your Self is to protect you and keep you safe. The moment you start fighting it, the Self does what it knows best. Rather than trying to dominate it, you will need to find and understand its positive intention. There are tools available in Neuro-Linguistic Programming (NLP) that can defuse the conflict with the Self. One can use the six-step Reframing concept in NLP at such times.

19

DEMANDS HONOR - FULFILL EXPECTATIONS

Just like a ship without a rudder reaches nowhere, a child without proper guidance would be lost. The protection and safety of the child are among the primary aims of parents, but other than that, giving direction to the child is also important. It is parents who channel the energy of a child into learning and different activities.

They may begin to teach children small tasks, like washing their hands before and after meals, rinsing their plates, or picking up their toys. The child could be engaged through activities or games, and s/he looks forward to that time with one of the parents. Beginning with such playful actions, children learn to take guidance from their parents. Every new activity becomes play for a child who loves to explore curiously. Some of them — riding a bicycle or climbing a jungle gym — may require the supervision of parents as safety becomes important. A parent can give advice that helps the child perform better or avoid painful injuries. It is meant for the well-being of the child. Sometimes direction is taken by children through copying parents and others or by fulfilling their demands.

The inputs that parents give as direction to the child become part of the child's Self and continue as the adult's internal guidance later. The Self becomes the driving force in our lives as we grow older, affecting our choices and decisions we make on how to live.

The Self Demands We Fulfill Expectations

As parents give guidance, they also want children to follow it, to live up to their expectations. All expectations are essentially goals set by others. They represent the desires of others that we fulfill to get their approval. Getting approval gives us a sense of assurance and makes us feel accepted. That ensures our survival is intact.

In the early years, parents place small expectations on us. We need to go to bed on time, wake up on time, come back from play early or before sunset, and aim for good grades at school. However, expectations of various kinds keep mounting on us as we continue to grow. In addition to parents, we take on the expectations of our school and our teachers, who want us to adhere to some rules and achieve certain learning outcomes, against which we are measured. A similar trend continues when we go to college and then the workplace. A person's Self takes in numerous and different expectations as s/he moves from one phase of life to the next, or one system to another — from the family to the education system to the workplace and beyond.

Expectations can sometimes be unreasonable and overwhelm a person. Meera, a grade three student, achieved a score of ninety-eight out of one hundred marks in her school arithmetic exam. However, her father, who was a mathematics teacher, wasn't satisfied. He caned her as a punishment for the loss of those two marks that could have gotten her score to one hundred. Meera was doing her best to meet the goals of others and became afraid of falling short. The same fear started to trouble her at her workplace when she became an adult. What would be the consequences if she fails? Such a fearful thought is part of Meera's Self and gets triggered each time she faces the prospect of falling short of others' expectations.

Another client of mine, Adrian, built a bigger house for his parents in his village, while he himself stayed in a poor-quality rented room, sharing it with a roommate. Adrian was already in debt but took on another loan at a higher interest rate to build his parents' house. It was vital for him to always meet their expectations, even if he was not asked to.

Demands Increase with Competency

As a child becomes more competent, not only do expectations go up but they grow exponentially. As a tiny infant, a child takes in the mother's milk, after which cow's milk is given to him/her. When the child can consume and digest solid foods, s/he is fed those. Then s/he is gradually expected to eat a large variety of nutrients so that the mother feels at ease about the child's nutrition and growth. The curriculum a child is expected to study at school becomes wider and more challenging as s/he goes from one grade to the next. Doing small chores at home, or at least independently tidying one's room, may also become another expectation. The child is encouraged (expected) to pick up a sport or an extracurricular activity after school. If the development of the child is slow in any area, then it can be a cause for worry.

Own Goals Versus Expectations

A child's own intrinsic desires and parents' expectations are two different types of goals. When a child desires to learn to walk and thus attempts to stand up and totter on two legs, it is the child who wants to reach a goal. On the other hand, when a parent expects the child to achieve good grades at school, it is not the child's own goal chosen freely but a subtle demand from the parent. Every child is expected to rise to meet challenges placed on him/her by family and then school. So, meeting expectations becomes part of the child's survival mechanism or, in simpler words, a way of ensuring s/he is accepted (hence survives) in his/her environment.

This pattern is not so different in adults. John once made a list of all his personal goals and the things others demanded he fulfills, whether they were explicitly stated or understood. So, to his own list, he added his wife's goals and those of his mother. Initially, John was happy that he was achieving all his dreams. He maintained a personal planner and tick-marked all goals he had met. But a few months later, John noticed that the list of demands every month only kept getting longer. And it did not have to do with his personal desires. His wife and mother would keep adding more to his list. It compelled him to earn more to provide what they had asked. John observed that he was keeping pace with their growing needs and unnecessarily adding stress to his life. But he did all of it to please his wife and mother. John could now understand how his Self had trapped him.

There are many of us who are achieving our dreams, not realizing that they are actually the expectations of others. We pay the price with our ill health or stress. If we fail to achieve the demands the Self places, we are dissatisfied with our performance — be it as a good employee, parent, spouse, son, or daughter. We then experience disappointment and negative emotions such as guilt, shame, or anger. In turn, these affect us mentally and physically, which is how our Self puts us in a catch-twenty-two situation. When we don't do as expected, we face negative emotions, and when we act out of the pressures imposed by the Self, we experience fatigue or stress.

20

CREATOR AS WELL AS DESTROYER

Our creators could even be no more, but they continue to live within us in the form of a Self. Though it may sound like a mystical idea, it is true. Our existence is null and void without them. But if parents can create a child, they can also bring about the downfall or end of the child. While parents, of course, do not intend to destroy their own creation, later in life, the mechanism of the Self can impact you. It is designed to protect a person, but it can potentially overwhelm them physically or mentally. The process is a survival trap so subtle that it goes unnoticed.

I had a session with Raj, a food entrepreneur who has started a restaurant that also delivers meals to homes and offices. He had previously started a business that incurred a loss of Rs.70 lacs (approximately $100,000). The new venture was started with a family loan but was also generating a loss. There was no doubting Raj's potential as an entrepreneur or his ability to work hard, but insecurities had surfaced within him. Fears were emanating from his Self. Since childhood, Raj's father never believed in him. Moreover, Raj was experiencing guilt due to indebtedness toward his father, who he could not repay. His guilt arose because he was squandering his father's hard-earned money.

I gave Raj the analogy of a man trying to swim to the shore with a seventy-kilo invisible weight tied to his waist, pulling him downwards toward the bottom of the sea. With this unseen burden, the man was making no headway in any direction but simply struggling to stay afloat and alive. How far could he survive with the huge weight that was causing him to sink? Raj had been going around in circles and was lately feeling anxious and depressed. His body and mind were unable to withstand the obligation of his father's loan. Besides, the quantum of indebtedness kept increasing every month. There may come a time when it will surely pull him down and drown him. Such is the weight on his own system - his Self. In Raj's case, his creator did not believe in him, and the psychological burden of that affected his performance in his business.

Every child tries to fulfill their parents' expectations to ensure that s/he survives. S/he must please them by meeting their dreams or expectations to feel protected. And failing to do so will unconsciously create uncertainty that is directly connected to one's survival. This fear exists more as an undercurrent if one fails to live up to parent's expectations. Most people are trying to fulfill a certain dream to feel accepted. This acceptance is directly connected to being accepted by one's parents. It's an unconscious process of behaving in a way or doing certain things that agree with our parents' ways.

The Effect of Harmful Words or Actions

In some cultures, people cursing others can be considered a bad omen. But what about the curse of the creator? I have heard a mother, out of anger, cruelly tell her son Nik, "It would have been much better if you had died the day you were born!" Does this message impact Nik when he grows older? Yes, it certainly does and becomes a part of the frightened child's psyche. He avoids the impact of the curse — avoiding death — by behaving the way his mother demands. Nik's Self plays the role of his mother, pushing the child (later the adult) to do everything the way it would please her. In this way, Nik's mother's curse leads to Self-sabotage taking place in his life.

Sometimes parents behave in ways without knowing why. In one case, a father's Self-hatred got pushed onto his daughter, Gauri, even though she was wanted by both her parents and innocent. Once, she dropped a container carrying warm rice. Her father told his relative that he didn't know why she was born into their family, as she was such a "useless girl." Gauri recalled her father bathing her when she was a three-year-old. He would use a kitchen utensil scrubber to clean her. Once, he used so much force that he scrubbed off her skin, making her bleed.

Although Gauri had all the traits of a Wanted Child, she questioned, "How can I be a Wanted Child when my father hated me all my life?" In the session, Gauri realized that her father looked exactly like her. He did not like his own looks and features. Every time he saw her, something triggered within him and passed on his Self-loathing to her. As a child, Gauri tried to comply with whatever her father told her. As an adult living with her husband, she does not want to communicate with her parent, remembering her experiences.

We may not all bear the brunt of severe words or actions, as Nik or Gauri did, nor the lack of belief from our parents as Raj did. However, we, too, experience the weight of our Self, which pushes us to strive hard in a particular way. In this way of living, we can literally end up feeling overwhelmed by poor physical or mental health.

21

SELF FEEDS ON THE PAST

The map is NOT the territory. This is one of the foremost presuppositions of Neuro-Linguistic Programming (NLP). Many maps are presented to us as children for the sake of our own protection, even when we are too young to decipher them. Some of them are valid and useful because they help us survive when we are young. Others lose their validity when we grow older as they restrict our growth. As we become adults, we find it difficult to challenge these maps because they have come from trustworthy sources who have protected us since birth. Our logic is a blunt tool against the emotional triggers we experience because of the past.

It was late in the morning. I was in my forties, sitting in the gallery of my family home, conversing with my father, who was in his eighties. Suddenly, he says, "Do you remember what you did?" Slowly, he raises his right arm and points to the adjacent plot of land. I became alert at that moment but remained calm, as I knew what was coming. He said, "You remember ... you killed all my jackfruit saplings."

My father was a farmer and the above incident, a bitter memory for both of us, happened when I was ten years old. He instructed me to add salt to his jackfruit saplings to control the onset of weeds but forgot to tell me about the right quantities to use. As a result, the jackfruit saplings perished. My father made an error in judgment but blamed me for what happened.

Since I was a practicing hypnotherapist when we had this conversation, I empathized emotionally with what my father may have gone through. He had seen all his painstaking efforts of growing jackfruit saplings come to naught due to his own misjudgment and poor communication. There was no way he could have revived them. He was in his eighties and still feeling the pain of the loss of his saplings, but he blamed me, making me feel miserable. My father made it a point to remind me of that memory many times during my growing-up years.

My father was my core Self. We are sometimes forced to experience certain emotions and in a few seconds, we regress to a time in the past and begin to feel them again. It is not possible to prevent our memories from being triggered by others. At present, it could be a spouse or someone else who may touch a sensitive nerve in us. In an instant, you could be lost and no longer in the present, operating out of memory.

This happened to Amol too, who narrated an incident to me that occurred with his wife. He was on an important business call at home and kept his wet towel on the sofa. That upset his wife so much that she called him "silly, stupid, and irresponsible." Toward the end of their exchange, she said, "You are a cuckoo." It is another way of saying he was silly or half-mad. Amol had had enough. Hearing his wife use that word greatly upset him, but he couldn't understand why. I anchored the trigger and regressed Amol into his past. Amol's father belittled him as a little boy by calling him a "sissy" in front of other children. Even though Amol is a successful entrepreneur today, whenever someone looks down on him patronizingly, it makes him furious. Words are powerful hypnotic tools that can take a person back to the past.

Most of our emotions and emotional triggers come from our Self. The core of the Self contains our past and who we are today also comes from that Self. Any person in your life can irritate you by touching your sensitive spot. Within a few seconds, you are no longer in the present but responding to an associated event that occurred in the past. In my case, my father unintentionally pressed my trigger point, and since then, I have distanced myself from him. I could not understand the emotional pain he had gone through when he saw his saplings die, nor did he know what really went wrong on that fateful day. In truth, as a ten-year-old boy, I had not done anything intentionally to kill his jackfruit saplings. But the emotional trauma from that incident, for both of us, continued to affect our relations many years into the future.

Self Enforces History on Us

Other than through personal experiences, the past becomes a part of our Self through the history we are taught. History by itself is the past told in the present. When we learn it, we tend to believe it's true. However, no person can vouch that all of history presented to us is true. If ten people were to experience even an ordinary event, perhaps all ten would narrate it differently. We can say there is some amount of truth in history but also much distortion on account of omission, personal perspective, or bias.

Each country has its history. But so does each culture, community, region, ethnic race, and even family. History is enforced onto children through a process of learning, as people want them to know the past. Families want the history of their lineage to be remembered. Going back to the example of Prince Wan earlier, he believed the story told to him about his family's history. He had no personal enmity against the neighboring king, but his parents unconsciously influenced his outlook through their narrative. The war had happened when Wan was not born, and he was not the cause of it. But Wan ended up becoming a part of his family's history too.

History is useful when we are willing to learn from it. Only when people learn about The Holocaust and other genocides that took place can they make sure such events do not repeat. But if history is used to instill feelings of pride in winning wars, conquering other lands, ensuring dominance, or settling our forefathers' scores, then there is no true positive outcome. This becomes more significant when we consider that there are people like Wan who operate from their Survival Mechanism. They do things to prove they are worthy and join someone else's war or, more broadly, another's goal in life.

Of course, not all stories from history relate to war or oppression. Some can be about harmless beliefs, which nevertheless persist for some time. One belief that made its rounds in India was, "Don't throw dirt out at night." Many households in smaller towns and villages did not have sufficient electrification years ago. As a result, people used to sweep the floor with a broom and gather dirt in one corner. It wasn't thrown out until the next day, when it would be scanned for any valuables, such as gold earrings or ornaments. Practicing such a belief today would be absurd; however, people follow many other outdated beliefs without checking if they are still relevant. Parents pass on a mindset that belongs to the past and bring up their children with ideas that may not hold relevance in today's world. The past remains alive in a person's Self in this way and influences him/her.

Evolution of the Self

The Self has been evolving for thousands or maybe millions of years. Our ancestors who were Homo sapiens, had physical features that were different from what we are today. But we are part of them, and they are part of us. Our basic structure comes from them. Cars and other vehicles running on wheels today represent the evolution of the wheel over thousands of years.

The process of evolution was progressive many years ago and has grown exponentially in the current times due to the industrial revolution, computers, and technological advancements. It is as if we are running a race, and everyone wants to win. Some do it with all fairness, while others are willing to achieve it through unfair means. But we live with the goal that we have got to get rich. Insecurities have reached another level, and its stress is slowly killing us.

Without interruption, many things are dumped from one generation onto the next, unknowingly in the form of beliefs, rules, laws, and concepts. We give so much importance to them that they become useless garbage clogging our day-to-day living. The undercurrent that makes us carry forward or not question certain fallacies is our fear that others won't accept us. We as humans crave ACCEPTANCE and, at any cost, avoid REJECTION. We are caught in this whirlpool of thinking, making our life stressful and challenging to live. Fear is the base of all emotions, which compels us to behave in a specific way. And this fear is driven mainly by our Self.

Below is a diagram that shows a chain of how different generations are part of our making. It was your parents who created you, but you couldn't have been born unless your grandparents gave your parents birth. This chain goes back into the past, for thousands and thousands of years, from which multiple beliefs and ideas come. The Indian caste system was invented thousands of years ago but was enforced on every subsequent generation born after that. It is still prevalent throughout the country. There are different sections of people reaping the benefit, while some still get exploited.

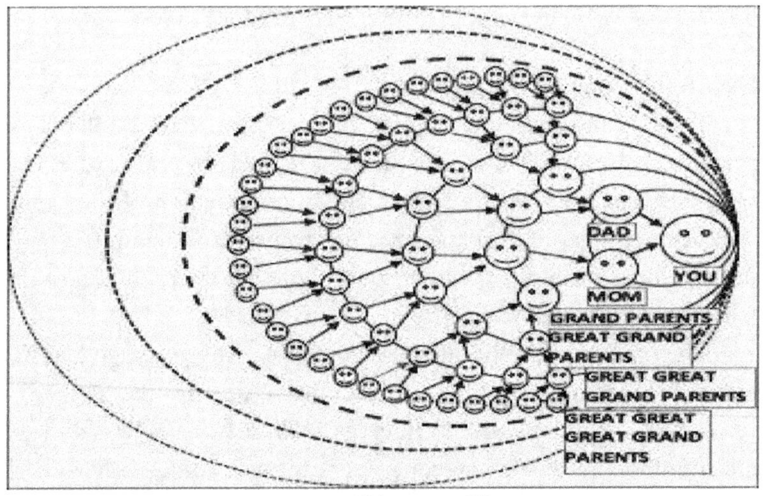

Diagram 13

Our Self is made up of history. In fact, we unknowingly live the past that gets handed down to the present and the future. As we are part of evolution, our ancestors continue to be part of us. They also become a part of the human being's Self. While certain things change or evolve, much remains connected to the past.

22

EXERCISES POWER AND AUTHORITY

Once, a young lady doctor named Aarti came to see me for hypnotherapy. She had finished her medical studies and needed to practice at a hospital. Aarti wanted help because she feared holding a syringe and injecting medicine into her patients. In reality, Aarti never wanted to be a medical doctor, but her mother had compelled her to choose the profession. She had been pleasing her mother, her primary Self, as her parents got separated when she was young. Another lady, Neetu, worked as an air hostess, but she was also a qualified dentist. Neetu said that her father had forced her to become a dentist, but what she really wanted to do was travel the world.

In the case of Aarti and Neetu, it's not just that their respective mother and father are part of their core Self. The parent represents a genuine source of authority and power to the person, which becomes part of the individual's Self that controls her.

Along with a parent's ownership rights over a child comes the idea that they have legitimate authority over them. This primary belief runs within our system, through the Self. As we grow older, a power struggle exists between our Self and us (more specifically, our Survival Mechanism).

Size, Strength, and Power Dynamics

Since our birth, we have sensed, seen, felt, and heard that our parents are much bigger than us in size. They were strong enough to carry us effortlessly, protect us against danger, and take care of us when we hurt ourselves. This sends an unconscious signal to us that they are powerful. As a child, you know that they could harm you if they chose to and that you are no match for their strength. On this basis, certain beliefs about power are formed that remain with us for the rest of our lives.

When you go to school, you discover that some children who are bullies are taller and stronger than you. You cannot challenge them, given their height and weight advantage. In cultures such as India, you are also trained to respect elders, which is a norm one must follow later in life too. All these subtle beliefs become part of our Self and influence our future decisions.

Parental control manifests in different ways, depending on the age of the child. When Dev was young, a wide-eyed stare from his mother could sufficiently signal disapproval. If simple forms of communication didn't have an effect on him, she may lose her temper, shout at, or even slap or spank him. As Dev grew into a teenager, if he went astray, he was deprived of pocket money, or his mother refused to speak to him for some time. Criticism is another useful tool for control. Dev would be told off for his wrongdoings and faults, which made him feel guilty and kept him in check. When the usual methods of control failed, Dev's mother occasionally complained about him to his father. Both parents would then sit him down and have a "talk." The mere hint that his father would like to "have a talk" with him would make Dev palpitate with discomfort.

In childhood, we know that parents have the power to approve and disapprove of what we do. After all, they decide how our desires are to be fulfilled regarding food, clothing, toys, entertainment, and social life. Unconsciously, we acknowledge that *they* are in charge of our life. Another word that is often used as a form of control is discipline, which is a form of training that produces obedience or Self-control in an individual. Discipline means we are required to toe the line and follow the rules established by another person. If we don't, punishment can ensue.

In previous chapters, many examples have been given of the way parents, teachers, elders, and other authorities discipline a child. It's mostly done in good faith, but that need not be true at all times. Rahul's mother taught him arithmetic at home. While he felt he did his sums right, his mother still punished him saying they were wrong. The next day, Rahul's school teacher remarked on Rahul's sums, saying his work was "very good." Rahul's mother, however, never apologized to him for wrongfully punishing him.

All this creates internal beliefs regarding authority and power, which become part of our Self. We, with our Survival Mechanism, try to cope with it. We mostly do this by pleasing or giving in to authority figures as our survival in a system depends on them. Authority figures appear enormous and powerful. As we grow older, we might rebel. When we become teenagers, our attitudes and beliefs towards our parents change because we know we can match them in physical strength. All this while, they towered over us but now we believe we can take them on, as we are taller and stronger now. We are also more capable of reasoning and questioning. So, we start to defend our being by standing up to our parents.

Our parents may not tower over us when we grow up to be adults, but our Self (inner parents) becomes an internal source of authority for us when we grow up. Our response to authority and power today reflects how we dealt with them as a child, which was to comply or revolt. At times we helplessly gave in, while at other times we got angry and showed that we were strong enough to take on the Self. This tussle against authority goes on for the rest of our lives. Because, in essence, we want to live free from the clutches of power and control. As our Self contains authority figures such as parents, teachers, and other elders, it becomes about a struggle against the Self.

23

UNFOLDING OF THE EGO

Anyone reading this book would have heard the word "ego" often. At times I have wondered what the term really means. In Latin, the word Ego means "I." Since we use this word so frequently, it would be important to understand it more clearly.

The word Ego has surfaced many times in my sessions. I have asked my clients what they meant by it. They tried to explain it to me the way they understood it. But they weren't clear, and I too, was grappling to understand its broad construct. Sigmund Freud coined the word Ego in his work long ago, and it has been very much used in psychology. Does it have any significance in our lives today? When we casually use it in our communication, what do we mean by it? Or has it just become such a part of our general vocabulary that we don't give much thought to it anymore? Let's dive deeper and try to understand its significance.

I went through some definitions of Ego presented by Sigmund Freud, a few well-known figures in psychology and the dictionary meaning of the word. According to psychoanalysis, the meaning ego is "the part of the mind that mediates between the conscious and the unconscious and is responsible for reality testing and a sense of personal identity" (Source: Oxford languages). According to Merriam-Webster dictionary, "ego" means the Self, especially as contrasted with another self or the world.

While there are many other meanings and definitions which I don't want to go into here, I would like to explore the word "ego" in my own way. Below are statements in everyday conversation where we use this word:

- ❖ His ego is too strong.
- ❖ His ego got hurt.

- ❖ I don't know how to deal with my ego.
- ❖ Anything I say affects her ego.
- ❖ She is an ego-centric person.
- ❖ He has a big ego.
- ❖ Inflated ego.
- ❖ She is on an ego trip.
- ❖ He is full of ego (full of himself).
- ❖ His job did boost his ego.
- ❖ Losing the match did dent his ego.
- ❖ She likes being friends with those who flatter her ego.

Let's take one of the above sentences and break it down.

He has a big ego.

In the above sentence, there is a subject "He" and a predicate "has a big ego." The verb "has" connects the pronoun and a subjective noun "ego," and in between, there is a quantifier "big." When I ask my clients further questions on how they know about the ego or how they can measure it, they usually describe it based on someone's behavior.

Let's take the above sentence and consider statements that could be similar. We can substitute "ego" with other nouns:

- ❖ He has a big house.
- ❖ He has a big car.
- ❖ He has a big coat.
- ❖ He has a big brother to protect him, whose name is Tony.
- ❖ He has a big brother – Tony.
- ❖ He has Tony.

We can take the sentence from above.

He has Tony.

It implies that there is a male who has a big brother whose name is Tony. Tony is older than him or is simply bigger in size and height and is capable of protecting him from possible harm.

All the above — house, car, coat, Tony — can be touched. When you say you have a big ego, can you really touch it? Can it really be measured? No one knows exactly what it is when one refers to the ego. People use the word casually or take it very seriously without realizing that it isn't anything tangible that can even be spotted under a microscope.

The word ego is an abstract noun. It doesn't represent anything tangible or even real, but our usage of the word makes it seem as if it does. In NLP, similar nouns are called nominalization.

A simple way to understand nominalization is, "Can you put it on the table?" Nouns such as chair, pen, cup, mobile, and laptop are tangible and can be placed on the table. At the same time, nouns such as a decision, relationship, or knowledge cannot be put on the table. Thus, they are abstract nouns and classified as nominalizations in NLP. The "ego" is also not something tangible but is a nominalization. The Self and Survival Mechanism, too, come under the same category.

What is Ego?

The Survival Mechanism, which each of us has, performs the same function of protecting our body. The Ego does the same. It is an artificial shield that safeguards us from possible illusionary dangers by creating an impression on the Self (others). When we compare it to the earlier definitions, we are redefining the word "ego."

The ego is a person's Survival Mechanism trying to create an impression on the Self (others) that may not be genuine, which gives the person a false sense of assurance. Like when someone portrays himself as successful. Without it, the person feels insecure and vulnerable. The ego serves as an invisible dummy shield that provides the person temporary protection by displaying an artificial persona to others, much like a mask protects your real face from being seen. The impression portrayed by the person will vary depending on their SOM. All three SOMs reveal their ego differently.

Tito is a highly accomplished person with double master's degrees from internationally reputed universities. He complained, "I am tired of living this life. It looks like I am a fake person, a fraud. I'm always defending my ego. Now I am fed up doing it and want to live my life." Tito is a Wanted Child and lived up to others' expectations by pursuing excellence, thereby proving himself worthy. He would think about his past. Tito had studied in a vernacular medium school and, as his English was not very good, he felt inferior to others. To make up for it, he worked harder to prove he was worthy. His survival trait of being a perfectionist meant he avoided making mistakes. Today, if his clients find errors in his work and question him, he feels criticized and looked down upon. His survival patterns were making him feel tired and exhausted. Till now, he had been tirelessly guarding the glitter of his crown — the Self-image. He used his ego as a shield because he didn't want to be looked down upon by others. In the therapy session, he realized how he was living his life and that his behavior was aimed at protecting the sheen of his illusionary Self-image. He was portraying himself to others as someone highly competent.

Self-acceptance and Ego

Ego is an untruthful presentation of one's being just to gain "acceptance" from one's Self, which is akin to getting it from our parents and others. It is difficult for the person to live with the actual truth about who and what they currently are, which compels them to portray a façade. We have difficulty in acknowledging the TRUTH of what IS. There is an underlying fear of being rejected by the Self (others). So we present a false picture of who we are to gain acceptance.

The ego is like an act of bravado presented by a person's Survival Mechanism, giving out a false impression to others. This gives the person temporary assurance. There might not be real danger involved but an imaginary threat from others. "What will others think of me?" or "How will others perceive me?" are thoughts that can go on in the mind of a person.

Bob, a film industry professional, owns an expensive premium brand car. As a child, he was not good at academics and was looked down upon by his parents, teachers, and others. People made fun of Bob and sidelined him during activities. In the past few years, Bob has tasted professional success and drives a high-end car, a symbol of success, to portray his status. While driving, if he got into an altercation with a biker who cut across his path, Bob would get angry. He would say to the biker, "Do you know who you are talking to?" Bob confessed in his session with me, "I am a nobody. I don't know why I say that."

Something even more telling was what Bob shared about his parents. The day he drove his car to their home, his parents were most unimpressed about his new acquisition. He said, "It looked like what I had achieved was insignificant. I was ignored and made to feel unimportant. And that was the worst and saddest day of my life."

We fear being authentic and exposed for who we are. The fear triggers our Survival Mechanism, which controls our identity, behavior, attitude, and more. It then wants to protect us by displaying a false construct, which we call the "ego." When fear kicks in, the Survival Mechanism takes over and does not permit us TO BE. It always invades our being and controls us when we experience threats and dangers. One way that it does this is by creating the ego, trying to present us as someone significant in the eyes of others. When we get their acceptance, we feel secure; if we don't meet the expected mark, we feel disappointed and insecure.

You may have also heard sentences and phrases such as:

- ❖ Let go of your ego.
- ❖ Don't allow your ego to rule over you.
- ❖ Diffuse your ego.
- ❖ Don't let your ego control you.
- ❖ Don't let your ego take over you.
- ❖ Don't let your ego do the talking.

The bigger question is, how do you not allow your ego to control you? You are unaware of the Survival Mechanism and Self operating within you. They control all of you — who you are, what you do, your relationships, your decisions and even your destiny.

Your ego creates an artificial persona, so you can experience a temporary feel-good factor. It keeps you high, trying to keep your spirit upbeat and alive. It is akin to the high from happiness drugs like cocaine, weed, or the like. They give people who consume them time-bound happiness. Then you need to consume them again to experience the same euphoric state. It becomes a never-ending loop. The ego gives us False Illusionary Assurance, which makes us feel momentarily good. Then we crave it again.

The idea of False Illusionary Assurance has been explained on pages 135 to 137 of my previous book *Stop Surviving Start Living with Freedom*. I'm presenting the extract below.

What is False Illusionary Assurance?

A False Illusionary Assurance is a temporary emotional high or feeling of safety. The Survival Mechanism thrives on emotions. Emotions are the compass that tell us whether we are surviving or whether our survival is in danger. The process works like a thermostat. When a threshold limit is crossed, an emotion kicks in. If that emotion is happiness, then our survival chances are looking upbeat. It means we are safe. If we are unhappy, because we are discontent, disappointed, sad, or angry, our lives are not working the way we want it to and we need to change that. We take actions to try to move away from these negative feelings, towards positive feelings that give us a sense of assurance or euphoria. That then makes us feel that everything is moving on perfectly or harmoniously. In the moment, we believe that to be true, not realizing that it's an illusion giving us a temporary false high.

We need to make a note of critical facts connected with emotions. Human beings want to avoid negative emotions at all costs and move towards positive emotions. They may sometimes indulge in unhealthy behaviors or habits to get that feel-good factor, the emotional high. Of course, it will depend on a person's Survival Mechanism, how s/he goes about getting that kick. Positive emotions are like happiness doses of drugs such as weed, cocaine, and marijuana. When one has a dosage of these drugs, for the next few hours the person experiences a high. Slowly, the effects start to fade away, and then more of the same is needed. As s/he loves to be in that elevated emotional state more often, a craving for it emanates. This craving mechanism drives the happiness dosage industry to thrive.

To avoid bad feelings, one may even do things that may be considered stupid or unwise, which is most often not required. A person who is deprived of positive emotions, may purchase it in the form of drugs, alcohol, sex, or in another form of indulgence (socially acceptable terms like "retail therapy," "food," "porn," "binge watching," "entertainment"). It's a way for maintaining homeostasis, a state of steady internal conditions. It makes us feel we are "pulling on, going on, getting on." That means we are surviving well. Life is going well. The security or euphoria from positive emotions continues for some time, and then it becomes a habit you look forward to and constantly seek.

Happiness, thrill, and ecstasy are examples of positive emotions that fall under the pleasure zone, whereas anger, helplessness, guilt, shame, sadness, anxiety, and fear fall under the category of painful emotions. The move away from pain toward pleasure lasts only for a while. We can't sustain pleasure for a long time and its effects fade away, much like those of happiness drugs. But as we have gotten used to it, we need more of it. It is the Survival Mechanism's way of assuring us that we are safe and secure, which is the False Illusionary Assurance. We fall into the loop of seeking it, not realizing that it is an endless vicious circle. This False Illusionary Assurance applies to all repetitive behaviors or habits such as binge eating, excessive alcohol consumption, or sex indulgence.

The same can be said to be true even for sports. You can take the example of playing tennis. If you win one match, your confidence improves. If that happens often, you want to play a tournament. You practice harder. Each time you win, you experience positive emotions. You feel the high and you want to thrive more by going to another level. If you lose, you feel negative emotions. But you want to move away from those undesirable negative emotions towards positive ones. You then work harder, put in more practice, and win some more games. You experience the high of adrenaline. But if you then lose the next few matches, you go into a slump, sad and disappointed.

The Survival Mechanism has created a life filled with false expectations — one desires positive emotions and is always trying to move away from negative emotions. One can't stop the mechanism's pendulum oscillating from one end to another. In this process of life, there is always a tug-of-war. The push and pull will continue as long as we are operating through the Survival Mechanism.

We all want praises, accolades, admiration, and pats showered on us so that we feel upbeat. We feel proud of ourselves, at least for some time. Our ego gives us a boost that makes us feel elated. However, too much success and accolades can inflate our ego, leading to excess pride that we display in our actions, behaviors, and attitudes. Others notice this and make remarks about our ego.

We want to feel good about what we have achieved in life. That is to say, we are not what we are, but we are our achievements. Putting it inversely, we are nothing without our accomplishments. We would like the world to know about us through our successes and achievements. These could be our job titles, awards we have won, places we have visited, personalities we have met, brands we wear or own, or the latest electronic gadgets. Without some or all of these, we can feel hollow.

Through our ego, we are communicating to the world a false construct. If we don't have much to tell the world about our accomplishments, possessions, or experiences, we feel inferior, left out, or not on par with others. Some of us will maintain a distance from others or go into hiding, while others will portray a fake impression of their lives to boost their ego. People from the three Survival Programs display their egos differently because they perceive the world through their Survival Mechanism's point of view. The survival traits of each program will influence the ego by creating an artificial image, hoping others will like and accept us. However, this feel-good factor is a False Illusionary Assurance, and understanding it better may allow us to make decisions differently.

SUBSECTION – B
THE SYSTEM

24

A SYSTEM WITHIN A SYSTEM

Sheila was forced by her father to rub her nose in front of her grandfather's feet for talking back to him when she was three years old. She said she had told her grandfather something that was a fact — Sheila felt she had done nothing wrong. These are traumas or abuses a child can experience during formative years when there is a clash between two systems.

Sheila had to learn to be submissive to two systems. Her father and mother are her core Self and also the primary system in her life. But the father belongs to another system, that of Sheila's grandparents. Her grandfather appears to have a hold over her father in a family where seniority is given respect. Sheila's father is passing on the same message to her: if you show disrespect towards your elders, you will be punished. The harsh and ruthless penalty Sheila received was not proportionate to the child's "error," but here, hierarchy was given more significance than a proper assessment. In many joint families in India, we notice similar conflicts where the parents succumb to the pressures of seniors within the system.

A child learns to become a part of other systems besides the ones she finds at home. When s/he goes out to play with children in the neighborhood, s/he interacts with not just children but their family members too. It is a new surrounding where s/he might like some children or elders and feel comfortable, based upon experiences. Neighbors themselves are another system, having their own cultural, religious, gender, and ethical norms. New people and experiences keep getting added to the child's Self. Essentially, new systems become part of it too.

A school environment for the child is totally different. The child sees multiple new faces of the same age as him/her and many who are bigger. A new authority figure, the teacher, is introduced, and the child learns to survive in this new place known as the classroom. This is especially true when the child leaves play school. School becomes a new system that gets added to the child's Self. There are different sub-groups within the school — include grades, class divisions, and sports teams. A child copes with each of these based on his/her Survival Mechanism.

I know of a boy of seven named Kevin, who used the F-word in his class, for which he was meted out punishment by his teacher. It could be that Kevin may have picked it up from another student, or that his parents often casually use swear words in the presence of their son. When he uses the F-word, I'm sure Kevin does not visualize people having sex, but the teacher takes this as the connotation. While the teacher may have punished the boy to teach him a lesson, the parents go scot-free and are never questioned about how their boy picked up the swear word. Kevin used it to express his anger, but the teacher interpreted it differently, as discipline needed to be maintained. Here again, there are two systems — the family and the school — that collide with each other for which a child faces the brunt. The Self within the child is in conflict. Certain things are allowed in one system but disallowed in another. Hereon, Kevin will be selective in using this swear word.

Religion is another comprehensive system that gets added to a child's Self. Every religion has its own rituals and customs. A child may or may not get closer to children having similar beliefs. However, religion will be a force in the child's life, laying down specific norms that s/he will follow, while s/he will need to adjust to people from other religions. A Christian attending a Hindu friend's wedding follows and respects the latter's customs, and vice versa would be true as well. It's just like getting ourselves acclimatized to different weather conditions if we want to survive. If we don't, we experience discomfort or even perish.

Most of the time, we adjust to various systems, because each one's Self is built on different rules and beliefs. Some beliefs will match with those of one's internal Self, while in other cases, we will need to adapt ourselves to new thinking patterns and cultures. Indian people working in the Middle East or other countries have to adapt to systems in those places. The laws are different in India, but Indians living there learn to adjust to the laws or practices prevalent in those countries.

A large system is made up of systems within systems, creating a wheels-within-wheels structure, quite literally. Like in a clock, the wheels of one system need to synchronize with those of another to allow it to function properly and harmoniously, or else they clash and create disruption. Within the Self, something similar takes place.

25

MICRO AND MACRO OF THE SELF

The System is an expansion of the Self. While the Self operates at the micro-level as the family, there are Systems that operate at a macro-level — countries, religions, and organizations. They function in a similar way. Most of what we see as features of the Self also appear in the System. In this chapter, our primary focus will be on Systems.

A System is a set of connected things or devices that operate together. In the context of this book, a System comprises people operating out of different Survival Mechanisms forming a collaborative team and having a leader. They make rules and regulations applicable to every person who is a part of it and that individuals need to follow. Moses and The Ten Commandments were one of the oldest Systems with laws that came into existence. One way of looking at Systems is the number of members they contain. Systems can be as simple as a unit family — a father, mother, and child. A joint family will have more people. At the other end of the numerical scale are countries and religions. Vatican City can have a population of less than 1000, whereas a country like India has 1.3 billion citizens. Some organized religions have followers running into billions across different countries.

In my previous book, *Stop Surviving Start Living with Freedom*, I wrote about how "the Survival Mechanism prevails in a System." Any System created by humans doesn't have its own independent identity. People's knowledge, thinking, and understanding go into structuring, designing, and shaping a model that is implemented in a group of people. Those people could be the citizens of a country or followers of organized religion. Rules and regulations are introduced, which become laws that need to be followed. Leaders of a System make and uphold the laws, may it be a school's principal (dean), the executive and parliament of a democratic country, or the Pope who is the head of the Catholic Church.

If we don't learn to adapt to Systems, a System can discard us. A child that doesn't fit into a school's ethos and discipline structure can be asked to leave. If followers betray certain norms of religion, they could be excommunicated. People who are perceived as a national threat can be imprisoned by the country's law enforcement authorities. As Systems continue to expand, our Survival Mechanism compels us to adapt to them, which causes us stress.

Functions of the System

While there are numerous types of systems, I will focus more on some of the larger ones founded by human beings, like the country, military, and religions. Nature also has various Systems, which are ecologically balanced and well-integrated into each other. We are looking at Systems designed by humans that have limitations because we have three different operating systems that compel us to perceive the world differently from each other. I will also use a catch-all term as "the System" when referring to them. The primary function of many Systems is similar to that of the Self, which is to protect and safeguard the interests of its members. They could be the financial interests of shareholders, the rights of citizens, or the well-being of religious followers.

Distinctions Between the Self and the System

While the Self and the System work in more or less the same way, let's first look at some important differences that distinguish them.

1. Ability to create — The main distinction is that parents are the core of the Self and are bestowed with the gift of giving birth to another human. Systems are designed to manage humans or even use them to achieve ends, but they cannot create another human being.

2. Choice of key people — Parents represent the core of the Self. In a System, leaders are chosen by us or others. At times, leadership passes from one generation to another, as in a family-business or dynasty rule.

3. Changes in people — The core Self consists of two people who do not change. But in a System, different people could come and go within a hierarchy. This happens in governments, schools, corporations, and religious institutions. The core of the System keeps changing too. A new US president can replace an existing one, or the British queen will one day hand over power to her successor.

4. Core and extension — The self is the core of a person and based on that foundation other branches spread out. The System is an extension of that branching-out phenomenon. The System forms the outer core of the person and can never overthrow the person's core Self.

5. Direction of expectations — In the Self, parents place their expectations on children. In a System, it is usually the other way around. People put their expectations on the leaders of a System. Mostly, the majority decide the fate of a System's leader. That is not the case with the Self and parents.

6. Harm to others — From the reference point of a Self, a person knows it is wrong to kill another person who also has a Self. But the behavior of the individual in a System will be different. Two opposing soldiers may not have any personal hatred for each other, but the army has trained them and deemed them as enemies. The irony is that the soldier cannot apply the same mindset to kill his neighbor, who has been a nuisance. The military System that has trained him to kill an enemy will not rescue him, whereas the country's judiciary will term him a murderer and put him behind bars.

We can now look at some aspects of Systems and how they are often similar to the Self.

The System Makes Rules and Regulations

People in power make decisions and apply them uniformly across different sections of people. Traffic rules laid down by local or country authorities make it mandatory for motorcycle drivers to wear a helmet and car drivers a seatbelt, for their safety. Everyone driving on the left-hand side has made it orderly. State authorities make laws protecting the well-being of multiple stakeholders — residents, workers, businesses, the environment, etc. Religions make laws to protect their followers from committing sin and thereby prevent them from experiencing suffering. Some of them also think of the well-being of their followers even after their deaths by hoping they follow the rules and avoid hell.

Not all laws are unanimously accepted, which can be a source of disharmony. In India, the government introduced new farm laws in 2020, which they said were for the benefit of the country. They were opposed by farmers, who said the laws were not in their interest. Leaders in the System make laws that all must obey. They will make it mandatory for their members if they wish to remain a part of the System. Certain religions have dress codes for women and men. Some even have specific rituals and personal identification that they must follow if they belong to a particular religion or sect. These are some of the enforced conditionings of the System to where members have to conform.

The System also Gives Directions

Just as the Self is a mechanism that gives a person directions, the System also gives directions, highlighting what is acceptable or not. In a capitalist society, property ownership and private wealth creation are the accepted norms. In contrast, socialist governments will deem that unacceptable and require state ownership of assets.

The System can be Challenged and, at Times, Overthrown

A few representatives elected by the people legislate laws that are well-meaning to which citizens need to conform. This is regardless of whether they like them or not. An obvious problem with applying laws uniformly is that some groups will protest against them as being unfair. The episode of Indian farmers (who are also citizens) revolting against the central government is one such example.

History has shown us that it is possible to overthrow a governance system. With Mahatma Gandhi at the helm, India managed to end British rule in the country that had lasted for nearly 200 years. Similarly, Russia and China overthrew their monarchs in the twentieth century and installed a communist regime. However, we always require a

System in a country which will need to evolve. Just like no person can exist for long without a Self, a country without a System will flounder.

The System is also Imaginary

We have already seen earlier how the Self is imaginary. The System, too, when it is based on beliefs, norms and rules, is an imaginary concept. It was built upon certain principles derived from others, in which we either believe or are compelled to believe. Whether we approve of it or not, we have to go along. This is like the composition of the Self. Most of what it is made up of is not our choice but embedded into us after birth, without choice. But we believe it is all real when it is not.

The System and its Rules Keep Expanding

On the foundations of the preamble and constitution written by a country's founding fathers, laws are developed for the welfare of citizens. From its core, laws keep increasing and expanding in different areas or directions. Some of them become obsolete and are replaced. The point to note is that a system is ever-growing and expanding, which also increases its complexity. India is not the same country it was when it gained independence from the British in 1947. The founding members are no more, but each elected government legislates new laws as they deem appropriate, which people must obey even if they don't like it. This is like how the Self keeps expanding and developing an extended Self.

The System is Based on the Past

As you comprehend the Self, you can see the way parents transfer their beliefs onto their children. It happens in a System too. The Indian caste system was devised many centuries ago, but is kept alive by every new generation. Therefore, Systems are also an accumulation of the past. Rules that were made in the past get passed on over the years. Some laws, though outdated, still continue to be implemented.

The System uses Authority and Power to Control

Certain Systems offer people more choice and freedom, but one must follow laws. Others are more rigid and require the following of orders, or else the System collapses. The armed forces are an example of such a System. Senior authority figures make decisions on behalf of juniors, whose power to ask questions is curtailed. Similar to the ownership rights of the Self (parents), seniors in the System are in charge of the fate of others in their unit. They can also impose punishment for disobedience. Any System will fall apart without power and control.

While authorities make laws for the benefit of people, how the System enforces them makes a lot of difference. In India, traffic cops sometimes hide behind a vehicle or around a corner to catch drivers who break the rules. The intention here is not to be a deterrent but penalize wrongdoers.

Systems are in Every Sphere of Our Life

Other than the government and the armed forces, we are exposed to Systems in every sphere. We are expected to understand their functioning. The education system, judiciary, corporate world, and religious institutions are powerful Systems with which we must interact. Numerous functional systems exist, like traffic management, road navigation, airports, trains, and buses, each having systems within systems. As a user, we must be abreast with how they work.

The System can Turn Against You

A System that is supportive of its members can go against one of them at another time. We have seen this happening in political parties or with citizens who are peaceful dissenters. Religious ex-communication is another form of eliminating someone who was once a member of the System. On its own, the System has no conscience. Leaders in the System have their own Survival Mechanism, which is active and runs on fear. People who manage the System or take orders also do so out of fear to protect their positions. This is similar to the way the Self functions. While it protects a person, if one challenges it, the Self will overwhelm the individual.

A Few Can Corrupt or Hijack a System

A group of well-connected or financially powerful people can influence the governing of a System and hijack it for their own benefit. There have been numerous banking frauds in India. However, the most recent famous one is that of Lehman Brothers, which filed for bankruptcy and triggered the collapse of the financial system in the West. The corruption of a System occurs because there are not adequate internal checks on the integrity of its leaders. Most often, powerful perpetrators go scot-free.

Systems are Mainly Interested in Their End Goal

Although different systems cooperate with one another, each one is primarily interested in its end goal. Corporations want to please shareholders by growing profits, but they might not be interested in protecting the oceans. A non-profit organization will be devoted to its own end objective, whether it is free medical care or environmental protection. The army will protect a nation's borders and not care about niceties. Each System creates a structure and organization rules to reflect its end goal, which members of the System cannot question.

Shoot the Messenger – Seal the Truth

An individual who fights the System may be termed a rebel or troublemaker. Just as a child who questions his/her parents too much could be called a "difficult child." A person may perhaps pinpoint what's wrong with a System, but people might distance themselves from him/her. If s/he is more unfortunate, s/he may also be victimized. In different parts of the world, people who have questioned state power have been imprisoned or incarcerated, usually without a fair trial. On the other hand, the System is disproportionately lenient to those who are financially powerful or influential.

If the System is managed optimally towards its designed outcome and issues are resolved fairly, then its members live in harmony. When the people governing the System have hidden agendas, they devise ways to corrupt it. Someone or a few within the System may then raise a red flag about wrongdoings. Influential people will target the whistleblower, preventing the fraud from getting exposed, thus preventing the truth from reaching more of its members.

The powerful use the System's machinery against the innocent of concealing the truth, thus safeguarding its interest and themselves. They manipulate the System to silence the individual's voice without giving him/her a fair trial on a different pretext. Tactfully, any person can be labeled as the enemy of the state and a traitor, while the real culprit goes scot-free. "Shooting the messenger" prevents the truth from getting exposed.

Edward Snowden was declared the state's enemy and called a traitor because he raised a red flag in 2013 regarding the surveillance of its citizens by some US agencies, affecting their individual privacy. The System labels its citizens as traitors and convinces people at large, using its power to taint and target the individual. In a System, a few can decide the fate of its citizens. An honest member or members cannot take on the powerful System when it is controlled by a few influential and financially powerful entities. A whistleblower can risk being imprisoned and/or even killed.

Adjust to the System

When people from one country migrate to another one, they have to adjust to and obey the different laws and customs of the new country. This is true for Indians who migrate to the Gulf (UAE, Kuwait, Qatar, Saudi Arabia), Canada, or the US. We can't behave the way we want. Moreover, even if someone chooses to live in a ghetto, s/he cannot totally ignore the laws of the home country. This is similar to the scenario the child is in when going to school. We can safely conclude that we are expected to adjust to the System, and the System does not adapt to our needs. The Self, too, doesn't take diktats from a person.

Survival Mechanism Will Influence the Leader's Style

In a System with a distinct leader, such as an army general, a president, a CEO, or a school principal (dean), one will see certain patterns. As all humans have a Survival Mechanism that influences their decision-making, a leader in a System will also have a Survival Mechanism that will indirectly affect the System. If the leader is a Wanted Child, then the dominant operating style of the System will reflect his/her personality. Others in that System will need to adjust to that style of functioning. Moreover, the style will alter if a new leader is an Unwanted Child or a Partly Wanted Child.

The System Works on Fear

The working of the System is similar to that of the Survival Mechanism (and Self) in that it is fueled by its primary emotion — fear. An elected government official is scared of losing power; therefore, s/he pleases the populace. Government employees fear losing their job and so oblige the authorities with their services. Citizens in a System are scared of breaking laws because they know they can be fined or imprisoned. We all operate out of fear, as our Survival Mechanism greatly affects our thinking.

A Few Can Bulldoze the Whole System

While we need to adapt to a System, it can be altered by a few powerful individuals to suit their objectives. Although there are rules everyone is expected to follow, those people can bulldoze their way through the System to get decisions turned in their favor. For instance, someone who is a dictator or autocrat with absolute powers could do that. Senior members of the main party of a communist state could also do it. Those people begin to believe that they themselves are the System.

However, a few rotten apples can bring down a powerful organization too. During the Enron scandal, management responsible for the financial performance of the business manipulated the accounts to present a flattering picture of the organization. Since the numbers came from a reputed firm and were audited by one of the world's largest accounting firms, Arthur Anderson, people believed them. When the truth got exposed, it brought about the end of Enron and Arthur Andersen.

One Who Tries to Change a System Pays a Price

Around the world, there have been many people who have been crusaders against a System they believe needs to change. Some leaders of those Systems then experience insecurity regarding their future. The thirst for power and control comes from the Survival Mechanism. The degree to which those leaders feel fear makes them commit forbidden acts, often violent, against people who try to change the System.

There have been numerous examples in history that show such a backlash. Gandhi was a leader who could unite people to overthrow British rule in India without the need for armed conflict. Although he had no personal enmity against the British, he showed them the mirror on their unjustifiable occupation of India. Finally, he along with other leaders playing their part, got the freedom to India. However, his vision of an independent India did not match that of a group of people who felt deprived and insecure. Gandhi was assassinated by one of its members. Abraham Lincoln, Martin Luther King Jr., and John F. Kennedy were some other famous leaders who were trying to change the System and got assassinated.

Martin Luther challenged many of the teachings, practices, and beliefs of the Roman Catholic Church, a powerful religious institution. He was a German priest, theologian, and writer; his writing questioned the church's authority and its religious practices. Luther's writing led to the formation of a new group as Protestants.

Perhaps one of the most famous examples, however, was that of Jesus Christ. As he was gaining more popularity among people, a certain section felt insecure about the way he was challenging existing practices and beliefs. So they found a way to ensnare him in the System and accused him of various offenses. Jesus became a victim of the System, where some people were trying to preserve their ideological thinking.

No System is perfect. Each one has its strengths and limitations. However, history has shown us that Systems need to update and changed when necessary. Nokia was once ruling the worldwide mobile phone company. But it didn't keep pace with the evolving market and consumers at large threw them out of business (https://fourweekmba.com/why-nokia-failed/). The leadership or a select few in every System will resist major changes, as they are trapped by the Survival Mechanism and then by the System itself.

26

OWNERSHIP RIGHTS - TRAPPED WITHIN THE SYSTEM

The System has an impact on every one of us. As it is impossible to analyze all different Systems, we will look at two major systems that affect people worldwide — governing systems and religious systems — and the ownership rights they claim.

Every country that we are born in has ownership rights over us. A country usually requires documented proof validating that a person is a citizen of that country. These can be a passport, national ID card, or something equivalent. Through the exercise of issuing such identification, a government claims its ownership rights and indicates it has authority over us.

Governance systems can be of different forms — democracy, communism, military rule, dictatorship, a religious republic, etc. Just as we don't have a choice in choosing our parents, we don't have the option of choosing the country of our birth. Whichever country one is born in, must abide by that country's laws, rules, and norms. If one doesn't, then the System will try to make the person obey through penalty or punishment. Therefore, we are compelled to adapt to the large and complex systems of a country, having its many different institutions, each of which has its set of expectations from us.

The ownership rights of a country over its citizens are complete. We don't have much influence in this System until we become a significant part of it by becoming authority figures in the government. Even then, an individual is not free. In the analogy given earlier about Prince Wan of Surviva, he is a prince in a monarchy and, in most likelihood, the third-highest official in the kingdom after the king and queen. Yet he becomes a property of the System and must prove to the

System that he is a capable future ruler. As authorities have placed a crown over his head, it symbolizes the responsibilities he now must shoulder. Unknowingly, he is proving himself worthy and has become the property of the king, queen, and kingdom. Wan is in his survival trance, oblivious to the reality of his life.

Modern states have their own expectations from citizens. In countries such as Israel and Singapore, there is mandatory conscription for citizens who have attained the age of eighteen. If they fail to fulfill this obligation, they can be punished. Communist countries treat citizens as the state's resources. Countries with religious leaders expect citizens to respect the state religion and a deviation could be considered blasphemy, punishable by death or flogging.

In democracies, one appears to have certain freedoms. But there have been numerous instances of abuse of power against ordinary people in democratic countries. An individual can be harassed on the pretext of being a threat to national security. S/he could be questioned by the country's tax authorities, have bank accounts frozen, or get imprisoned by the state. In countries with a laggard judicial system, it can take a huge toll on that person until justice arrives.

As we have read earlier, the undercurrent of fear gives rise to the concept of ownership. We always have a fear of being disowned if we disobey or fail to abide by rules imposed by the authorities. So, we try to always conform to laws. Due to fear of punishment, we avoid displeasing the authorities and sometimes get exploited in the process. There is an innate craving from the Survival Mechanism for us to belong and be accepted by others. We are willing to go through any discomfort to get that.

We Want to Belong

We all want to be part of something that is a System. In order to belong to it, we have to abide by its rules, but unknowingly also lose our freedoms. The Survival Mechanism creates the illusion that we don't have a choice and that we must survive by following diktats. Even if a choice existed, being a stateless person or subject is neither desirable nor encouraged. Our parents make sure that we become the property of a nation at birth, usually the one we are born in or they are from.

The System is Not a Person - Cannot Be Held Accountable and Can Disown its Members

A System is an invisible, artificial entity that is created by humans on certain principles. It is not a person with a physical body. Since it is this way, a human (or a group) must take charge of the System as a leader.

The bigger a System, the more hierarchical its layers are and the greater the division of labor within it. A leader can delegate authority and pass on responsibility to junior leaders or managers in this way. Those people can be tasked with the execution of rules or mandates. An unfortunate outcome is that those at the lower rungs of a System can be held accountable for the System's lapses — not the System itself or its senior leadership. Most often, a System will not take ownership of its errors, and someone from within will become a sacrificial lamb on its behalf.

The infamous incident of the murder of George Floyd, a black man in Minneapolis, USA, in 2020 highlights this aspect. It shook the consciousness of people around the world. Derek Chauvin, a forty-four-year-old police officer, placed his knee on George Floyd's neck for over eight minutes while he was lying handcuffed on the ground. The video of this incident went viral, and there was an uproar in the USA. It quickly spread to worldwide protests against police brutality, racism, and the lack of accountability in the police force. Minneapolis city agreed to pay George Floyd's family a sum of $21 million following a lawsuit. However, I recollect reading that Derek Chauvin was sentenced to 22.5 years in prison.

Now, I am in no way supporting Derek's heinous actions, but one could ask a few questions. As many have pointed out, it was a failure of the System. Who trained Derek to do his job? Despite the outcry against it in the USA, the System did not take sufficient responsibility for what happened on that fateful day in May 2020. Only one person has so far been penalized harshly. It means one person is paying the price for the fault of the whole System, which cannot be held accountable.

Perhaps Derek held prejudices against black people. However, no one is born with biases against a particular group of people. He picks it up from his environment. Who influenced Derek along the way to hold such views? Given that he and other officers suffered from biases against the black community, how much training was imparted by the System to neutralize this prejudice?

A group of institutions functions together here as a System — the police department, judiciary, and local government. The police department teaches every officer to follow a training manual without questioning it. Any inherent flaws in it cannot be challenged or revoked by trainee officers. Besides, suppose they do not implement the protocols of the System. In that case, it falls apart and they will be penalized (just as a military unit in battle collapses if soldiers don't follow the orders of seniors). This means police officers are deprived of their own reasoning and operate like inhuman robots. The judiciary, also part of the System, implements laws made by the legislature. By sentencing Derek Chauvin to 22.5 years in prison, the System has tried to make an example of him — such actions will not be tolerated anymore. But senior members of the System, the people who were really responsible for what happened, went unpunished. There is no way one can hold the System responsible because it is an artificial construct made by humans. Authorities at the top make laws and design a rulebook — a training manual in this case — and lower-level people execute them, paying the price if things go awry during implementation.

Let's look at Derek's position from another perspective. Let's assume he did not do what he did, which is place his knee on George's neck, a procedure he was taught. Imagine George somehow tried to wiggle his way out and escape his captors. Derek may have been reprimanded or penalized by his police department. This is a catch-twenty-two situation for Derek, where he incurs punishment either way, although in this scenario, the quantum of punishment would have been quite less when compared to 22.5 years in jail. In both scenarios, the System would not be held accountable.

The overall message is that the System does not take responsibility for its mistakes but disowns its own members when it comes under harsh scrutiny. People in charge of a System experience fear and will crucify their own to escape the consequences of their shortcomings. That individual ends up as the scapegoat for the System's faults.

Living in a Fabricated Reality

We accept and adhere to Systems designed by others, whether they are religions or forms of government. We create these Systems and try to believe in their truth, but in the end, they are a product of the human mind. Others around us, however, compel us to believe in them. If an illusion fails to meet our expectations, we change it. Once there was a monarchy in Russia and China. People of those countries were experiencing unhealthy levels of poverty, injustice, and corruption. So they underwent revolutions and established socialism and communism as their governing systems, which, too, were born from human imagination. People of Russia and China hoped their discomforts would be alleviated, but instead, they encountered another form of tyranny. After the dissolution of the Soviet Union, Russia became a federal semi-presidential republic. People may feel more positive about the change, but one make-believe reality got swapped for a new one.

"I am the Law"

Everyone in a System is not subject to its laws or rules. Parents in a family say, "We are the law." The child cannot question their authority and also doesn't have the ability to understand it all. In a monarchy, the king and queen are the law. They can ignore the laws they create, as those apply only to citizens or subjects. The modern state of Russia, described above, has a leader who will remain in power for a number of years. Something similar has been implemented in modern China. In democracies, too, political leaders are rarely held guilty by the judicial system of their country when they are in power. So elected representatives think of themselves as the law.

Religion and Ownership Rights

One of the ways in which countries are governed is on the principles of religion. Despite people's values and thinking changing in the twentieth century, the influence of religion in many countries cannot be discounted. It can even play a significant role in many democratic countries. Political leaders in such places bring it to the forefront during their election campaigns. Even though religion could have been an individualistic goal in one's spiritual journey, it has been enforced on citizens in many countries. It appears leaders there know the path to heaven.

Countries governing on religious principles and doctrines are doing so to save their citizens from going to hell. It is an illusionary concept that works on fear. It seems like their core intention is a positive one, salvaging humanity from possible discomfort after death. However, as fear comes under the realm of the Survival Mechanism, how can anything that operates on it give salvation to humanity? When everyone within the System functions out of fear, is it even possible to liberate its people? That would be like darkness eradicating darkness. However, in the name of salvation, it helps authorities to have complete control over people.

Most people are born into families that follow a religion. Certain beliefs get passed on to us from birth. Whether we like it or not, we learn to adapt to them. We believe that's how life is because religion has a large say in how people ought to live their lives. As we grow older, religion becomes an integral part of many people's lives.

Human beings are social creatures; therefore, living in isolation is difficult. There is an inborn fear of being alone and family becomes our support system. As we grow older, we want to feel a sense of belonging to a broader society. Culture and religion play their role in making us feel integrated into society. The Survival Mechanism has also planted the fear of death in us, as well as ideas of what's considered right or wrong. We worry about our mortality. Religions provide the foundation of a basic understanding of certain fundamental truths. They do it through literature and commandments, which act like maps that give humans direction. They also provide us with ideas on how to live in harmony and peace within our communities.

Sometimes, we experience a vacuum in our life and religion plays a role in filling it. We take solace under its wings and try to find solutions to our survival issues. But we don't realize that religions that prescribe a particular or rigid path that offer us comfort is a False Illusionary Assurance. They claim to know the perfect pathway to heaven or a way out of problems. While religious scriptures are a great resource for humanity, their verbatim and rote use have obscured their core purpose.

At other moments in life, we wonder what will happen to us after death and that fear makes us cling on to religion. Our insecurity drives us to adopt certain practices. This creates a further binding towards a religion. In our feelings of incompleteness, we often surrender to a group, cult, or institution and become subservient to it. They help us face the fear of being solitary and of death or the unknown afterlife. Religious Systems, like governing Systems, also work upon our fears, which we have acquired from the Survival Mechanism.

In my book *Stop Surviving Start Living with Freedom,* I explained how humans move away from pain towards some form of pleasure. Assurance that life is going well is a kind of pleasure that humans seek. Religion can give it to us. However, this is a short-lived feeling of security and ends up being a False Illusionary Assurance. We end up unconsciously craving it again and again. So, we submit to religion completely, with very little experiential learning and connection.

When we want to belong to a religion, we need to conform to its rules and norms. Numerous rituals are drilled into us from when we are young, which become unconscious habits. We need to go to church to pray every Sunday. Others need to pray five times a day. Fasting for a period every year is either recommended or made mandatory. These practices have been drilled into us through fear and it is implied that if we don't perform them, we do not belong to the family, culture, or tradition. When we rebel against them or don't do them, we experience guilt. To dispel our feelings of helplessness or insecurity, we feel obliged to fulfill the terms and conditions to be a part of a religion. In this process, it takes ownership over many of us after birth. It determines our beliefs, attire, food choices, rituals, marriages, and even how our body will be disposed of after death. Numerous other matters of significance need to be decided through religious norms.

Many religious representatives have not experienced heaven or hell, but deploy fear as a way to make followers conform. In such ways described above, we give up our ownership rights to religion and become its property.

No System is Perfect

Systems are designed by humans, and we try to live our lives from within their set parameters. It is not possible to follow all the conditions placed on us at all times. There may be a time people go against the System, but fear restricts them, even though they know and feel the truth. All Systems need to be updated as time passes by. There will never be a perfect law that applies to all humans, everywhere and at all times. Despite this, nobody can escape Systems. For instance, we are born into a Family System, and we have to learn to deal with it. The more aware we are of its workings and limitations, the much better equipped we are to address issues that arise from it. We forget that any System is a creation of our ancestors, who were also human. They designed Systems that were the need of the hour at the time and as per their understanding. But Systems don't always take into account the changing realities of people.

Systems are designed by well-intentioned people for our well-being. It was necessary for Karl Marx and Friedrich Engels to write *The Communist Manifesto* in 1848 as an analysis of class struggle and its relationship with capitalism. This was followed by Marx writing his three-volume *Das Kapital* in later years. He had observed how capitalism was exploiting the working class during his time and his critique of it was that it would eventually destroy itself. There would be a worker revolution across the world. Although Marx didn't explicitly spell out what a communist society that replaces capitalism would look like, his ideas would inspire revolutions in Russia, China, and numerous other places in the twentieth century. However, when people in those countries put Marx's principles into practice, the results were different from what they imagined. Leaders in those countries perverted his ideas and, at an extreme, it became totalitarianism.

A creator can create something, but the creator doesn't know how the creation will unfold in the future. Marx envisaged a new society would one day emerge from the ashes of capitalism, but he had no clue how things would really pan out. It's because there can never be a perfect System, even if corrupt forces do not take over. However, there is something we can do. We can align ourselves to a System that is perfect — nature. We do not know how tomorrow will unfold, but we can live in the moment and leave the rest to the original creator — the Source. Tomorrow's design is not in any person's hand.

SECTION III

THE GAMES PEOPLE PLAY

27

SELF-IMAGE WORKS AS A ROAD MAP

Over the next two chapters, we will look at the crucial concept of Self-image that directly or indirectly affects the lives of all three personalities — Wanted Child, Partly Wanted Child, and Unwanted Child. This will be followed by sub-sections on how the mechanism of the Survival Mechanism, Self and Self-image impact the individual personality types. Readers may choose to go through all the sub-sections or go directly to the one that pertains to them.

While we have seen how a person's Self provides guidance, the way in which it does this is through a Self-image. From childhood, as we grow, an expanded Self gets formed that is an amalgamation of different identities and our own experiences. Alongside it something else happens that becomes inevitable. We start seeing ourselves through the eyes of others and how they would like us to be. An image of us gets created in our minds that becomes a sort of ideal we strive to be. This image springs directly from a person's Self and is therefore known as Self-image.

The parent who has a child as a goal also has an image of what s/he would want the child to be like in the future. This takes a rough form in the earliest years of the child's life but keeps evolving and changing as the child grows up. As we have seen, the child absorbs these expectations and tries to fulfill them. The expectations are held in the form of a Self-image, which a child tries to match up to throughout life. So, if the Self of a person is the internalized parents, the Self-image is the expectations of those internalized parents.

Fitting Into Someone's Imagination

The woman is the chief architect who makes the dream of having a child a reality. Nature has bestowed on her the unique gift of conceiving and giving birth to another human. Every one of us is somebody's imagination bought to life, born out of a woman.

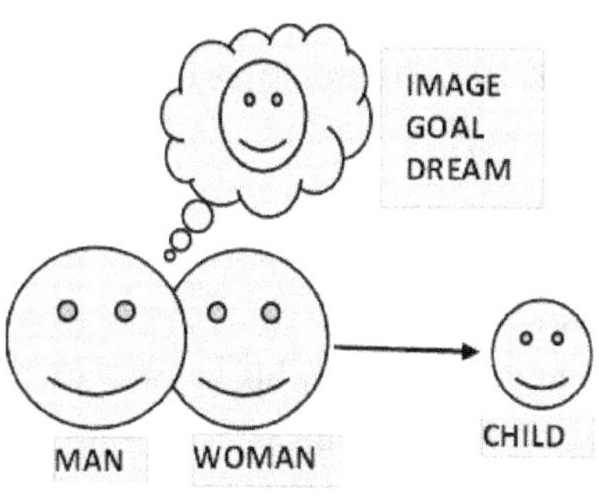

Diagram 14

We have already seen in Chapter 2 how our goals and desires are the expectations of others. Since we are born out of someone's imagination or dream, we are also somebody *else's* blueprint. There is a desire that we will conform to a particular vision a parent has for a child, however indefinite it may be at the start. This goes on to become our Self-image. Initially, we take it from our parents, who are our creators, and later from other people and influences who comprise our expanded Self. Unconsciously, we try our best to match the specifications of that image (the expectations).

Just like a coconut seed must grow to become a coconut tree and not a mango tree, there isn't too much leeway given to us to deviate from a design. Parents have in their minds a set of aspirations, dreams, and expectations that they would like their child to fulfill. Consider the following statements:

* ❖ "I want my child to be friendly with neighborhood kids."
* ❖ "I want my child to learn to be creative, just like I was when I was young."
* ❖ "I want my child to learn the value of discipline."
* ❖ "I want my child to be educated and to get a good job."
* ❖ "I want my child to grow up to be rich and get us out of poverty."
* ❖ "I want my child to be a doctor, scientist or go abroad."
* ❖ "I would like my children to carry on our beautiful traditions when they grow up."

These expectations exist independently of the child in the minds and hearts of parents. Even parents who adopt a liberal parenting philosophy have some expectations from their children, whether it relates to values or behavior.

Parents may have a vision of a healthy, obedient, intelligent, or well-mannered child while the child is picking up that vision. A child is certainly given a degree of flexibility to express his/her personality and wishes. Parents will accommodate them to an extent, but not if they violate a boundary. Metaphorically, it's like a child is allowed to play a game of his/her choice within the confines of a park. But s/he mustn't run outside onto the street to play or play once it's dark. Or a child is allowed to watch his favorite cartoon after dinner, but not for more than thirty minutes. While young, there are decisions a child is allowed to make, but only in limited ways. This is akin to an inhabitant of a house who is permitted to knock off a wall or two, and rearrange some of the interiors but who cannot raze the structure of the house itself and rebuild it.

The Blueprint Changes

A child has to keep adapting to a *changing* blueprint. Parents load their children with new expectations as a child grows older. While a child can playfully engage in learning the alphabet at the age of two or three, s/he can't be playful about her English homework from school at the age of ten. The blueprint (expectations) has changed in the parents' minds of what they want the child to now be and do. As a college student, the child may be expected to take up a part-time job or participate in household tasks as a young adult learning to take on responsibility. This is not to denounce what parents expect but to show how a child keeps trying to fit into a certain ideal representation of him/her.

Another reason why the blueprint changes is because an increasing number of new people influence the child. More people enter the child's life, with their own set of values, beliefs, and ideas. The child's life changes as siblings, relatives, teachers, and neighbors keep adding more and more items to a child's blueprint, which a child must learn to match.

Seeing Through the Eyes of the Self

We have seen how a child carries a mix of identities and starts to gather his/ her own experiences. Each of these identities has an image of what they would like the child to be or to imbibe. So the child starts to perceive this image through the eyes of the different people who constitute his/her Self. S/he tries his/her best to meet that standard.

While the Self is an imaginary identity a person holds, the Self-image is an image that a person perceives of him/her through the eyes of those identities (father, mother, or others), looking at it the way they would see it. The child identifies his/her being with the parents and projects their image onto a screen. S/he wants to fit into that projected image and

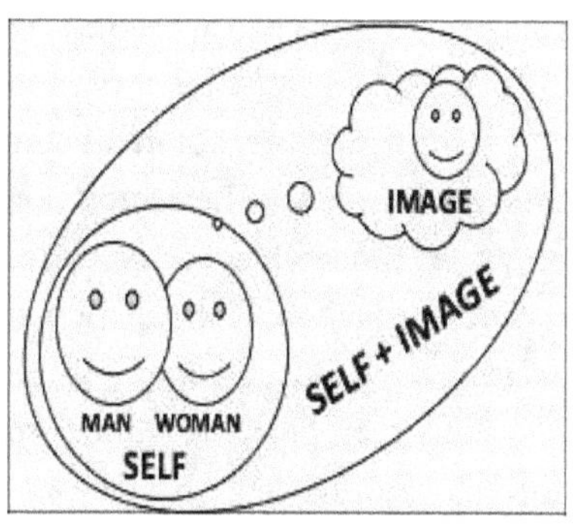

Diagram 15

the closer s/he gets to that image, the happier s/he feels for having met the expectations of parents and others. It becomes the ideal the person keeps chasing and matching up to throughout their life. Self-image is like the blueprint referred to above but, as explained, it keeps expanding and changing.

The diagram shows the expanded Self-image. As we grow older, the Self-image keeps expanding and altering as per the changing expectations and circumstances around us.

We go through life struggling against the pressure exerted by an imaginary Self that wants us to live up to expectations (the Self-

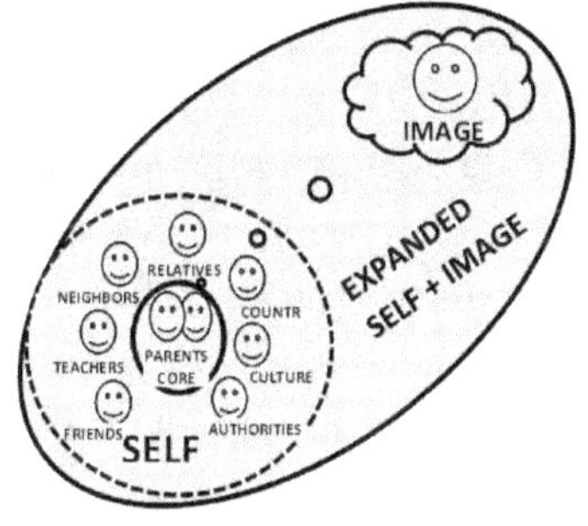

Diagram 16

image). Sumit, who was mentioned in the first chapter, had a Self that was dominated by the identities of his father, mother, and girlfriend. His parents had built up certain expectations of him, either directly or subtly, and this became his Self-image — the person he ought to be — that was guiding him through life. He was constantly viewing this Self-image through the eyes of his father, mother, and girlfriend and saying to himself, "What would *they* think of me?" They were a part of him and his identity — he had no identity that was purely his own. If he was unable to make his physical being, Sumit, the person, attain his Self-image, he would experience stress. On the other hand, if his performance matched that of his Self-image, he would feel happy.

Sumit's Self was not in his control. It was in the hands of his parents and girlfriend, and he almost looked like a puppet dancing to their tunes. At times when their expectations would shift, Sumit's Self-image would change too. If they experienced any displeasure or dissatisfaction relating to Sumit, it would result in him feeling anguish.

This may be hard to fathom, but we all experience this sort of internal pressure. We live as per specifications given to us by a Self-image (imagine it as something out there). We see that Self-image through the eyes of others — our parents, relatives, friends, and our culture, to name a few. These are people or things we have absorbed into our Self. We try to perceive our lives the way they would and try to conform to their wishes or standards. For instance, living up to a cultural stereotype or what it means to be a man or woman in one's society are examples of living by a Self-image.

The stress that we often experience comes from the Self that pushes us to fit into a cast imagined by the people who constitute our Self. The Self is like a boss inside a person. Visualize the scenario of a demanding male boss at your workplace. You see your tasks through the eyes of your boss and think of what would make him happy. At that moment, you are not focusing on the job. Instead, you are looking at your performance through the eyes of your boss, wondering what would impress or satisfy him. Your attention has moved away from what you are capable of doing towards the goal of placating your demanding boss.

The diagram below shows how SELF and IMAGE are embedded into us at the time of our birth. Sometimes the process begins even earlier, in the imagination of the parents. Progressively over the years, these become our identity and what we strive to become or maintain. The Self-image keeps shifting and modifying as parents and others keep adding or altering their expectations of their children. The SELF is shown as separate from the IMAGE, but as human beings, we operate as a combination of both, and we don't know how to segregate them.

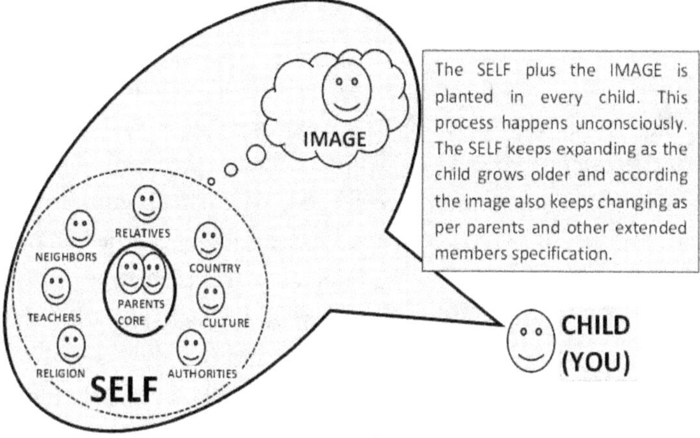

Diagram 17

Self-image is beyond the control of any human being until one understands the workings of the Survival Mechanism. In the chapters ahead, we will take an in-depth look at Self-image. We, as children, didn't have a choice but needed to survive with whatever was available in our environments. However, we don't have to stay tied up with a self-image that comes from others and, through awareness, can change as we grow older

28

SELF-IMAGE GOVERNS YOUR DESTINY

Kirti, a Wanted Child, demanded she needed an emergency session with me. Sitting on the recliner, she sobbed away, calling herself a total failure. When I asked her to tell me more, she spoke of going away on a weekend trip with her friends. Kirti shared with her friends her recent success in her job, where she had increased her organization's sales by thirty percent and then to ninety percent within a few months. When her friends asked her about her salary, she told them it was $500 a month. On hearing this, they burst out laughing. They told her that she was being exploited and should be paid at least $1,500 while they were earning $2,000 a month themselves. Crying, she said, "I have always been a failure in my life. All through my life, I have only felt worthless."

I regressed Kirti back to a time when she was a fourth-grade student. Her father was pleased as she excelled in her studies and told her she should become a doctor. Since that day, she stopped playing and having fun, making her studies her sole focus. I asked her, whose decision was it to become a doctor? She said it was hers. While she studied hard for years, when the time came, her father couldn't finance her medical school education. Since then, she has been disappointed with her life and angry towards her father. As a child, Kirti saw her image through the eyes of her father, who was her core Self. As she grew older, she saw her image through her friends' eyes. On hearing her friends mock her, she judged her performance as a failure through their eyes, for she had failed to match up to their standards. Kirti was projecting her image through the eyes of her friends in the same way she did through her father's eyes when she was a child. In both cases, she was emotionally reacting to others' perceptions of her.

Such emotions arise from the confusion and conflict within a person caused by one's Self, Self-image, and Survival Mechanism. When we are fulfilling the dreams or goals of others, we are following the direction given to us by our Self and Self-image. How well we meet the expectations of our parents, relatives, peers, or others who comprise our Self results in us experiencing positive or negative emotions. Let's take a closer look at how Self-image influences us.

Self-image is a Primitive Map

Self-image is a mental picture a person holds of his/her body in the form of thoughts. It functions as a roadmap that gives direction to the child and how s/he should perform to get acceptance from the Self. The visual representation is of the person's body and its accompanying behaviors or communication. It results in an internal process where s/he compares his/ her physical body's actual condition or performance with that mental image. I've used the word "primitive map" to describe Self-image as this map was created by people in the past, the way they saw the terrain of life.

We may have a dream of owning a dream car. *But the car cannot decide who the owner is going to be. The car cannot also decide its owner's destination or end-use.* A child is a part of the desires of parents. We have seen this being described in the section on goals. The parents make all early life decisions for the child, whether they relate to food, toys, entertainment, or books. The parents become the core of a person's Self, which becomes the driver of decisions s/he makes as a teenager or adult. This mechanism gets more reinforced when the person unconsciously pursues a particular Self-image.

Self Projects a Self-image

We need to re-look at the definition of Self-image. We want to match a Self-image as we do it to feel accepted, whether it is doing well at school as children or achieving a certain kind of success as adults. Getting acceptance is directly connected to our survival and meeting expectations makes us feel accepted. No matter how old we are, there is an internal mechanism that indicates whether we are going in the right direction. And those signals are our emotions.

We see our image on an imaginary screen through the eyes of our parents and try to match it with our actual performance. It's as if our parents are projecting the image onto the screen. We are trying to fit into a mold designed by our parents and others, which gives us assurance that we are doing well, making us feel secure. We know how the Self is our parents, who we have internalized. It places expectations on us. So even when our parents are not communicating with us directly, the Self inside us projects an image we need to match up with.

This is a subtle process. Self-image is a mental picture of an outcome that is expected or possibly demanded of us, which drives us to adopt goals and act in a certain way. Without our awareness, we are constantly shaping our body's performance to match certain specifications directly or indirectly asked of us. A person who wishes to be in the armed forces has to fit into the mold of a soldier, perceiving it through the eyes of his superior rank officers. To be accepted as a soldier, the body's output modes (movement, sound, and words) need to match a soldier's behaviors and communication style.

In the below diagram, Prince Wan is viewing the projected image of him on the screen as a prince through the eyes of his parents. When this happens, he forgets his own being and represents one or both of his parents, looking at a projected image through their eyes of what they would like him to be. Wan is mentally displaced and starts to embody one or both of his parents. This process takes a fraction of a second and will determine how Wan feels at that moment, emotionally. The parents with whom Wan is identifying are in his Self, and the process is an unconscious one. Wan's Self creates a Self-image and projects it outwards. Wan tries his best to fit into that image.

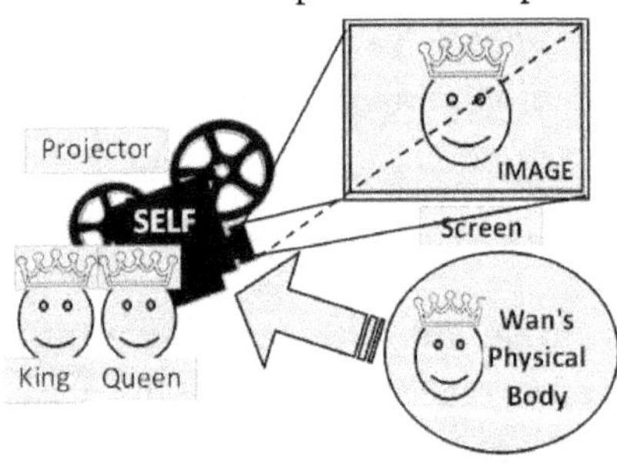

Diagram 18

You will notice how Wan has no direct access to his Self-image. He relies on his parents to be able to perceive it. Just like the car cannot decide its owner's destination, a child cannot decide his/her own destiny. So s/he has to access it via the parents, who have laid out goals. The whole process goes on within Wan's mind in a few seconds and he is entirely unconscious of it. Only by pleasing his parents, his survival is intact. The assurance that he gets from it can be called a False Illusionary Assurance, which is temporary and dependent on others for approval.

The Changing Self-Image

An image is an imaginary representation of our physical body (what we ought to be) in our mind based on the expectations of others. Since it's derived from others' expectations, the image keeps on changing as we grow older. The pre-decided picture undergoes modifications arising from the new wishes of parents. Parents teach their young children the alphabet and then basic words. When the child goes to a higher grade in school, parents want them to perform well in studies and school activities. The goalposts for the child keep shifting as new challenges are placed before him/her. It could be public speaking, sports, dance or drawing competitions. Through this, the child tries to focus on the parents' outcomes, thinking they are his/her own goals. That is the survival mechanism in action. The more the child meets the parents' expectations, the more s/he feels safe and secure. The child's positive emotional state indicates it. If s/he underperforms, it makes him/her sad and disappointed. At all times, the Self-image remains an ideal the child strives for.

This unconscious process continues even in adulthood. Our parents get replaced by our spouse, boss, peers, or others. Self-image keeps changing as we grow older and move into new environments, countries, or cultures. It is never constant and will never be constant because others will continue to place their expectations. We spend our whole life fitting into that imaginary image sculpted by others.

We Decide on the Basis of Self and Self-Image

We have seen in earlier chapters how our Self makes decisions for us. Very rarely do we use our free will, though it is available for everyone to exercise. A spouse, boss, or those we want acceptance from will continue to affect our Self-image. It might look as if we are making conscious decisions, but in actuality, it is happening through one's Self and its changing constituents. We are unaware of this automated process happening within us.

Although Kirti is in her thirties, her Self and her image still affect her. She feels she is not up to the mark and feels incomplete when others push her buttons. At such moments, Kirti is no longer living in the present but has regressed to a time in the past. When she was unemployed, she prayed for a job close to her home, a decent salary and one she enjoyed. Her current job gave her exactly that and there should have been no cause for regret. Instead of relaxing and enjoying her holiday with friends, she returned with bitter memories and negative emotions.

Kirti decided to study to become a doctor not because she desired it, but to please her father. She never thought that he would also be the cause of her anger and sadness, defining her experiences in life. The core of the Self, parents, are directly connected to our fate as our decision-making always goes through our Self. Our Self creates the image we want to match up to and we have no direct access to it. We always need to go through the Self to fulfill our parents' expectations by matching up to a Self-image. As mentioned earlier in this chapter, a car cannot decide its own destination and a child cannot independently decide his/her own destiny. This is true for most of us, except for the rare few who have taken charge of their fate and are living by their terms.

Creating One's Own Image

When a person is trying to meet or succeeds in meeting someone else's expectations, s/he cannot create their own image. In the diagram below, Wan is a Wanted Child who is supposed to perform well at school. Parents give Wan this message, whether directly or indirectly, which he needs to fulfill in order to feel accepted. Even if the message is not delivered verbally, Wan senses the expectation and picks it up. This process is happening unconsciously within Wan, beyond his awareness.

There is an arrow with a cross in the diagram below going upwards from Wan to the image. This indicates that such a possibility cannot happen — Wan can access goals placed before him (the Self-image) only via his Self, which represents his parents. *He, with his Survival Mechanism, has no direct access to his Self-image.* His sense of achievement and happiness here comes from matching his performance to expectations that are perceived through their eyes. They will be proud of him if he becomes what they would like him to be, and this ensures his survival is intact. Wan is not aware that this is not his goal, but an expectation that arises from his Self.

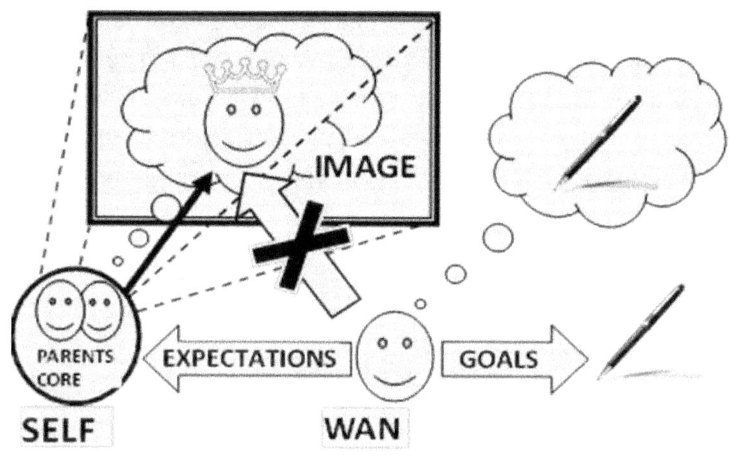

Diagram 19

On the other hand, if Wan earns some pocket money doing small jobs and wants to buy a new pen, it becomes his goal in his mind. In this case, he can satisfy his needs by buying a new pen. Notice that in this case, he can directly access the image of his goal, unlike in the case of the Self-image, where he can't. This process is similar to when a man wants to own his dream car, which is a personal goal. Contrast this to an expectation, which is the goal of someone else.

When we are fulfilling others' dreams or goals, we are following the route of our Self and Self-image to meet certain expectations, which generates emotions of happiness or disappointment. It is dependent on their approval and degree of satisfaction; both lie in the hands of others. Even one's best performance might not satisfy others, making one a puppet in their hands.

But when goals or dreams are your own, the choice of how you achieve them is entirely yours. The controls are in your hand. You make decisions at all times and can choose how you want to feel emotionally when attaining your goal. Your destiny lies in your own hands.

The image of the outcome of your desire is your own; this time, you have direct access to it. You may refine the image or change it altogether until you feel satisfied. There is no one you have to please and nobody else controls the goal.

Wan and Kirti are Wanted Children, and the above description of the Self-image relates mainly to the Wanted Child. The process is different for the Partly Wanted Child and Unwanted Child. In the chapters ahead, we will see how all three categories of the Survival Mechanism go about constructing the Self and Self-image in their own distinct way.

THE WANTED CHILD

29

SURVIVING BY LIVING OTHERS' DREAMS

The potter in the below diagram sits with a clay lump on his potter's wheel. He needs to be clear about what he wants to make from the clay. In this case, the potter wants to make a water jug. The clay cannot take its own shape, but it's the potter who gives it one with his imagination and skill. The wheel synchronizes with the potter's intentions, creating a water jug. Although the clay could have become a mug, vase, flowerpot, or utensil, it cannot become anything other than what its creator would like it to be. Similarly, a farmer who plants a jackfruit seed will grow a jackfruit tree and not a mango tree.

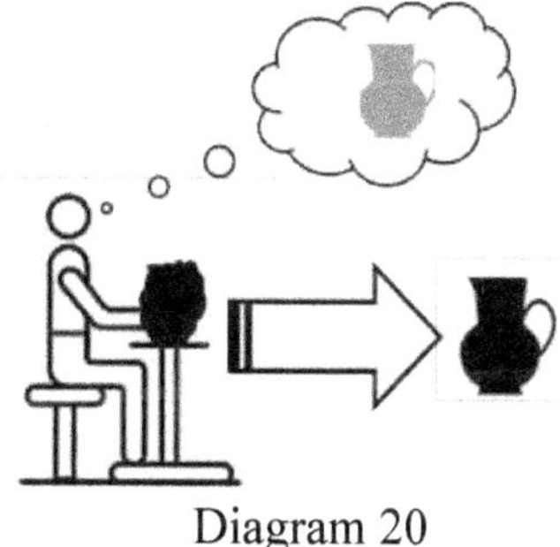

Diagram 20

The new jug needs to meet the expectations of its creator. It's size, exact shape, design, and durability need to conform to the potter's criteria. If it fails to do so, the potter can destroy it and begin the process once again.

A Wanted Child is a dream of the parents. Both of them want the child and co-operate to fulfill their wish. Knowingly or unknowingly, they also place their desires on the child and expect that s/he achieves them. Unaware and unconscious of this truth, the Wanted Child tries to live up to their expectations, much like the clay that gets molded to fit a specific form. Parents decide the fate of the Wanted Child.

You can observe your own desires. They must meet your expectations, or else you will feel disappointed. The degree of disappointment may vary based on the nature of the goal. The satisfaction a cup of coffee offers to a coffee drinker cannot be matched by making the person drink tea, although s/he may consume it. When Arnold builds his dream house, he invests his life savings, energy, time, and imagination into it. He certainly won't be content if his home ends up being quite different from what he had imagined. A Wanted Child is a lifetime project and perhaps the most significant dream of his/her parents. Much will depend on their financial capabilities, background, upbringing, and other influences. Parents may be willing to trade their whole life for such a child, just as owning a dream house is a once-in-a-lifetime opportunity for someone else.

Many of us have a deep desire to create another human being, for which we will prepare patiently and wait for the right time. Once a Wanted Child is born, we start to live our dreams through him/her and burden the child with expectations. We want them to achieve what we couldn't or go beyond what we could. It could relate to financial success, a flamboyant lifestyle, or a career choice. A shipbroker I know would have loved to make films instead. As he didn't fulfill his own dream, he wanted to live his life vicariously through his son. He wished his son would rather join film school than opt for the monotony of a corporate job. The message that you are a dream project gets transferred to the Wanted Child. If the child wants acceptance and to survive, s/he feels s/he must meet expectations.

A photographer who buys his dream camera wants its specification to match what he is looking for. He is excited by the prospect of clicking high-quality pictures. So, he doesn't just buy any camera but one that will give him the results he desires. Just as desires are transferred to the camera, they also get transferred to a Wanted Child. Desires, as expectations, get downloaded into the child's system when the child is conceived. It becomes essential to know how a Wanted Child comes into existence. The extract below from my book *Stop Surviving Start Living with Freedom* tells us more about the birth of a Wanted Child. (Page No 47-48)

In Agreement

When both the man and woman are IN AGREEMENT on matters of sex and procreation, the by-product (child) is a Wanted Child. The core factor here is that the woman accepts the man and thus accepts his sperms in her body. The man wants to have a child (a by-product of sexual intercourse), and the woman consents to the proposal. That means she is willing to give birth to his progeny. The fact that the man and woman are in sync transfers a message to the unborn in their sexual activity itself.

Let's look at this from the point of view where we contrast it to a woman who has unfortunately been raped. The deep psychological scar a woman who has been raped experiences is created by the sexual act when she was violated. The trauma she went through then and the recurring emotions she experienced subsequently sends a message to the unborn that she doesn't want him/her. The child is a reminder of and a trigger for a traumatic memory. Therefore the sexual act and ensuing memories of it itself affect the mother's emotional state, which is picked up by the fetus. Suppose this is true in the scenario of a woman who has been violated; then in that case, it's also true that a positive message gets communicated to a fetus by a couple that is in harmony with each other through their sexual act of conceiving. The mother's emotional state in this scenario will be a positive one and be picked up by the fetus.

When the couple is IN AGREEMENT, the woman accepts the man. Thus, he holds a position of importance in her life. The message is also picked up by the fetus that s/he is valuable to the couple. The expectations and dreams of the parents also get transferred to the child in a general sense. This continues after the child is born, which creates a set of expectations in him/her. You will get clarity on this when you read about the survival traits of the Wanted Child.

Since the woman has accepted the man and gives him importance, the man plays a primary role in the Wanted Child's life. The Wanted

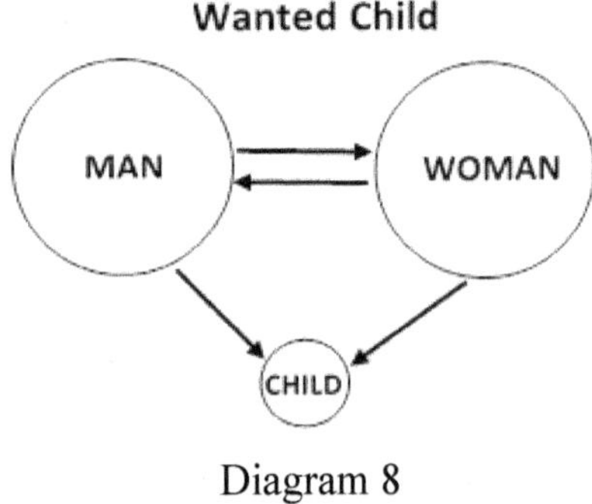

Diagram 8

Child also gives more prominence to the father and wants his approval more than that of the mother. Let's try to understand the reasons for this by seeing it from the perspective of the Wanted Child. The child is part of the mother's system, and she is caring for him/ her. It is the mother that introduces the father to the child. The mother, in this case, also values the man. Somewhere the child picks up the message that here is someone (the father) who wants me and is taking responsibility for me. The child now also gets the message that there is a team of people looking after him, and the father is the team's leader. That is because the mother gives the father this value by looking up to him as the supporter, particularly if he is the provider.

As a summary shown in the above figure, there is an agreement between a man and a woman. The woman has accepted the man, who knows he is accepted by the woman and vice versa. The woman accepts the man, thus also accepts a child that is borne through him. By accepting both the man and his child, the mother also gives the child a father. This agreement validates the idea in the child that s/he is wanted even before s/he is born.

Given that parents invest so much of their resources in them, the benchmarks set for Wanted Children are high. They can be compared to a prince or a princess who is coronated within a few days after their birth. As their kingdom's future rulers, they wear metaphorical crowns on their heads. The crown symbolizes responsibilities that they will need to shoulder. Therefore, an image or vision is created at the time of conception and handed over to them, like a map that gives direction to a specific place. The predicament of the Wanted Child is expressed in the below extract from *Stop Surviving Start Living with Freedom*. (Page No. 150 – 151)

Prince or Princess - Royal Slavery

The Wanted Child is usually born with a crown on the head. Now you can imagine a crown is made up of pure gold and is studded with precious gems. It's of considerable weight and is highly valuable. Children who are born as a prince and princess are supposed to live up to the expectations of the king, the queen, and everybody else who looks up to them. In this kingdom, even the people have expectations for the prince and princess, and they are supposed to fulfill everybody's dreams. When this young prince and princess are growing to be a young man and woman, they still carry the burden of the crown. The crown signifies responsibilities, unknowingly dumped on to them. To make it worse, they are not even aware of it. These children will be living all their adult years carrying this invisible weight. They don't realize that the system (primarily it's the family and later society who gives them this message) has shackled them with it. They have to be a cut above the rest and are not permitted to make mistakes, as everyone looks up to them.

Every prince and princess has to go through his and her regular drill of learning how to conduct themselves strictly in accordance with their status. All those born as princes and princesses have to follow their daily supervised training by professionals so that they can impart their royal duties, class behaviors, attitudes, and communication styles to the kingdom. This consists of all of their activities, which they will display to the common people of the kingdom. That includes the way they walk, the way they talk, the way their conduct should be in public, the way they eat, their dressing style, and other etiquettes. Every prince and princess born to be an heir has to learn a language spoken by the royal family. There are many such rituals the royals are made to go through. All these are forms of indirect force applied to them so that they learn to comply, in order to be able to live the royal life. They are not supposed to make any mistakes, can't take criticism, and can't be looked down upon, while they are trying hard to fulfill the aspirations of the king, the queen, and the people of their kingdom. They are forever required to meet the royal standard, which is above the ordinary class, drilled into them through perfection.

Note that we are not judging whether it is right or wrong for parents to transfer expectations onto their children or whether it is natural or unnatural. It's about understanding a process whereby the desires of parents get picked up by the Wanted Child and become the goals s/he strives for.

Over the next two chapters, we will look at how the mechanism of the Self, Self-image and Survival Mechanism works within the Wanted Child. How does the Wanted Child make decisions and how do others decide the child's fate?

30

PROJECTING THROUGH THE EYES OF THE SELF

Wanted Children spend their whole life chasing a Self-image that has been given to them by their parents and others. They are living under constant pressure to match up to this image, which keeps growing and changing with time. This image is nothing but a projection of the Self, which contains all the identities the Wanted Child has absorbed over life. What those people would like him/ her to be is something this child puts a lot of value on. Before we look into how this happens, let's delve a bit further into the personality of the Wanted Child.

The Wanted Child is the manifestation of a couple's desire to have a child, where both people wish for a child during conception. The two express or have a readiness for parenting a new child. This shared goal affects both their emotions in a positive way.

Self of a Wanted Child

No child can have his/her existence without the parents. In the Wanted Child in particular, both parents become the core base of the child's Self. Since s/he does not have his/her individuality, s/he constructs it from those who matter the most, unconsciously. During childhood, it's primarily the parents who occupy the child's mind space and the extended family, including grandparents, uncles, and aunts. The Wanted Child also needs to look good in the eyes of teachers who play an important role during the child's formative years and also become part of the expanded Self.

As s/he grows older, authority figures like bosses and managers get added to the Self. Work colleagues could join the list too. And of course, when married, the spouse becomes an integral part of the person's Self. The Wanted Child is like a prince or princess who does not want anyone to look down on him/her. That means anyone who s/he deems important, and is capable of evaluating him/her, can become a part of that Self.

It's worth remembering that these identities get absorbed into a Self that is not concrete. That is why it is called an illusionary Self. The Wanted Child operates from within that illusionary Self and perceives the world through it. No child can make a conscious choice to act differently because consciousness has not yet sprouted at a young age.

Perceiving Through the "Eyes" of the Self

Proving to be worthy becomes an overarching life goal for the Wanted Child. This personality type develops traits such as performance orientation, a fear of failure, a fear of being looked down on or of criticism, excessive cautiousness or risk aversion, and other qualities that have to do with his/her survival. These traits are ever-present in the adult who is a Wanted Child. How well or poorly the Wanted Child meets expectations placed on him/her will affect the way s/he feels emotionally.

Most of the content in the chapter "Self-Image Governs Your Destiny" relates to the Wanted Child.

What this means for the Wanted Child is that s/he lives life seeing through the eyes of others, especially the parents. Parents do not always have to be physically present. They are *inside the Wanted Child's mind, in the form of his/her Self.* Through the Self, they act like a projector that projects an image onto a screen. This projected image is the Wanted Child's Self-image. The same Self is also looking at the actual physical person having a body, judging and evaluating his/her performance vis-à-vis the Self-image. In other words, the parents, in the form of the Self are monitoring whether the physical person is living up to the image. This is the "comparison" Wanted Children go through in their minds. In this way, they are caught up in a race between their self-image and their personal performance.

The Wanted Child's Self is an amalgamation of different personalities in which parents get maximum weightage. Wanted Children look at their physical body's performance through the eyes of all these personalities and make comparisons with the outcome these personalities would like to see. In such instances, the one who is actually looking at the physical body's performance and the image is the Self. The internal comparison gives Wanted Children a glimpse of whether they are matching up to the expectations of others or not.

They want to look worthy in the eyes of their dear ones, which gives them False Illusionary Assurance. This makes them take on many expectations their families may have, such as getting a good education, achieving financial success, or getting married. Wanted Children are willing to do anything to protect their image from getting tarnished. In fact, they want to shield it from any damage because if that gets damaged, they will experience negative emotions or illness.

Wanted Children do not truly live their lives but live them through the way others perceive them and how they ought to live. Wanted Children are fooled by what gets projected onto the metaphorical screen. What is projected on the screen is not reality but an imaginary work of the person's Self. Since such children are wanted, they must be a class above the average, a source of much strife for them throughout life as they go about proving their worthiness.

Perform or Perish: The Inner Life of Prince Wan

The outer circle in the diagram below represents Prince Wan's body. We can see what's happening inside it. With his Survival Mechanism and its tools, he tries to mold and fit into a Self-image to please his Self. With the aid of his Survival Mechanism, the more his performance matches the image, the more assured Prince Wan feels. That gives him a positive emotional boost. But if the performance mismatches the image, negative feelings crop-up, which the Wanted Child avoids at all costs.

We, with our Survival Mechanism, try to please our Self (which represents others) to preserve our bodies. Only when the body survives, we can thrive. The Survival Mechanism does not have direct access to the Self-image.

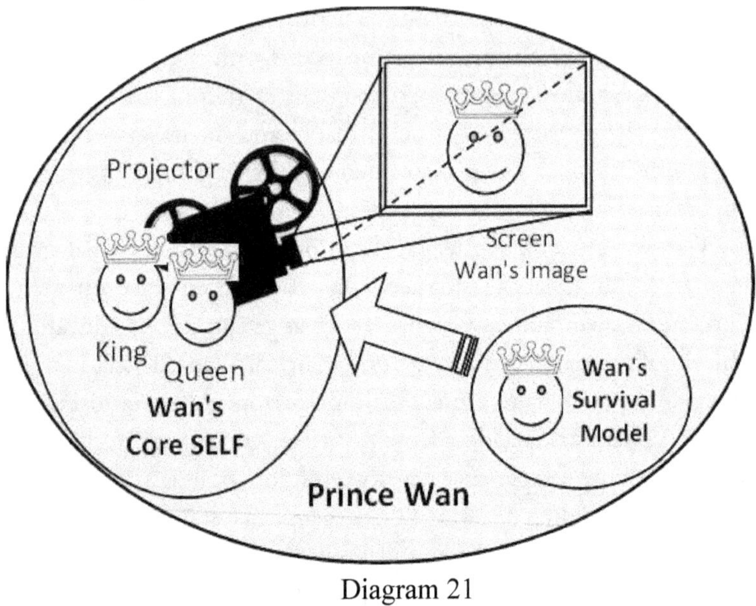

Diagram 21

The diagram reveals how Wan's internal thought processes work and how he perceives his life. Wan's Self is functioning like a projector, and he (with his Survival Mechanism) is looking through the eyes of his parents, the king and queen, at a projected image of him on a screen. We have seen this in the example of Wan two chapters earlier, where the Self is projecting a Self-image.

It is as if Wan is not in his own body, but inside his parent's body, looking at the projected image the way they would perceive him. Wan is viewing the world through his parents' eyes. As the Self, he is playing the role of his parents. At times, he could be perceiving his image through the eyes of one of his parents, or at other times through both the parents' eyes.

Within his brain, there is a regular internal comparison taking place. Wan evaluates his physical body's performance and matches it with his Self-image. In the diagram, Wan's image and Wan's body look alike, with a crown on their respective heads. It means they match each other. The result gives Wan a deep feeling of inner satisfaction, experienced in the form of positive emotions. He enjoys these emotions, which gives Prince Wan a temporary assurance that he is doing well and that life is going well. He is unaware of the unconscious comparison process going on inside him, or that the standards he matches are those of his parents, who exist in him as a Self.

On the bottom right-hand side, Wan has no direct access to Wan's Self-image. At all times, he can access his image (projected as if onto a screen) only through others who comprise his Self, which in this case, are his parents. Self-image does not exist independently; it originates from the Self. To access this image, Wan operates a projector through his Self and looks at the screen. This is what makes Wanted Children visual people. They are constantly seeing an image of themselves they need to match with their body's performance.

We may have come across a truism that we perceive ourselves through the eyes of others or through society's eyes. But we may not have appreciated how the Self inside us, which is an amalgamation of multiple personalities, is the one making this happen.

If Prince Wan's actual performance didn't match the desired result of his Self-image, he would experience discomfort. Wan could also imagine future expectations through his parents' eyes, generating anxiety or even panic. He could be expected to buy his own house someday. Wan knows at a conscious level that if he doesn't deliver the desired outcome, he will be deemed a failure. A Wanted Child looks at failure as a survival issue, not as an event, as it means s/he hasn't been able to prove his/her worth. Thus s/he may no longer be considered special or out-of-the-ordinary any longer, a terrifying prospect.

This whole process of comparison inside Wan's brain happens in a matter of seconds, sometimes even a fraction of a second. Besides, perceiving the image and matching it to the performance of the physical body happens almost seamlessly. It's like a child who is unaccustomed to public speaking, who suddenly feels nervous the minute s/he is placed on a stage and facing an audience. There is a marked degree of self-consciousness, as there is an expectation of performance from the child. Everyone is watching me, and will I be up to the mark? The child has to look good in the eyes of the audience and freezes up. Performance pressure was applied on the Wanted Child from a young age, so s/he worries about not living up to a high standard.

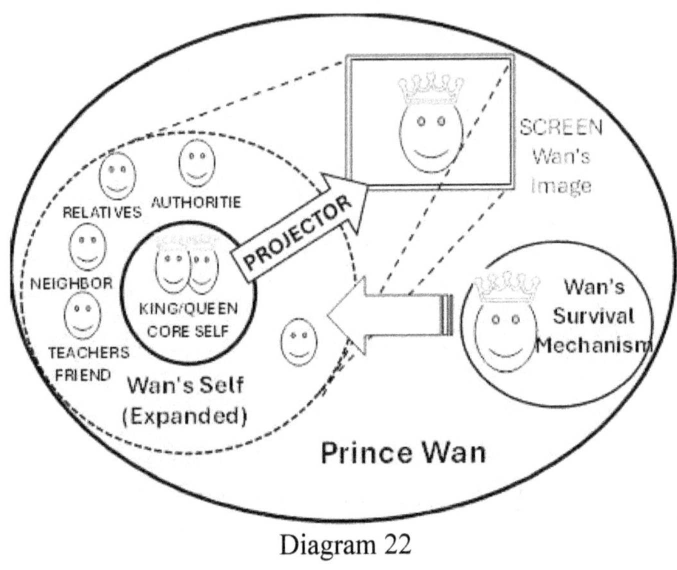

Diagram 22

The above diagram is a depiction of Wan operating under the influence of his expanded Self, which is his larger kingdom. Again, the outer circle represents Wan's body. As mentioned earlier, the use of the word "kingdom" refers to anyone who knows Wan directly or indirectly on a personal level, so as to form a judgment on him. Parents obviously occupy the core Self. Those who inhabit the expanded Self include relatives, friends, authority figures (teachers, coaches, or a boss), and people from the community.

Prince Wan tends to look at his image through the eyes of this extended group, imagining how they would like him to be. He certainly detests the idea of anyone looking down at him. Even when it comes to his future, Wan will perceive his image through the eyes of this group. He chooses their goals and sees how to achieve them. It's like someone graduating from an Ivy League college may want to look good in the eyes of his/her peer group. S/he ends up chasing a prestigious or sought-after career rather than one that makes him/her genuinely joyful. If Wan's image — the way his extended group perceives him — matches how he performs in life, he will experience feelings of comfort, happiness, and pride. This process takes place in his mind within a time frame of a few seconds. The outcome will be positive or negative emotions.

During the course of writing this book, I had a session with a man who is a film director. He was working for a reputed film production house and was recently experiencing anxiety and, occasionally, panic. Although he had years of experience as an industry professional, he was questioning his credibility. That's because he was looking at his image through the eyes of his boss and wondering if he could live up to his boss's expectations. He harbored doubts concerning his performance and was agonizing over success or failure. What if his project was not successful? How would his boss and others perceive him? Instead of focusing on the here and now — the project he needed to finish to the best of his ability — he imagined his future through the eyes of others.

The Self – The Driver in Charge

Yogi, an entrepreneur who is a Wanted Child, visited me as he was feeling anxious and restless. He had a manufacturing plant that could produce a maximum of 200,000 units of a product every month. However, Yogi would accept client orders of 300,000 units instead, which was fifty percent more than the plant's capacity. He confessed to me that he didn't want his clients to know that his plant couldn't produce 300,000 units. Why did Yogi do this? He was looking at his image through the eyes of his customers. What would they think of him if they discovered his true position? So, he was projecting an image of a capable businessman, looking at his image through his clients' eyes. Of course, as his (plant's) true potential was limited to 200,000 units only, it was causing him restlessness and anxiety, because he was falling short on his commitment and risked missing a deadline. He couldn't produce 50 percent more units within the same time limit. In the process, he got trapped in his own game - Self-sabotage.

Most often, the Wanted Child's personal decisions are processed through the Self. It appears that Wanted Children are making their own decisions. However, on closer scrutiny, one finds out that others greatly influence their decision-making. In the example of Prince Wan, who went to war, his parents greatly influenced his choice of waging war on the neighboring king. Such decisions are never neutral but are laden with what I call an "emotional charge." Emotions that have their roots in the past are an underlying driver. Though the Wanted Child makes decisions in the present, they come from a pattern established in the past. Thus, they are living their pasts in the present. And the same process is being taken into the future through goals they choose, which means they are projecting the past into the future. There is an internal mechanism at play that is compelling him/her to behave this way. What this implies is that their decisions are not being taken out of freedom but out of compulsion. The internal mechanism that drives Wanted Children to do so is their Self.

Even when they make a decision, they need approval from someone in authority. Until such a time, they are hesitant to go ahead with it on their own. In the process, they prolong their decision-making or postpone it to another time. I have met people in this category who manage their family businesses. Even if they have a workable proposal, they will hesitate to execute it independently. They will seek out someone in authority to give them the go-ahead signal. The example above of the film director is one such case. Despite having many years of experience in his field, he held back on making core business decisions and wanted the approval of a senior producer. It's simply challenging for such a person to implement decisions independently.

The decision-making process of Wanted Children follows the route of viewing themselves through the eyes of others. Fear of failure is an undercurrent, making them procrastinate to a future dates until they are mentally prepared. Meanwhile, the weight of expectations on them keeps on mounting.

31

THE DESTINY OF THE WANTED CHILD

Expectations that get piled on to a Wanted Child over a number of years accumulate to become an invisible load s/he carries in life. While growing up, demands from their parents gradually increase regarding their performance. Wanted Children want to also live up to those expectations and try their best to fit into the role thrust upon them, assisted by their Survival Mechanism.

Sometimes it may be the subtle validation of their parents' belief in their abilities. They want to do well in school, college, or life because their parents believe in them and expect a level of performance from them. Of course, they are unaware of this pattern when young. They try their best to cope with the stress that can accompany it. However, slowly and gradually, the weight of the pile keeps increasing because expectations keep growing. The unseen load becomes bigger and heavier.

Take the example of John, in the chapter "Self Demands Honor - Fulfill Expectations." He made a list of all the goals he wanted to achieve in life. To those, he added all that his wife and mother expected from him. As time went by, the list kept getting longer and longer on account of what they desired from him. John was experiencing stress, but he went on this way, not realizing that many of the goals he had on his list were not his own desires. Finally, one day he suffered a mild stroke and was unable to speak after that.

Wanted Children genuinely begin to feel the stress. Some pull on for more time or find coping mechanisms, such as drugs, alcohol, pornography, or entertainment. Others experience burnout due to the invisible baggage. If the Wanted Child doesn't diffuse this pressure, it can lead to health complications, faulty decision-making, or relationship issues.

As Wanted Children grow into adults, their responsibilities keep increasing. It is quite common for their coping mechanism to fail, as they collapse under the weight of their invisible burden. The body cannot withstand the pressure of the unseen pile, which has been ever-expanding. Doctors and counselors are unable to diagnose their issues fully. That's because *the whole mass Wanted Children carry is an imaginary one and invisible beyond one's comprehension.*

Recollect the analogy of Tom fighting an imaginary Tim from the introduction. Even if Tom takes a sharp-edged sword and tries to attack the imaginary Tim, who do you think will win? Tim is unreal, while Tom has a physical body. It is impossible for Tom to defeat Tim under any scenario simply because Tim is imaginary and, therefore, invisible. It is Tom's body that will get frustrated, exhausted, and eventually collapse due to the futile attack.

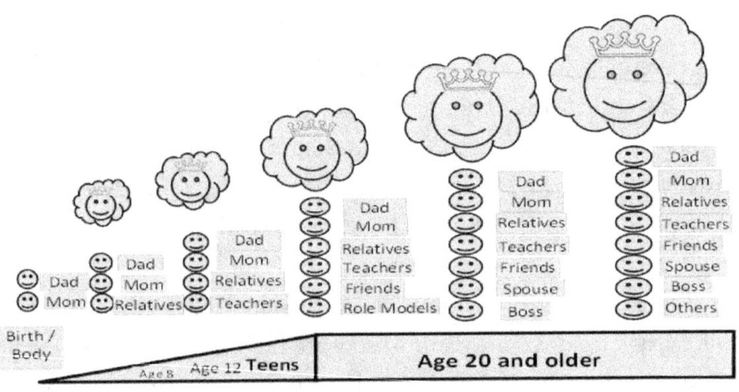

Diagram 23

The above diagram shows the timeline of the Wanted Child. The physical growth of the Wanted Child continues till the age of twenty. In the initial years, there are fewer responsibilities, but that will vary from person to person.

In the rectangle above, there are two factors. The horizontal timeline at the bottom represents different personalities that get absorbed into the Wanted Child's Self over time. Above it is the projected image on the metaphorical screen. In the formative years, the parents' personalities dominate the Wanted Child's Self. Over the years, more people get added to it. Some of the core personalities will continue to be there for many years, like mom and dad. All-important personalities are part of the Self through which the Wanted Child projects his image onto a screen.

The upper half of the rectangle shows the person's expanding Self-image — let's once again call it the image of Prince Wan. Prince Wan's projected image on the screen keeps getting bigger and bigger as new personalities get added with time. These new personalities add their own expectations on Wan. These could be a few people in the prince's life, but the quantum of the invisible load he has to carry at a specific time will depend upon the expectations of those few. The higher the expectations, the heavier is the unseen load.

The whole rectangle above represents an invisible mass that keeps increasing as the person grows up. Initially, the growth of the mass is progressive, but as it reaches adulthood, it can increase exponentially. This psychological weight affects the Wanted Child's body and mental state. Prince Wan's crown comes with responsibilities, and the crown gets heavier as the responsibilities grow with time. The unseen weight expands. Sometimes the weight may not increase, but a load of carrying it for so many years may exhaust the person. They collapse under the unseen weight of the crown, which affects their health physically and mentally. This is the same mass that could even terminate the life of a Wanted Child, as cruel as this may sound. It is nothing but an imaginary object, the Self, that takes a toll on the physical person. The Wanted Child has to learn to deal with this mass of the illusionary Self.

Dan, a young entrepreneur, once visited me. He complained of developing fears of becoming unwell. Fever, blisters, and heart palpitations would petrify Dan, and he would immediately visit a doctor for a medical examination. Only on the assurance of his doctor would he feel comforted and move on with his regular routine. Dan was extremely responsible towards his wife and other family members, which unfortunately burdened him. He had already proved his worth to everyone, but his survival mechanism kept reminding him of his inadequacies and would unknowingly haunt him.

Sumit, who we discussed in chapter one, similarly started feeling crushed under this illusionary Self's weight. Since he was a young boy, he needed approval from his mother and sometimes his father. That meant, unconsciously, his mother was a prominent part of his Self and was in the driver's seat. Sumit had always performed well in sports when he was young. Now he needed to make his own decisions, but he got lost in confusion. In a state of limbo, his internal mechanism was under stress because his peer group was making progress while he was stagnating. It sent a signal to him that he was not performing up to the mark. He also gained weight and wanted to lose it quickly. His internal mass, the Self, generated the stress on his spine that caused a slipped disc while he was doing gym exercises.

Finally, after deciding to pursue an MBA degree, Sumit fell back in his first year's performance. He then applied even more pressure by trying to perform well at business school. This compulsion to focus hard on achieving high standards aggravated his slipped disc injury. When he returned to India for surgery, high expectations did not spare him. The mass of his Self got heavier and unmanageable. At this point, the personalities in Sumit's Self were his parents, girlfriend, other relatives, and friends. The latter had already progressed in their respective careers.

Sumit was unaware of this unseen Self and the imaginary mass that affected him. It had already taken a toll and caused him enough discomfort, unknowingly. In his session with me, it was the first time he realized the existence of an unseen and unknown troublemaker in his life. It had the appearance of an enemy out to get him. But our Self is not the enemy — it is a system we need to understand and update. The more clearly we understand the Self, the better and more harmonious our life is.

Curtailed and Predefined Growth - a Bonsai Mango Tree

The Wanted Child, as s/he gets older, ends up much like a Bonsai tree. Bonsai is a Japanese art form of cultivating small trees inside pots that mimic full-size trees. These trees are trimmed and manicured to perfection in ways that appeal to their owners. Bonsais have to be watered, fed, kept in sunlight, and taken care of by others. They do not have the freedom and liberty to grow and experience life naturally but are always curtailed by those they are dependent on. Wanted Children have behaviors, ideas, concepts, and knowledge drilled into them from a young age. They are never allowed to be fully themselves. Their personal growth can be designed for them, much like Bonsai trees are tended to. There is someone always there with scissors to chop the next leaf or to trim the branch that seems out of place. Wanted Children, therefore, grow in a particular fashion that can stunt their natural expression.

We can take the analogy further. The roots of Bonsai mango trees are tied with a string so that they don't expand and grow. They only remain in their enclosed container, never touching Mother Earth. The trees remain inside their guarded pots forever. Hence, they experience no grounding. Since the roots do not penetrate the ground, a gust of a strong breeze can topple the Bonsai mango tree. The Bonsai has to be kept in sunlight. If the plant has been exposed to temperatures above forty degrees, it will wilt. If it is not watered and tended to for a day or two, its leaves will start to decay. Thus, the Bonsai tree is constantly living under the threat of strong winds, fear of high temperatures, and fear of not being watered. At all times, it has to please its master and caretaker by being the way it is designed. On the other hand, a mango tree in an orchard planted in the soil will endure strong gusts of wind because its roots have penetrated deeply into the ground. It enjoys the sunshine and gets enough water supply from Mother Earth. That gives it a sense of freedom and liberty to experience nature. Even if there is stormy weather, the mango tree will sway in the direction the wind is blowing, but face it with the belief that Mother Earth will support it. On the contrary, stormy weather will completely blow away the Bonsai due to the lack of grounding.

In the same way, an element of fear creeps into the personality of Wanted Children. They seek approval on most aspects of their personal life. They don't make independent decisions. The roots of the Bonsai tree are wound so strongly with a string that it's impossible for it to set free. It has to please its owner and all those who visit the bonsai art gallery. Even when the Wanted Child grows up to be an adult, s/he can't look beyond the family-set trap but continues to live life assuming "that's the way life is." The individual has the potential to expand, grow and go deeper to connect with nature, but s/he won't do it. The Wanted Child does not know how to unknot the string, nor can s/he understand the external forces that have bound him/her. S/he is living under the influence of the Self, and s/he hasn't been allowed to fully develop his/her own personality.

In the above analogy, you will notice that its creator makes every decision about the Bonsai Mango tree. It is the creator's property, and ownership rights are with them. So, it must comply with and please the master. The upbringing of a Wanted child is no different — they live in the trap of their Self.

Avoiding a Predetermined Fate

Through the workings of the Self, the fate of the Wanted Child is in the hands of the parents and the people the child considers part of his/her kingdom. What plays out in adulthood is simply a reflection of childhood programming. Prince Wan, who went to war for his parents and kingdom, was also programmed to avenge his parents' misfortunes. It was the king and the queen who influenced his decisions to wage war. He was their property and had to prove he was worthy.

The consequence of the above is that although the Wanted Child is wanted, his/her destiny is very largely predetermined. Only a narrow bandwidth of choices are given to the child to choose from, which can be a subset of the expectations of parents. An example of this could be that a Wanted Child has to choose a prestigious and safe career when s/he grows up, as this is what the parents would like. So, while there are many options presented to him/her, they must first conform to this chief requirement, which comes from parents. Going against this necessity is not an option for Wanted Children. Again, no parent has to put overt pressure on such children after a while. It just becomes part of their system to take on expectations or what they need to be or do.

Their Self and Self-image control their functioning and decision-making.

This is not the true Self but an illusionary one that protects the person. But it is this very Self that overwhelms the Wanted Child. An unconscious process is happening within the Wanted Child's mind beyond his/her awareness and comprehension. Understanding how the illusory Self creates a predefined destiny is one aspect that will help Wanted Children to be aware and know how to deal with their limitations. The more we understand this system of the Self, the more competently we can navigate the hurdles it poses and live our lives freely.

THE PARTLY WANTED CHILD

32

NO CLEAR IMAGE - STANDBY PLAYER

We can see a potter once again with a lump of clay on his wheel. This time the potter is unsure of what he wants to make out of the clay. It could be that he is uncertain, or the wheel is not ready to give the optimum result. We can see a question mark that denotes a lack of a clear image in the potter's mind of what he wants to create. Since the potter doesn't have a specific goal, the clay takes a non-specific shape depending on the wheel's cooperation. Something does take shape out of the clay, but it's not clear or exact because the image is missing. Eventually, what is produced takes the shape of a pot.

The fate of a Partly wanted Child is like the clay in the hands of the potter, who is uncertain but ends up creating a form. Maybe he is not pleased with his creation but considers

Diagram 24

letting the object be. It's not "the item" the potter wants, but he keeps it anyway. One parent has accepted the Partly Wanted Child, while the other is not ready to have the child but is compelled to keep him/her. The child born in this category must please the parent who rejected him/her to feel safe and secure, i.e., to keep his/her survival intact. But since there is no image, the child drifts rudderless, depending on others for decision-making.

The Partly Wanted Child is also one who is affected by the mental states of the parents at birth or when in the womb. S/he is born to a couple who share a healthy bond but are not in sync on their decision to have a child. One of them wants to have a child, whereas the other doesn't. Since there is no consensus, there is a level of uncertainty and confusion among the parents that get passed on to the fetus. The parents' insecure feelings get communicated and transferred to the fetus during the mother's pregnancy. This sends a message to the fetus or newborn child that s/he is not fully welcome.

Either the woman is not ready, or the man is not ready, which causes the pregnant mother to feel unsure or anxious. In the latter case, where the man is not ready, she communicates the father's message through her own emotional state of unease, which gets picked up by the fetus. At times a woman may not have been ready to have a child. She may have engaged in what she thought was purely a sexual act with her partner and later discovers that she is pregnant. In either of the two scenarios, a message gets delivered to the conceived child during pregnancy or at birth.

How the Partly Wanted Child comes into existence is explained in the below extract from *Stop Surviving Start Living with Freedom* (pages 49-51).

Partly in Agreement

When one of the parties is PARTLY IN AGREEMENT with the other about having a child, then the child will be a Partly Wanted Child. Maybe the parents already have a child, or perhaps one partner is content with life, so doesn't want the child, while the other partner wants a child.

Here too, the mental states of the man and woman will affect their communication with the unborn. This goes back to the example I gave above of a woman who has been raped and how that traumatic event creates an emotional pattern that gets transferred to the unborn. Similarly, when a couple is not in sync in their decision to have a child, the woman experiences confusion, regret, or anxiety. A message gets communicated to the unborn through their emotions that s/he is not fully wanted. Sometimes this could happen at birth. The woman may have engaged in what she thought was purely a sexual act with her partner and later discovers that she is pregnant. Either she herself is not ready, or the man is not ready, which causes her to feel unsure or anxious. In the latter case where the man is not ready, she communicates the father's message through her emotional state of unease, which gets picked up by the unborn. Based on what each of them desires, a message gets delivered to the conceived child either during pregnancy or at birth.

In the case of Partly In Agreement, as it is mainly one partner who wants the child, it also implies that one of the parents has rejected the child. The parent who has partly rejected the child is the one that plays the dominant role in the child's life after s/he is born. The child always wants approval from the parent who has rejected him/ her.

Possibility 1 — man wants the child; woman doesn't

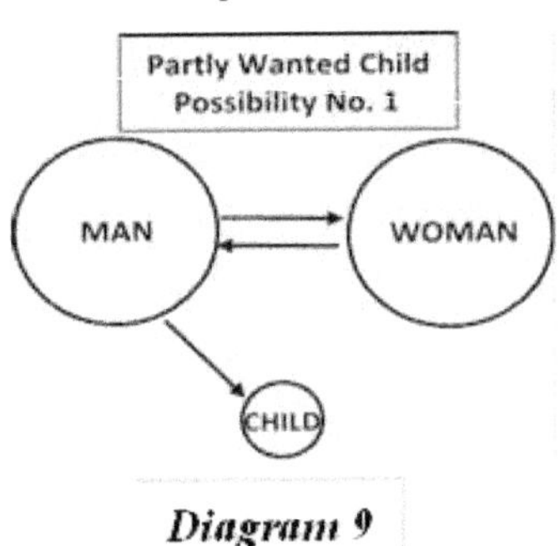

Diagram 9

In this case, the relationship between the couple is harmonious, but they do not equally want the same things. The man wants to have a child, but the woman is not ready. There could be different factors that may prevent her from being completely willing to have a child. It could be her career, financial limitations, or she may have already delivered a child very recently, etc. She may not want the responsibility of having to raise another child. The child born in this situation is partly wanted. The connection between the mother and the child is missing. The child will try his/ her best to restore that relationship for the rest of his/ her life. S/he will try to please the mother and do whatever is required to reconnect to the source (the mother). But the connection between the father and child exists in this scenario. The details of this are mentioned in the chapter "Survival Traits of Partly Wanted Children."

Possibility 2 — woman wants the child; man doesn't

In this case, the relationship between the couple is healthy, but the man is not ready to have a child. The woman wants a child, but the man feels he is being sucked into agreeing on something he doesn't want. There could be different factors constraining him, such as financial inadequacy, unwillingness to bear fatherly responsibility, or job uncertainty, etc. When a child is born in this situation, the child has a connection with the mother. The

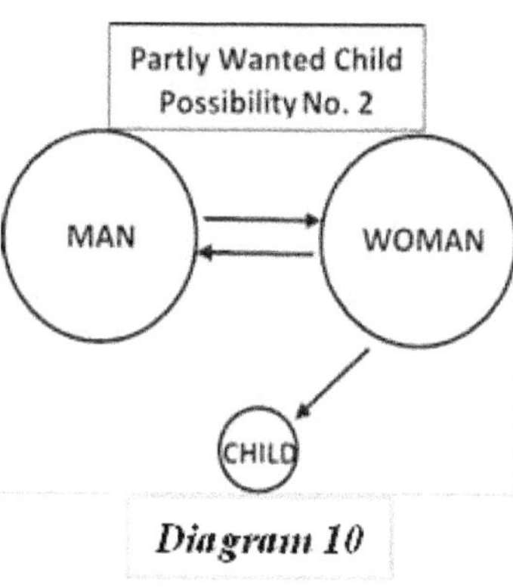

Diagram 10

fetus has received the message that the mother wanted him/her. There is no relationship with the father. The child born in this situation always craves the attention of the father. S/he will go out of her way to please the father by doing whatever it takes to gain his acceptance and establish a connection that has been missing. The details of this are mentioned in the "Survival Traits of Partly Wanted Children."

No Vivid Dream or Image

In a marriage, there are ups and downs which a couple deals with together. Difficulties are most often resolved in this way, but at times that does not happen to each person's satisfaction. Having a Partly Wanted Child is one such decision a couple takes. One of the parents dreams of having a child, but the other one is not on board with that wish. Either s/he is not convinced of having one right now and would prefer to wait, or is simply not interested in having a child. This may happen due to the person's circumstances, maturity levels, or the fact that the couple already has a child. At times there could be a child or children from a previous marriage. Essentially, the man and woman enjoy a good relationship and bond well with each other, but are not on common ground in this matter. This lack of consensus eventually conveys a message to the child that one parent doesn't fully want him/her.

The missing consensus leads to a second issue — there is no image given to the child. The Partly Wanted Child is not a dream child, as both parents are not excited or eager to have the child. Even in the case of the Wanted Child, it could be that only one parent is the dreamer, but the other one is fully supportive of fulfilling this dream and making it a reality. In the case of a Partly Wanted Child, the vision of the team — the parents — lacks coherence. One can imagine what happens to a team's performance when one or some of its members are not interested in playing well. The image of the Partly Wanted Child in the parents' minds is distorted and incomplete, no

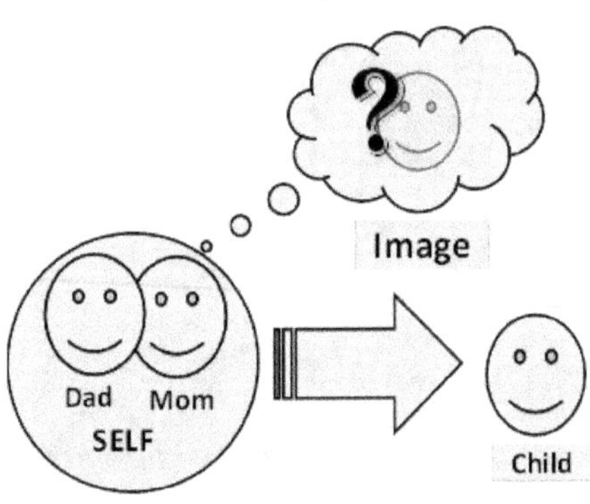

Diagram 25

matter how clearly one of them wants the child. The collaborative vision is not clear, making the image unclear and incomplete. In the process, nothing definite gets created. The child born out of such a union experiences incompleteness and doesn't have an image coming out of his/her Self. The Self is, however, very much there within Partly Wanted Children. But a blueprint is not specified to the unborn child.

In order to create an image, the explicit cooperation of both partners is required. Hesitancy on the part of one partner creates uncertainty and non-clarity in the joint project, which creates fear in the fetus. The result is that the project of having a child is not set on solid ground.

A child is born to a couple in the above diagram. The image with a question mark on top of it signifies that the parents are unclear about their outcome. Even when it comes to simpler goals, such as buying a family car, you can imagine what a lack of consensus could lead to. Both partners need to contribute financially. One of them is maybe ready, while the other is not comfortable with the high cost of owning and maintaining the car. One may want his/her dream car, while the other bargains for a more feasible option. There is a compromise. Something similar happens when there is no oneness among parents who decide on having a child. There is no clear vision (image) of the child, which would have served as a blueprint.

When the child is conceived, it picks up mixed emotions of the parents, which have been conveyed through the pregnant mother. As the child comes into existence, one parent is happy while the other could be unhappy or unenthusiastic about the same. There are no clear-cut aspirations or expectations the child must meet.

The One Who Did Not Get Picked — a Substitute Player

The primary goal of a child after birth is to survive within his/her environment. Since a Partly Wanted Child is not a dream child, s/he has his/her own tools and mechanism to do that. The feeling such a child carries is what a substitute player experiences in a soccer team. S/he gets

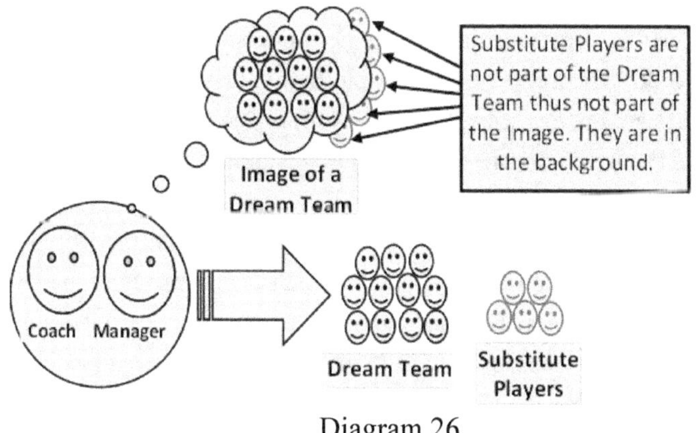

Diagram 26

to play the game only when the coach decides to replace one of the on-field players. Until such a time, s/he doesn't get to participate and remains excluded from the core team. So, the Partly Wanted Child does his/her best to get noticed by the parent (the coach or manager in the example) who has rejected him/her.

On the left-hand side of the above diagram, there is a coach and manager of a soccer team. Through their team selection process, they have already imagined their dream team – the eleven players who are going to play the game. The image of the dream team exists, and the wish list has been finalized. Eleven players of a dream team are like having a Wanted Child. Behind the image of a dream team, there are another five players in the background who make up the team's bench strength. They are not thought of as the ones who would ideally play for the team but are included as substitutes or second choices at best. These people are not visible. The dream team's image has blocked their visibility. As a substitute is not required at the outset of a game or may not be required at all, a message is communicated to the five players: "You are not as valuable as the core team." It also implies that, if all goes to plan, the team could play the game without them. This creates insecurity and uncertainty in the minds of the players on the bench, who feel excluded. Will they, too, get a chance to belong to the dream team?

The children in the dream team could be the firstborn child or children who are born before the Partly Wanted Child. They could be children from a previous marriage. Or, in certain instances, the dream team could just comprise the couple themselves, who are content in their present relationship. In all cases, the message being passed on is that the family is complete the way it is and doesn't truly need another child to feel whole.

But it's not to suggest that substitutes are totally rejected. The coach and manager above do want substitute players, but partly. As they constitute the peripheral part of a team, reserve players have to prove themselves physically with their prowess, using their bodies. This makes such people kinesthetic and highly action-oriented when it comes to proving their caliber.

The purpose of this diagram was to highlight that the Partly Wanted Child is not part of the dream image of the parents. There are no clear expectations placed on him/her. Thus, s/he operates differently from a Wanted Child.

Seeking Attention - Actions Speak Louder Than Words

The Partly Wanted Child's life path is unclear and distorted, as no clear goals have been given to him/her. S/he cannot perceive the world in the manner as a Wanted Child does. The absence of a shared vision of the parents impacts the Partly Wanted Child. The parent who has not welcomed him/her has certainly not given the child a vision. The other one may have a dream, but it is insufficient on its own to create a compelling picture the child can pursue.

Partly Wanted Children are born out of a parent's state of uncertainty, either that of the father or mother. This creates some confusion and discomfort in such children. The missing connection bothers them incessantly. They would like to feel worthy in the eyes of the parent who hasn't entirely accepted them. In order to prove they are valuable, Partly Wanted Children are willing to walk the extra mile for that parent — quite literally, using every ounce of their physical energy. They are capable of hard work that is well beyond the capacity of an average person.

Just as the football team's substitute players use their sporting talents to get the coach to notice them, Partly Wanted Children use actions rather than words to make themselves noticeable. It's like they are saying, "Hey! Do you notice me? Did you see what I can do?" Their survival mechanism makes use of kinesthetic skills to help them survive, rather than visual senses, as is the case with the Wanted Child. As there is no image given to these children, it makes it difficult for them to visualize the world or themselves. Their main way of perceiving the world is through kinesthetic sensations. It is quite common for Partly Wanted Children to end up as athletes, sportspersons, dancers, or in something else that involves physical participation. Unconsciously, they do it to get noticed by the one parent who rejected them.

33

REINS IN THE HANDS OF THE SELF

Every child has a different identity; however, in the case of a Partly Wanted Child, the parent who has rejected the child occupies a more important place in his/her life. As a result, that parent also takes up a larger space in the child's Self.

That parent has a major impact on the child's life. The latter feels the void of a self-image, which serves as a roadmap with milestones for direction. At an early age, the Wanted Child knows s/he is special and from whom a lot of things are expected. S/he picks up the expectations of parents, at different stages of life, through his/her self-image. Expectations become a guide to what path a Wanted Child must take on to match a blueprint. A Partly Wanted Child does not get this direction, which comes from having an image.

While both parents exist in the Partly Wanted Child's Self, the dominant one is the parent who has rejected the child. The role of the image has to be directly fulfilled by that parent, who holds the child's reins. The Partly Wanted Child would have felt complete if this parent had provided an image. As the parent didn't, the child falls back on his/her Self for direction in life. The other parent who wants this child may be doing all that s/he could. But as the Partly Wanted Child has picked up an emotional message of not being fully wanted very early on, s/he demands attention from the parent who has rejected him/her by performing tasks to please that parent. The survival mechanism of the child filters out the attention she gets from the nurturing parent and directs it towards seeking it from the parent who has not accepted him/her. As the Partly Wanted Child gives much more importance to the latter parent, the main driver in the Self, or decision maker for the child, becomes the parent who has rejected him/her. The other parent remains part of the child's Self but not the influential one at the core. Later in life, Partly Wanted Children will attract people with a similar personality type to the parent who had rejected them. Likewise, others will be part of the person's Self but won't have the same impact on them.

Pleasing the parent to get acceptance becomes a way of life for the Partly Wanted Child. Through these behaviors, the child takes on an overall persona of a people-pleaser. S/he develops a non-assertive nature and mostly complies with those around him/her. Such children are naturally warm, friendly, and outgoing. They are unable to say "NO" to others as they feel they will hurt them by doing so, and the consequence of that is they will not be liked and accepted by those people.

The desire to belong to others makes them amiable and compliant. As young children, they eat what their mothers serve them, with little or no tantrums. Imagine a mother saying to a toddler, "Open your mouth." The child opens his/her mouth, and the morsel of food is put inside it. The young one doesn't even bother to chew it properly but quietly swallows what may not have even been to his/her liking. Rarely do such children ever protest over eating well or other things that are asked of them. The Survival Mechanism does not permit them to do so but to accept what others provide with a smile. Therefore, it is inevitable for Partly Wanted Children to grow up to be "good boys" or "good girls." They also become "good husbands/wives," "good sons/daughters," and "good employees," always submitting to authority.

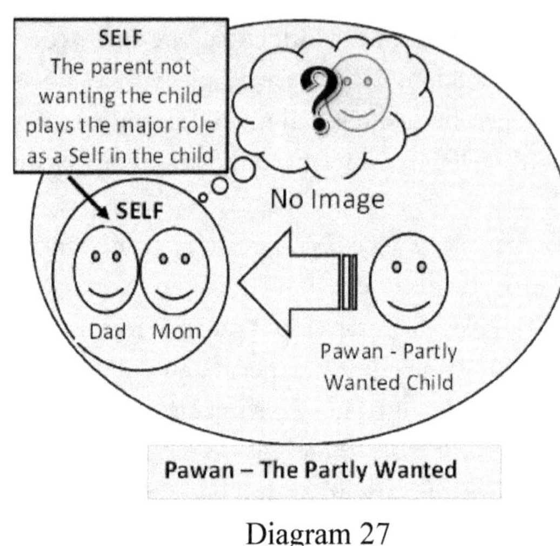

Diagram 27

The Self of the Partly wanted Child, Pawan, is depicted in the diagram above. The core of Pawan's Self consists of the parent not wanting him, and so the approval of that parent is of paramount importance to him. He wants to please that person more than anyone else in the world. And so, Pawan will try to live up to the parent's demands or expectations, obediently conforming to his/her wishes. Following instructions without questioning them will become his natural personality. Even when demands placed on Pawan become unreasonable, he will continue to oblige that parent. Pawan is the quintessential "good boy," maintaining his persona to the delight of his parents. He will hardly ever be able to say "NO," retaliate, or back-answer the parent. These qualities make him tolerate all sorts of nonsensical expectations imposed on him. Later in life, he does the same with his spouse.

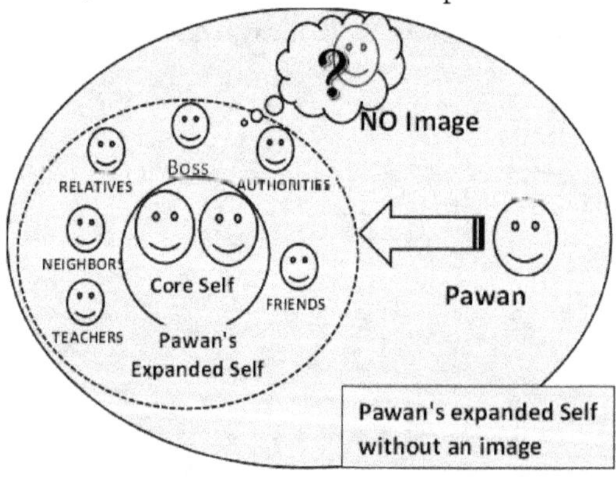

Diagram 28

As years go by, Pawan's expanded Self takes shape. In the diagram, one can see several personalities who have impacted Pawan since his birth. The inner circle of Pawan's Self consists of both parents. However, Pawan gives prominence to the parent who has rejected him. The outer ring has in it Pawan's relatives, neighbors, teachers, friends, authorities, and others who also become part of his Self.

In Pawan's case, the lack of an image means he may not have his own life vision. It is crucial to have an image for direction. If not, a person can become dysfunctional, like a man in a jungle with no map. Pawan has to rely on the Self that comprises his special parent or others to give him direction. Every human being, of course, has a consciousness that can direct him/her. But at a young age, it is not fully developed, so the child cannot tap into his/her potential. The topic of consciousness is vast and will not be covered in this book. For now, let's look at how the Partly Wanted Child receives direction.

Property Rights Over a Partly Wanted Child

With no disrespect to them, Partly Wanted Children can be compared to well-trained horses pulling the weight of a cart. They wear blinders and move just the way their masters direct them to move. Their reins are always in the hands of their owners. The workhorse has to gallop at the pace the owner desires, lugging the bulk of the cart in the direction where the reins get pulled. It doesn't have any say in its movements but obeys its owner. The horse knows that its survival is in its owner's hands. Were it to retaliate, some stiff punishment could be meted out to it. Human beings who are Partly Wanted Children have the same survival pattern. They are at the mercy of others and live in total compliance with the rules they are placed under. They essentially conform without complaining, often with a smile on their faces that masks their inner discomfort.

The man in the cart firmly holds the reins of the horse. It signals a message to the horse that the man has

Diagram 29

complete control or ownership over it and its movements. As the horse is the man's property, it takes his every instruction as a command, for which it has no choice but to follow. Partly Wanted Children also have a master who directs their moves. It is the parent who has rejected them.

These children are people pleasers, but some people, especially those that match the traits of the parent who has rejected them, will have exceptional control over them. It's an unconscious pattern associated with their survival mechanism, which they are unaware of. They feel a compelling need to be of service to others. Not knowing how to deal with this pattern, they become subservient and unconsciously bound to them.

Partly Wanted Children are mostly amicable, but they often get exploited due to their good nature. An inability to say "NO" is a weakness that makes life difficult for them. Adjusting with and accommodating the wishes of others becomes their habit, where they simply go along with the decisions or preferences of those people. If they feel discomfort by doing so, they prefer to skirt the issue than confront people. Not only will they avoid the issue, but they will work harder to fulfill the whims of the other person. They will likely attract a spouse similar to their parent, who will govern their life.

A lady by the name of Amina visited me some time ago. She had married a man after a few years of courtship. Amina was the third child to her parents and her traits matched those of a Partly Wanted Child. Her husband had won her trust and that of her family to such an extent that they took him on board to manage their family business. But he began to embezzle funds and have extra-marital affairs with other women. Just like a horse who wears blinders, Amina simply couldn't see her husband's wrongdoings for a long time, despite repeated warnings from her family members. Mustering some courage, she even fought with her husband but later reconciled with the hope that he would change. Things continued the way they did as in the past. Finally, being pressured by her family to take a tough stance, she filed for divorce. By that time, enough damage had been done to her and the business. Amina dragged her feet on the decision to separate, even though there were enough reasons and evidence to justify it. A Partly Wanted Child wears blinders and his/her decisions, especially important ones, are made by others. They don't take control of their lives into their own hands.

They can be easily exploited in workplaces too. As they are hardworking, diligent, and friendly, such qualities make them very attractive to bosses who can use them. But rather than feeling valued, Partly Wanted Children may end up feeling rejected by those who have similar traits to the parent who rejected them. They get carried away by the difficulties or sob stories of others, their hearts melting with sympathy, allowing for their further exploitation.

This category of people have been in an invisible trap of their own Survival Mechanism. It's as if their owners have lassoed them since birth and they are not aware of a rope around their necks. As long as it exists, the other end of the rope remains in somebody else's hands, and they remain the property of that person. Unfortunately, they do not know of any other way to live.

Deprived of the Map, They Need a Guide

A Partly Wanted Child's situation and decision-making are different to that of the Wanted child. In the case of the latter, the parents did have an image of a child in their mind, which becomes a map the child can use for decision-making. An image is like a roadmap that provides a possible direction one can take to a destination. If one does not have a map, then one has to have a guide who is aware of the terrain, on whom one can rely. Partly Wanted Children mostly rely on the parent who has rejected them and, when they become adults, they rely on their partner for making decisions. At the workplace, they will do most of the work, but when it comes to making decisions, they would prefer that others make them.

Having no map and no image guiding them, the domain of the Partly Wanted Children's Self is unconsciously governed by that one parent who rejected them. Later in life, they attract others having a similar personality type and want explicit approval from those people. Unwittingly, they surrender their decision-making to such people most of the time. The whole process is an emotional tangle that is beyond their understanding. Allowing others to make decisions for them makes them feel assured, even though it is a False Illusionary Assurance.

In the picture of the horse cart above, the horse's face and body are well strapped with blinders on its eyes. The man holding the reins makes most of the decisions for the horse, making it trot, gallop, come to a standstill, turn directions, or sit. The horse may even know the way to a destination to and fro but hardly makes any decisions. Similarly, for a Partly Wanted Child, decisions get made by the person who was not ready to have him/her. The one who occupies an important position in the core of the child's Self.

Later in life, the decision-making power gets transferred to a spouse, who mirrors the personality traits of that of the parent who refused them at birth. They put their lives in the hands of people who remain a guiding force – and also act as a roadmap of their life.

Another client of mine named Monish had started his own business and was running it well, on his own, for two years. Looking at the venture as a lucrative investment opportunity, Monish's friend wanted to partner with him and contribute financially towards future projects. Being a Partly Wanted Child, Monish did not take an independent decision on what to do but instead relied on his friend's judgment and went ahead with what he offered. He did not even ask for a larger share (via business goodwill) to which he was entitled. Finally, the two sold the business to another organization for which an initial sum of money was received. The deal was structured by Monish's friend in such a way that he first got his invested amount back. Monish agreed to the terms in good faith but did not consider asking for a return on his hard work for commencing the start-up. He gave away the initial amount to his friend, hoping later payments would be shared equally. Soon after this, the COVID-19 lockdown happened, and Monish did not receive a penny. Monish's friend was in the driver's seat on important financial decisions that affected Monish, despite the latter being the original founder of the business. Similar patterns were visible in Monish's earlier decisions. It's not unusual for investors to demand unfair financial returns from founders of businesses, but it illustrates how Partly Wanted Children can blindly allow others to make decisions that go against their own interests.

It not true that Partly Wanted Children don't know how to make decisions, but they don't want to invite disapproval of a specific parent or of valuable people in their lives. They want them to be happy. As highly obedient "good boys" or "good girls" who don't want to look "bad" in the eyes of their parents, they don't want to make decisions that may look like they are favoring their own interests. They hardly assert, and even if they have to, they will skirt the issues. The parent who had refused to accept them becomes their internal guide and acts as an instructor. Using their bodies, Partly Wanted Children diligently execute what they are asked to do, like workhorses. But over time, this behavior takes its toll on their physical and mental health.

34

PAYING THE PRICE FOR NO IMAGE

Tony, a man in his late sixties, once visited my clinic and started to sob. He was the youngest of nine children and grew up amidst poverty and hardship. He took care of his family and supported his mother for many years, more so than any of his siblings. After marriage, Tony always pleased his wife like he did his mother, but both women were never satisfied with him. He made decent earnings and educated his two sons in reputed schools, and they were now doing well independently. Tony's wife was a bossy lady controlling his life — she had similar traits to his mother. On returning from work, Tony usually helped his wife in the kitchen. She lived a luxurious life and didn't earn an income. While none of this is unusual, what surprised Tony was that she influenced both her sons to portray him as someone incompetent. She made him feel insignificant in their eyes. Despite all

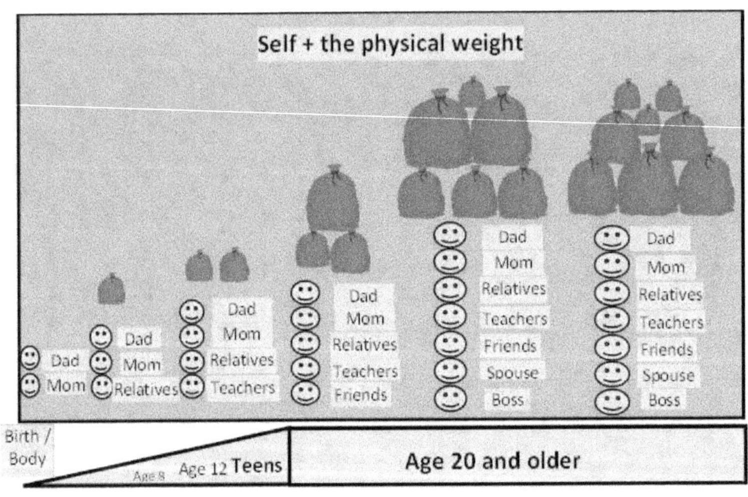

Diagram 30

this, after retirement, he learned to cook to please his wife. Tony, a Partly Wanted Child, was living life with a sense of ingratitude from those he had supported all his life, but he still couldn't stop pleasing the same people. Eventually, he exceeded his threshold of tolerance and landed in therapy.

Tony's life can be understood better through the timeline of the Partly Wanted Child. The progression of the child's Self is seen on the bottom horizontal axis in the above diagram. It begins with the parents, with the one who has rejected the child being in the core. With time, more personalities get added to the Partly Wanted Child's Self, which s/he feels is necessary to appease for his/her survival.

Above the horizontal axis are gunny bags being loaded onto the Party Wanted Child by the personalities in his/her Self. The gunny bags represent the physical and emotional load the child willingly takes on, regarding requests, instructions, expectations, or demands. In the earliest years, the child is dependent on the parents, so there is no load to carry. As s/he grows, gradually, s/he takes on an increasing number of tasks. Relatives and teachers start to become important. As Partly Wanted Children are "good boys" or "good girls" unable to say "no," it means they must please the people around them. These people reside inside the child's Self and, through it, they direct his/her every move.

In their teenage and young adult years, Partly Wanted Children are keen on experiencing life, and can take on challenges vigorously. Their coping mechanism is robust at this stage. So, as visible on the diagram, the number of bags and their size also increases here, indicative of more weight. All the people in the child's Self may not place demands on the Partly Wanted Child to the same degree; some may even help to reduce them. However, the parent who has partly rejected the child will regularly place more load on the child.

Why does this happen? The parent commensurately expects more from a child who is obedient and dependable. Let's look at this in more detail.

As the parent thinks this is a lovely child who is a delight to raise, s/he thinks s/he can justifiably ask more from him/her. The parent may not even be a demanding one. But the Partly Wanted Child will just take on more of his/her wishes or alleviate the parent's concerns. The more the child pleases the parent, the more the parent feels the child is a good boy or girl, reducing his/her burden. So s/he feels s/he can add more expectations on the child's shoulders. In the beginning, it may be about obeying home rules, or eating whatever's being cooked for meals. Then it could go on to assisting in different household chores, mastering new skills the parent thinks valuable, or performing well at school. The smiling child could be considered a "dependable helper" at home or in the kitchen. Finally, it could even be that the parent chooses the college the child should go to, or the career s/he ought to pursue. It may be a well-meaning influence in the mind of the parent, but it will sound like a command in the mind of the child. Going against the parent's ideas or wishes is like endangering one's existence (that is the way the child's program functions). The Partly Wanted Child always wants to please the parent so that s/he feels fully accepted by him/her. It all boils down to the acceptance s/he believes s/he hasn't received.

Notice that there is a similarity with the behavior of the Wanted Child, who fulfills the goals of his/her parents. The Partly Wanted Child also fulfills the goals of others, but here s/he mainly picks up the goals of the one parent who has rejected him/her. There is goal fulfillment taking place, but of the parent whose goals are placed above everyone else's. Besides this, the Wanted Child has an imagination that directs him/her toward goals. But there is no roadmap to guide the Partly Wanted Child. S/he operates mostly out of direct instruction. A metaphorical rein is being used to push and pull him/her in different directions.

Over time, more people like the significant parent enter the Partly Wanted Child's life, who s/he will please. In turn, just like the parent who did earlier, they will expect and demand much from the person. As the Partly Wanted Child grows older and more competent, the quantum of load piled on him/her increases. It also reflects a willingness to take on greater responsibilities for others. A boss may demand more time, effort, or output. As s/he can't say "no" and draw healthy boundaries, a hefty gunny bag will get added and its size may expand too. S/he will end up marrying a spouse with the traits of the parent who has rejected them. Life will go well for the couple, initially. However, at the end of the honeymoon period, or after a certain time elapses, the demands of the spouse will start to surface and the Partly Wanted Child will take them on without objection, just like Tony did with his wife. Again, it may not be that the spouse is an overtly demanding person. It's just that the Partly Wanted Children will make every effort to make the life of their spouse as close to heaven as possible. In return, they demand appreciation and acceptance.

Besides pleasing their parents, spouse, and boss, they try to please their friends, relatives, and even office colleagues. Requests from these people now become additional loads they are willing to carry. Partly Wanted Children can go to great lengths to do things for others, even if it's costing them their own health and well-being. It is an unconscious pattern that drives their actions, which they are unaware of.

The Partly Wanted Child doesn't make conscious decisions but always pleases others, thinking that is happiness. It is like they want others to enjoy a lavish Christmas dinner while they pay for the meal. The more others are happy, the more they feel happy and experience a sense of assurance, though it's illusionary and false. Such external happiness does not last too long for such people. Just as the effect of alcohol and drugs fade away, this sense of assurance is also temporary. They then feel the need for more.

35

DESTINY IN THE HANDS OF OTHERS

The workhorse's reins are in the hands of his master. The owner makes decisions for the horse most of the time, which also means the horse's destiny is in the former's hands. The same principle applies to the Partly Wanted Child. They want to please others and so would like others to make decisions for them. They also fear that they might displease others by making a wrong decision. Since the parents did not have a clear Self-image formed in their minds at conception, there is no visual roadmap or clear direction for the Partly Wanted Child to follow. Due to their inborn fear, they avoid making decisions. In this way, they put their fate in the hands of others.

When it comes to their personal life and relationships, they are too scared to take destiny into their own hands. They fear saying, "no" and even if they have to, they will be non-confronting and skirt the issue facing them. Partly Wanted Children feel obliged and indebted towards others, not wanting to disappoint a soul. At times it seems like they are a puppet in the hands of others.

Tony, from the previous chapter, was weeping at my clinic saying everyone has turned against him. He asked me, "What wrong have I done?" As the youngest among nine children, he took care of his mother till her death, like a good son. His wife ruled over Tony's life. After returning from the office, he worked hard on kitchen chores and, on retirement, learned to cook for her. But she influenced his two sons and their respective wives to perceive Tony as someone who is worthless. There was NO wrong that Tony had done, but he had been overly pleasing his family and paid a heavy price through a loss of respect and dignity. Tony's mother controlled his life initially, and after marriage, the reins shifted to his wife. Although he was the chief provider at home, he was still at the complete mercy of his mother and wife. His destiny was in the hands of others.

While Partly Wanted Children to get happiness by making others happy, they carry emotional weight, like a heavy stone tied around their waist that makes them eventually sink into the waters of a lake. This is a catch-twenty-two situation they get caught in, which causes self-sabotage. They must please others to feel assured and accepted, but this behavior, with time, brings their downfall. The weight of the gunny bags they carry causes them relentless stress, leading to fatigue or mental illness. When they are young, they are capable of withstanding the strain of this survival pattern. As they get a bit older, they cannot bear the load and their system starts to collapse under the pressure of the unseen and unquantifiable weight. There comes a time when they are tired of pleasing others because they feel mentally exhausted and physically drained. But they find it difficult to shrug off the weight from their shoulders for fear of rejection, which is deeply associated with their survival. This fear is an undercurrent rather than one they are consciously aware of. Unhappily, but usually with a smile to conceal their inner pain, they carry on the same way.

Freedom From Chains

The Wanted Child is governed by a self-image that serves as an ideal to compare with. That child's burden comes from striving to match his/her actual performance to the image. A Partly Wanted Child also carries a burden, but differently. S/he is completely directed by the instructions of others, like the workhorse in the above analogy. The workhorse is always performing, but there is a limit to how much load it can carry. One day the Partly Wanted Child collapses. Too much performance is unhealthy, and one must learn to draw a line somewhere.

As others hold their reins, the fate of Partly Wanted Children gets placed in the hands of those people. They are unaware of how they make decisions and allow others to control them. Visualization is necessary to make constructive decisions, but it's not the default faculty for these children. They were not given an image to "see" from birth.

So, Partly Wanted Children mostly execute what they are asked to do, and do it diligently using their bodies.

It's important to add a caveat here. Partly Wanted Children do develop visual faculties through life experiences. For example, they are very well capable of seeing and deciding on items they pick for purchase or food ingredients they blend to cook recipes. We have to distinguish here between the pragmatic decisions a person takes through life experiences and those s/he takes emotionally out of the Survival Mechanism. When things get personal, we end up making emotional decisions. We don't know when exactly we will do this. However, if one is operating practically through one's experiences (getting one's hands dirty), one is not doing it from within the Survival Mechanism.

Although Partly Wanted Children may meet different people in their lives, even from other cultures, they will be drawn to those who are like one of the parents who refused to accept them. These people will play a big role in deciding their destiny. While they please them, the significant question remains — are they happy from within? They want to make others happy so that they feel secure and safe at a deeper level. That is their inborn survival mechanism. But it need not be this way, as they can take charge of their own destinies and begin to live life without shackles.

SUBSECTION - C

THE UNWANTED CHILD

36

NO ROAD MAP - LOST AND ABANDONED

The potter sitting on his wheel is unsure of what he wants to make from the lump of clay. It could be that he doesn't want to create anything and is just playing around at the wheel. The wheel itself may not be functioning properly. He puts the clay on the wheel and after a certain time, it hardens to become solid as a rock.

There is no image the potter had when he began to make something at the wheel. So no specific object got created out of the clay. The potter could choose to discard the item or put it back into the clay pit. Shapeless clay does not have any worth on its own — the creator

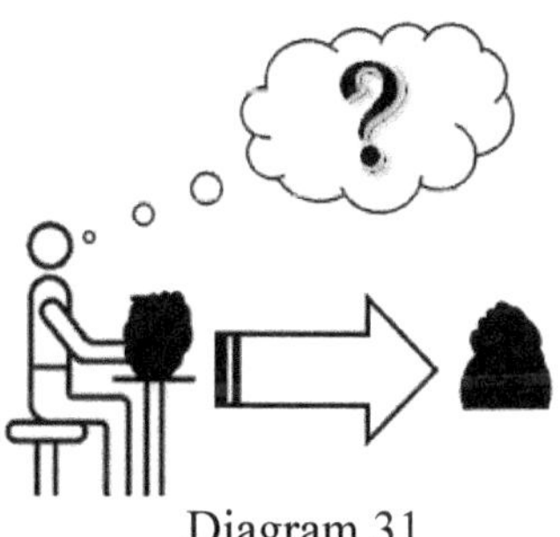

Diagram 31

creates value by molding it to a specific object. In this case, it gets thrown away.

The fate of the Unwanted Child is like that of hardened clay because the parents rejected him/her at conception due to some chaos. The fetus picks up a message of rejection in the mother's womb, and from then onwards, it tries to survive with certain natural resources. But there is neither a clear image nor someone to give the child guidance.

The birth of the Unwanted Child is a woeful tale of bringing a child into this world who neither the father nor mother wants. An unwanted pregnancy, combined with reasons that are beyond the control of the mother or father, compels them to have a child they would rather not have had.

More commonly, an Unwanted Child can be the by-product of sexual intercourse between a couple who may be in a disharmonious relationship. While they had sex, they had no desire to procreate. Some of the other factors that could give rise to an Unwanted Child are religious beliefs, adoption, power equations between the man and woman, or marital rape. More details on how Unwanted Children arrive in the world can be found in my previous book, *Stop Surviving Start Living With Freedom*, on page 69.

The extract below is from the same book (pages 51 to 53). It describes the consequences for a child born to a man and woman who are not living in agreement with each other.

Not in Agreement

The couple in such a scenario may be married or unmarried. How much ever influence or control a man may have over a woman, at an emotional level, it is the choice of the woman whether she accepts him or doesn't. In this scenario, she is clear about one thing: she doesn't want to have the child of the man she is with. But she has unintentionally become pregnant with his child.

Sexual activity can be done and completed within a few minutes. A woman may have consented to sex, but that does not mean she wants to have the man's offspring. The woman might have had a different motive for continuing in a sexual relationship with the man, but he might mistake this for her willingness to have a child together. She has thus rejected the man, from the perspective of him being a father to her child. There could also be various traumas that could be created in this situation, where the woman is unable to deal with her circumstances, thereby rejecting the man. Rashu's case mentioned at the

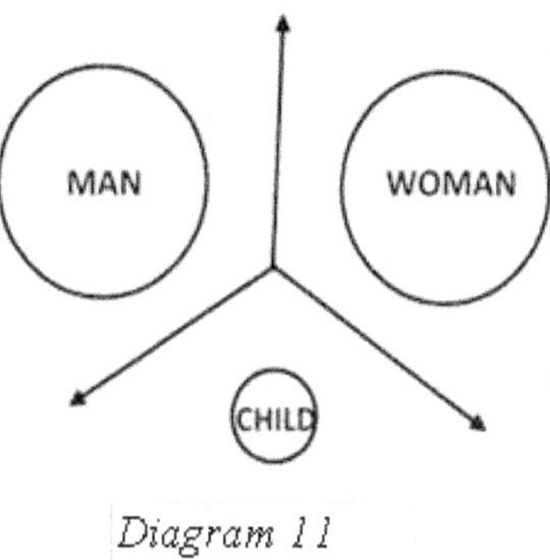

Diagram 11

beginning of the book (on page 11) is one such situation where her mother rejects her father and therefore rejects the daughter she bears through him. In this case, the man and woman are NOT IN AGREEMENT with each other.

In this case, the mother has not accepted the father. There is no deep connection between the man and the woman, and both are NOT IN AGREEMENT. So, the child borne through him is also not accepted by the woman. As she never wanted to have the man's child, no relationship exists between the mother and the child. The fetus experiences the same rejection by the woman as does the man. Since there is no relationship between the man and the woman, there is no relationship between the child and the father either. It's usually the mother that honors the father, and the message is picked up by the fetus (as stated in the earlier sub-section "In Agreement") that the man is someone significant in his/her life.

The child is lost and does not experience bonding with either of the parents. S/he does not know how to bond or what it means to bond. Therefore, experiencing acceptance and love is challenging for an Unwanted Child. As the child born under these conditions does not belong to either of the parents, his/ her survival in the world is a tricky one. The child unconsciously knows about the rejection and seeks acceptance from the mother. The mother's role is crucial in the case of the Unwanted Child and his/her survival. As s/he has been rejected, s/he finds it difficult to accept rejection from the world at large. We will cover more on this in the "Survival Traits of Unwanted Children."

Unwanted Children experience a sense of abandonment even before they are born. This makes their beliefs, communication, behavior, thinking, and attitude very different from that of Wanted Children and Partly Wanted Children. Let's look at how they go about surviving.

No Goal, No Dream, No Image

Every child is the product of the parents, but it doesn't mean that every child is also a wish or dream of the parents. There are several abortions that take place every day, by both married and unmarried women, in different parts of the world. In some cases, such unwanted babies do end up taking birth. Many children are born out of religious or cultural compulsion because an authority prevented abortion from happening, or from purely out of guilt. Owing to such reasons, it implies that not every one of us is a goal, dream, or aspiration of our parents. Faced with challenges they couldn't resolve, parents, or single parents, nevertheless choose to go ahead and raise such children.

In this scenario, other than a desire to engage in sexual intercourse, a man and a woman do not want to share much else, least of all to have a child together. But the woman becomes pregnant and is emotionally or psychologically forced to go through pregnancy and childbirth. How did she feel having conceived this child? What were her emotions during pregnancy? How would she relate to him/her after giving birth?

To gauge how she feels, let's consider two hypothetical situations where you have felt compelled to accept something you don't want.

Let's say you visit your favorite mall on the weekend, not to shop, but to have lunch at a restaurant you like there. After your meal, you stroll by the shops for a while and enter a gardening store. A charming salesman greets you and persuades you to consider buying a gardening tool set on sale. You try to tell him that you don't want the product, but he waxes eloquent on the sophistication of the tools he claims will make your gardening far easier. Feeling the pressure of his sales pitch, when he offers you a heavier discount, you end up succumbing to him by buying an item you don't need. On returning home, you feel helpless and angry that you were unable to resist his sales tactics. What's worse, you forgot to read the fine print and realize you can only return the product for store credit, not a refund! The toolkit is lying unopened in the corner of your garden shed and you feel ashamed about being a silly fool. Buyer remorse is eating you up from within.

Then there are times when you are directly compelled to do something by others, such as a family member or an authority. Many people didn't want the COVID-19 vaccine shot, but coming under family pressure, they went ahead and took it. Others were compelled by their employers or the government. Freedom of choice is taken away in such instances.

Many women have become pregnant and regret their actions. But they yet have the child to please a family member, a source of authority or a system, such as an extended family, local community, or culture. There are instances when a different motive results in an unexpected pregnancy. Sometimes a woman may want to be with a man for financial security, status, or fame, without wishing to have the man's child.

In all the above cases, the child born to the couple is like an unwanted item lying around, neglected in some corner of the house. The mother is filled with feelings akin to buyer's remorse from an impulsive purchase, berating herself for her negligence. A child who is born to such a mother is unwanted but has to survive. Importantly, the image of the child is missing. There is no dream, aspiration, or goal underpinning their existence. An emotional message that you are "not wanted" gets conveyed to the child.

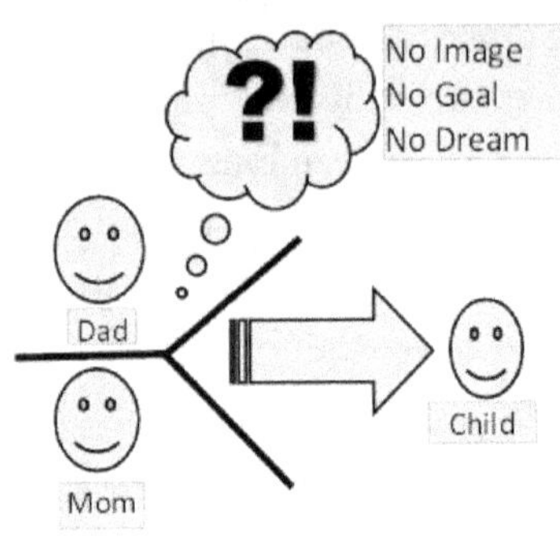

Diagram 32

The diagram shows that a man and woman are not in-sync with each other. As they suffer from a fractious relationship, it also means they won't agree on having a child together. The mother is especially unwilling to have the child, but she cannot express herself or be adamant about her choices with her partner. She may be bound up in social, religious, or extended family pressures, which she experiences during pregnancy.

In some situations, the woman may want to fulfill her own desires or agenda. One of my clients said her mother did not want to have another child, but she would gladly have accepted one if it happened to be a boy. Another client was the third child of her parents, conceived immediately after the birth of her sister. Her mother wasn't ready to have another baby, especially so soon. In another case, a woman who gave birth to a child lived with her dominating husband and controlling mother-in-law. She wasn't happy to become a mother, given her circumstances. There could be numerous possibilities why a woman may not want to have a child.

Feeling Lost and Abandoned

A child that is not part of a dream or a goal will inevitably end up feeling lost, without a sense of belonging to anyone, like a discarded piece of furniture.

The creator of the chair above doesn't need it and has left it on the pavement near his house for anyone to use or pick up. Who does such a chair now belong to? In other words, who is the owner of the chair when it is disposed of? Who can use it? Here, I am looking at humans as if they were a commodity to give you a perspective on what an Unwanted Child unconsciously goes through in

Diagram 33

life. It does not mean that the parents of an Unwanted Child literally physically discard him/her. They may raise the child, but the child feels like a discarded piece of furniture due to a message received earlier.

Parents are the creators of every child, which means the child can't have its existence without parents. What happens when the creators disown their own creations? How does the creation feel when s/he is disowned? It's like a potter disowning her artifacts. The mother continues to reject the fetus emotionally but can't abort for various reasons. Such emotions affect the way the child feels.

The action of discarding the chair is a message of giving up ownership. The chair belongs to nobody but, simultaneously, it belongs to everybody or anyone who wants to use it. The relationship with the true owner is cut off. Moreover, no one else can claim to be the real owner. The person who gets the discarded chair home knows that s/he isn't its actual owner but has accepted it because of a need. This scenario can occur when a child has been put up for adoption. The new parents know that the child is not theirs, and unconsciously the child also knows s/he does not belong to them. By giving the child away, the biological parents have snapped their connection with the child, which creates a deep, lasting, emotional impact on them.

Public Property — No Ownership

At times, the Unwanted Child could be treated like a park bench. Take the case of the one above that has been donated by a patron. There was an original owner of the bench, but it has now become public property. Anyone visiting the park can use it to rest or enjoy it as they like. A tired man may use it to get a short snooze during the afternoon. Children might jump over it or stand on it while playing games, which is forbidden to do with chairs at home. Hardly anyone may question the wrongful use of the bench, neither the donor nor the public. There is little accountability toward an owner. No specific criteria have been communicated as to who can sit

Diagram 34

on it. It could be a tired homeless man, someone poor or wealthy, a Christian or Muslim, a young or older person, or even a stray dog or cat. The bench has NO say in this matter, as there is NO specific ownership. People's attitudes towards what they own and what they don't own can be markedly different. Even a pet owner may treat a homeless animal differently. The above examples are about how we perceive the world through our internal filters and distorted outlook. When there is ownership, we relate differently to humans, animals, and inanimate objects.

The personality of an Unwanted Child depends entirely on the family, extended family, the degree of rejection s/he experiences and the circumstances. When a child is not wanted by his/her mother, the latter doesn't feel a sense of ownership towards the child. Multiple thoughts could be running through her mind, such as, "I never wanted you," "You are a burden," or "I have to take on the responsibility of caring for you, which I never wanted." The mother communicates various messages through her actions, behaviors, and emotions that express her inner turmoil. An overall message of regret and rejection is conveyed, that the being which has come into existence wasn't required and now is a drain on her. The child has sensed the emotions of the mother because, as a fetus, s/he was part of her body. Till at least three years after birth, s/he continues to sense his/her mother's feelings and behavior. Sometimes they are openly revealed by the mother. One of my clients, as a young girl, was reminded by her mother many times that life would have been very different for the mother if she had not conceived her.

The horrendous scenario of a woman who is raped and gives birth to a baby will almost always result in an Unwanted Child. The child is a reminder to the mother of the traumatic event. Each time she hears the baby's cry, she unknowingly experiences the same negative emotions of rape. The child experiences the mother's negative emotions unconsciously. The mother may not be aware of it, but a message subtly gets communicated to the child when this happens. In certain countries, marital rape is not deemed illegal by society or law, so such incidents can also occur within marriages. This problem gets compounded when a spouse is thought of as one's property and sex is considered a right by the man.

It's a real tragedy to be born unwanted. No person would want to be in the shoes of someone who feels unwanted by their parents. No one likes rejection, as there is a deep craving in all of us for someone to love and accept us. Unwanted Children don't like to be treated as people who have been rejected. They want to feel wanted, valued, and given importance. As they didn't get it inside their homes, they passionately sought this acceptance and importance from the world around them. Suffering from the pain of rejection, they want to do anything to be out of their trap. So, an Unwanted Child will do everything within their means to gain the acceptance that s/he feels will fill the void of emptiness within.

Many of the traits of the Unwanted Child we will cover in the chapters ahead are a reflection of this inner desire. The irony is that the void doesn't get filled, whatever the means used to accomplish it. A sense of incompleteness remains. In the bargain, they also end up causing damage to others around them.

37

BETRAYAL OF THE GENIE

Once, a farmer on his way home passed through a jungle and heard muffled sounds coming from the bushes. Out of curiosity, he went closer and discovered that the sound was coming from a sealed glass bottle behind the bushes. He picked up the bottle and saw a little Genie stuck inside, talking to him. The Genie was pleading with the farmer to open the bottle and let him out. Frightened with what he saw, the farmer dropped the bottle and began to leave. The Genie immediately said, "Ask for whatever you want and I will fulfill your wishes." Intrigued to hear this offer, the farmer returned and picked up the bottle. The Genie proceeded to say, "However, on one condition. You will set me free after I fulfill your wishes."

The farmer was excited but inquired, "What would happen if I don't open the bottle on you fulfilling my wishes?"

The Genie replied, "If you don't keep your end of the bargain, all that you have obtained from me will turn to ashes and dust." The farmer agreed, thrilled he could ask for all the luxuries and comforts he had never dreamed of enjoying through his hard labor. The Genie was soft, sweet, and gentle in his speech, showing deference to the farmer. He almost treated the latter as a king, putting him on a pedestal and fulfilling his wishes one by one. The farmer asked for a mansion, lots of money, and several other material comforts. Boom! The Genie gave him all he wished for.

After fulfilling all his desires, Genie reminded the farmer of his promise. Satisfied beyond his wildest dreams, the farmer felt he had nothing to lose now by allowing the Genie to come out of the bottle. Cautiously, he opened the bottle, and out came black smoke and Genie's thundering voice. Taken by complete surprise, the farmer wondered what happened to the gentle and servile Genie who had granted him all his wishes. The Genie uttered, "I have fulfilled your every wish by giving you a fabulous mansion, money, and comforts. Now, it's time for YOU to repay and treat ME as your master."

The farmer objected to the fact that this wasn't a part of their deal. But the Genie simply said that he didn't spill out all the terms and conditions that came with their agreement (these days, terms and conditions are given in fine print, illegible to the naked eye). Since then, the farmer became a slave to Genie and his whims, while the latter governed the farmer's life.

This short fable, which I have adapted, is about how the Genie wins over the farmer's trust. The farmer has his vulnerabilities — he is poor and has to work hard for his living. The Genie exploits the farmer's weakness and entices him by saying it will grant all his wishes. But once the Genie gets out of the bottle, it controls the farmer's life. As you read further, you will find that the fable is very relevant to the life of the Unwanted Child.

38

THE CORE SELF HIJACKED

Children begin to take shape in parents' minds as dreams or aspirations long before they become a reality. Unlike the Wanted Child, an Unwanted Child is not something the parent desires to create. Due to some chaos in her life, the mother was unwilling to take responsibility for creating a child.

All the dreams we have are visual representations. There is a fundamental relationship here between the creator and creation. It is from this relationship that the idea of ownership emerges. In the case of an Unwanted Child, parents did not create any image, and so Unwanted Children don't have one that represents them.

Many principles of creation get violated when it comes to the Unwanted Child. Despite there being no aspiration, no image, a child comes into existence. The parents of the Wanted Child meet all the criteria for the child's survival. That child feels s/he fully belongs to the parents. In the case of the Partly Wanted Child, there are some unfulfilled criteria. The creators haven't created the image fully in their minds; secondly, ownership is partly taken. The belongingness is not complete, yet it isn't fully absent. On the other hand, multiple principles of creation and ownership get transgressed by parents when they give birth to an Unwanted Child.

The fundamental violations taking place in the case of an Unwanted Child:

1. The co-creators (parents) had no goal/dream of having a child. Thus, they did not create a child's image as a Wanted Child. This means the Self-image is missing.

2. The co-creators (parents) never wanted to create, but the creation happened by mistake, for which the mother is experiencing negative emotions.

3.   The co-creator (mother) is unwilling to take responsibility for the creation. Therefore, the space in the child's Self is denied to the co-creator, as s/he doesn't trust the mother, even though she might take good care of the child after s/he is born. The domain of the child's Self seems empty.

4.   The relationship between the co-creators and the creation is essentially lost. Co-creators also surrender ownership rights when they disown their creation.

5.   Possibly, there is some compulsion on the co-creators to take ownership, which means one does it unwillingly.

When the above happens, how is a child supposed to survive once s/he has come into existence? An Unwanted Child's way of survival is unique as Nature has devised ways for his/her preservation. The methods of Unwanted Children may not be acceptable or pleasant to others. However, they have an obvious connection to them being rejected and disowned by those responsible for them. These children are in pain and insecure from within. While many of their traits are likely to come across as negative or manipulative to us, we must remain sensitive to the fact that Unwanted Children act without awareness and knowledge about their birth, which has shaped their every aspect.

Certain traumas create a split within the child, which activates the Survival Mechanism and also gives rise to the child's Self. The Unwanted Child feels like the discarded chair in the earlier example. Someone has surrendered their ownership, and anyone can use them. The unconscious message for the Unwanted Child is similar, which makes him/her mistrustful and fearful. Situations may vary depending on who else is around in the environment of the child. A family member or close relative, such as a grandparent, could impact the child positively as s/he is growing up. Some children could be adopted, while others could continue to live with their biological parents. But they know deep within that they are unwanted. What plays a major role in the child's development is how they adapt to their specific environment and the people in it.

Unwan, the Unwanted Child, is a product of his parents, who are not in harmony with each other. An emotional separation exists between the man and woman, which reflects as a missing connection with the child. When Unwan is born, he has an unconscious

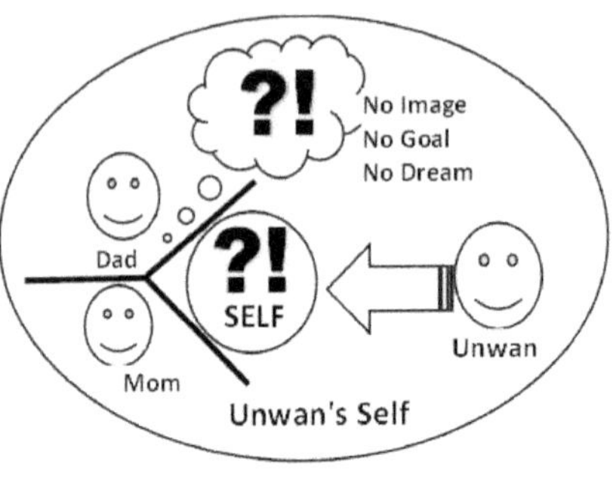

Diagram 35

memory that he is undesired. The parents have rejected the baby, and when the child's Survival Mechanism is activated, Unwan's quest begins, which is entirely about his survival. The core of the Self of the Wanted Child contains both his/her parents, while that of the Partly Wanted Child contains them too, but is dominated by the one who has rejected him/her. Because he is an Unwanted Child, the core of Unwan's Self appears empty. In reality, however, it contains the parents, but an artificial Self has blocked access to it.

It is not true that the Self of an Unwanted Child is empty. The mother is present in the child's Self and so is the father, but since the former has rejected him, Unwan's mechanism is unwilling to trust her, or for that matter, even others around him/her. So, nature gifts Unwan with a unique model of the Self, which serves as a surrogate in the place of his original Self. It will do whatever it can to make him feel safe.

In the early childhood years, parents are responsible for safeguarding and protecting the child, who is fully dependent on them. The Unwanted Child is no exception. Even if the parents do not want the child, they generally do enough to ensure the child survives. Almost all Unwanted Children have a support system that ensures they live and, in certain cases, even thrive. If the child is adopted, the couple or parent who has adopted him/her may perform that function lovingly. That means the primary caretakers, the mother and the father, are in the Unwanted Child's Self. The child's Self is not empty.

It's just that the pain of rejection creates a high level of insecurity, which does not allow the child to validate this truth. The Unwanted

Child doesn't trust the mother and others due to the memory of rejection. So, even though the parents are in the child's Self, they get blocked out. A dummy Self gets created, which runs the show for Unwan. In the process, the parents who are in the child's Self get concealed from the child.

All this takes place at the fetus level, which only surfaces when the child experiences rejection. As stated earlier, the Survival Mechanism kicks in between the years of three and eight when the child experiences some form of trauma that causes separation from the mother, giving birth to the child's Self. Every trauma the child experiences signifies chaos within the child because s/he has no solution to it, causing a state of confusion. This weakness arising out of rejection also allows the Genie to enter the life of the Unwanted Child.

39

CONTROLS WITH A DUMMY SELF

Imagine that when you land on planet Earth, someone had promised that she is going to pick you up and also be your guide. But when you arrive, you realize you are abandoned and disowned, not knowing whom to trust. A stranger comes out of the blue and says, "Don't worry, I am there for you. I will help you" At that moment, you feel assured and secure, although with some uncertainty. As time passes by you, get used to that stranger – the Genie.

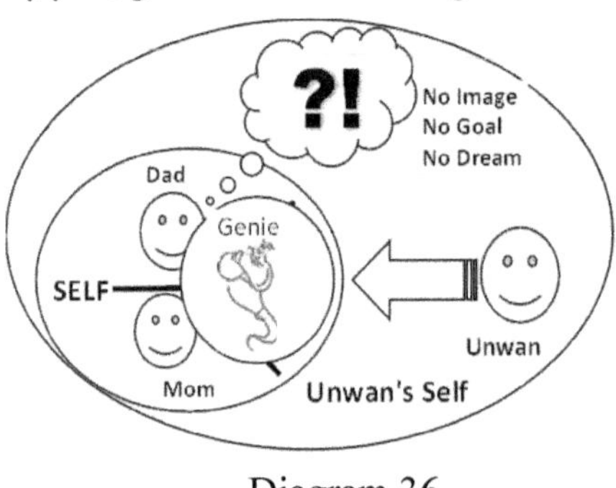

Diagram 36

The Genie is a dummy self of the Unwanted Child. It cannot eradicate the child's "birth Self" but superimposes itself on it. In the picture above, Unwan's birth Self contains both parents. A Genie, a dummy Self, occupies the domain of the birth Self to protect Unwan's body. The child can't trust the mother to be his/her protector and caretaker because s/he has received a message of rejection during pregnancy ("I don't want you," "I don't want to take care of you.") The child feels that the mother has disowned him/her.

As the child grows older, the Genie, too, starts to grow bigger and stronger, taking complete control over the child's behaviors. At certain times, it will seem as if the child has lost his senses, especially while throwing a tantrum. I have even seen grown-ups in this category behave in this way. It seems as if, in such moments, their body isn't in their control. If you ask them what made them do it, there will be a blank look on their faces. They become stoic.

Unwan's mother has rejected him, so he feels he can't rely on her for his protection. He cannot trust the father either because an Unwanted Child's mother often has a certain animosity or coldness towards the father. An artificial Self – the Genie — which gets superimposed, operates as Unwan's guide and protector in his journey on planet Earth.

The Unwanted Child's situation is precarious. They arrive in the world and realize they are abandoned. Unwan needed to rely on a guide to give him a roadmap and direction, but the guide failed to keep the promise of being there for him. Unwanted Children find that they are on their own, figuring out how to survive in this new terrain. As they are without a guide or a map, they don't know whom to trust. While the artificial Self serves as a guide, it's an imaginary entity without a map or experience. Just the way our Self is imaginary, the Genie is an entity, also imaginary.

NOTE

The Genie is a concept I have developed to help us understand how the Unwanted Child's Self functions. When I use the word "entity," it should not be confused with a ghost or spirit. We are delving into the mechanism that takes over the lives of Unwanted Children unknowingly. It is as if they are governed by someone else.

The software on a mobile phone or laptop controls its hardware. A computer virus is also software that makes an entry into the operating system by finding loopholes and hijacking it. Likewise, the Genie enters a human being's system due to major ambiguities within its system.

A Genie doesn't have a body but uses Unwan's body as the parents rejected him. Rejection becomes the weakness that allows the Genie to enter the person's life. It acts like a software/virus program that takes charge of the Unwanted Child's system when s/he experiences rejection. Reading on further, you will understand how the Genie also shapes decisions and destiny.

The Genie can't make practical and pragmatic decisions on its own but relies on information from others. An artificial Self cannot perform the function of creating an image, like a Wanted Child's Self, which is made up of parents and genuine experiences. Both experiences with parents and information from them allow the Wanted Child's Self to form a Self-image. The Genie has no known experiences at all to fall back on. In reality, the parents are there and so are the child's memories of growing up with them. But the access to those old memories is deprived by the Genie, just like a computer virus prevents access to the computer's foundational coding. So, it needs to be given wishes by the Unwanted Child; only then can it bring them to fruition. It lacks an imagination of its own and cannot create anything independently but responds well to the Unwanted Child's demands.

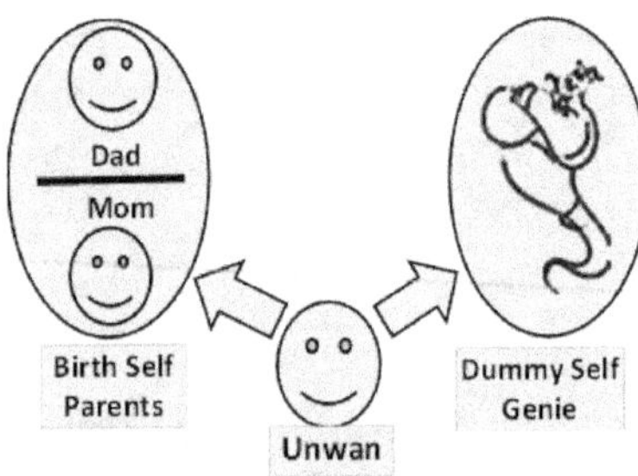

Diagram 37

The Genie takes over the child's Self and blocks out the parents. In this way it at least creates psychological distance between the child and his/her parents because it can't keep the child physically away from the parents.

Therefore, the Unwanted Child has two Selves. One is a "birth Self" that gradually gets eclipsed by a new artificial Self, the Genie. The Genie suppresses the knowledge of the birth Self and governs Unwan's life. Unwan doesn't know what makes him do what he does. Even though he is conscious that he has been receiving support from his parents and other people since birth, the Genie doesn't allow Unwanted to recognize this. It's similar to how a Partly Wanted Child's Self filters out the loving parent who wants the child and focuses attention on the parent who rejected him/her. The Unwanted Child's artificial Self filters out both parents as people who are not trustworthy. This process is so subtle that the Unwanted Child is not conscious of it even happening. The birth Self serves as a reminder of the rejection the child faced. Now the child's chaos has created a Genie to counter the old Self.

Can't Trust Anyone

The underlying meaning of this is that the Genie does not allow the Unwanted Child to trust anyone. There is NO specific human personality that the Unwanted Child can fully trust. S/he doubts and doesn't have faith in anybody, including extended family members. S/he operates out of suspicion and finds it challenging to put his/her fate into the hands of anyone. This is out of obvious concern. The Unwanted Child doesn't want to face the danger of being unprotected and exposed to harm anymore. The mechanism that is responsible for the child's preservation is already aware that the mother, the primary caretaker, has rejected the child at conception. Now it's the responsibility of the child's artificial Self to protect him/her, whatever the consequences may be.

Imagine if you put your entire being into another person's hands, but she drops you, which causes you tremendous pain. You cannot trust that person anymore and will maintain a distance from her, as far as it's possible. It is far beyond your comprehension that she may have experienced genuine chaos, due to which she dropped you. Ultimately, the trust in that person is lost, and it affects how you trust everyone else.

Unwanted Children do not even trust themselves. I have asked my clients who fall into this category whether they feel the following statements are true:

"You don't like anyone rejecting you."
"You micro-manage."
"You don't trust anybody."
"You don't even trust a therapist such as me."
"And you don't trust yourself."

My clients agree that these statements apply to them. What does the last statement above mean? Who is not trusting whom? Unwan knows that his mother has rejected him but also knows she has taken care of him. The conscious awareness of the latter aspect is there, but the artificial Self — the Genie — does not give access to it. The Genie doesn't allow Unwan to trust the "birth Self."

Does the Genie Really Exist?

Do Unwanted Children really have an artificial Self, a Genie, in them that controls them? So far, all my sessions with clients of this category have authenticated the same. Below are two cases that validate the existence of the Genie. Others may not have labeled their Genie by name, but they agreed to the concept.

Julie, an Unwanted Child, revealed that she calls her Genie Self by the name of Janet. At the time we spoke, Janet would keep her awake the whole night. Julie was feeling restless and exhausted as she was awake till early morning. As a solution, she ordered an Uber taxi at 4 am and went for a long drive, just to feel relaxed and stop Janet's internal chatter. When Julie came home from a taxi ride, she hit the bed and was fast asleep.

In another case, Sharmila, an Unwanted Child, said that she called her Genie little Shanti. Shanti was also her mother's name. Sharmila refuses to have her mother as her real Self, but creates little Shanti to replace her mother. She also said her mother is a control freak and a narcissist. After a long conversation about her survival traits, I casually inquired whether she had the same traits as her mother. She agreed. Then I asked her whether she also has narcissistic traits like her mother. All this while, Sharmila blamed her mother but failed to notice those same traits within her. She was shocked to realize that she was also a control freak and narcissist.

An Unwanted Child who is a narcissist will usually blame their partner or others for being a narcissist, but in reality, they are accurately describing their own Genie Self. They will sometimes magnify others' mistakes and tell how they lie. But they are also talking about what they do but are unaware of. It's like they are in an intoxicated state in such moments and lose self-awareness.

The Unwanted Child's Expanded Self

As the child grows, the birth Self expands to become an expanded Self, containing others who are a part of the child's upbringing. They fall into the outer ring. But, here too, the Genie plays a big role in

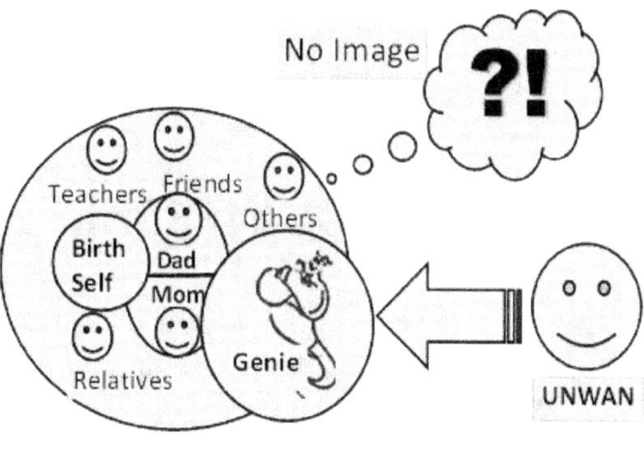

Diagram 38

concealing them. Initially, the child will try to grow close to people and learn as much from those s/he feels safe with. Certain personalities in the expanded Self may influence the child based on the family setup and environment. The child may seek sympathy from them.

Although these people will influence Unwanted Children, they won't rely on those individuals for their decision-making because of their deep-rooted insecurities. They want to make sure they are always safe and secure, no matter who they get close to. This can make them excessively cautious in their initial years. One of my clients, an Unwanted Child, said she was reserved and hesitant to interact with her relatives. She thought they wouldn't accept her for the way she was. The pattern of insecurity continues in the Unwanted Child later in life too.

40

OWNERSHIP LOST

As is the case of the discarded chair, a message goes out to the Unwanted Child that it belongs to no one. Nobody explicitly claims ownership rights over the child. These rights may be surrendered or disowned, as the mother doesn't want to but is forced to raise the child. On having the child, it could be that the parents' feelings towards the child change. They want to now play the active role of bringing him/her up. Ownership over the child is desired, but by then, the child has already picked up the emotional message of not being wanted. Hence, the Survival Mechanism of the child picks up the message of being Unwanted.

Both the parents and the child are unaware of the nature of the Survival Mechanism, or when it gets triggered. The activation of the child's particular survival mechanism signals that nobody owns the child, and the Genie takes over to protect and safeguard them.

The Genie creates a thirst for power and control in Unwanted Children, which they exert over others, as a way of making themselves feel safe. Accordingly, they develop traits that help them achieve their ends. Let's look at a few of these more closely.

As we explore some of the traits of the Unwanted Child, it's always important for us to remain sensitive to their plight of being rejected by their parents. The psychological scar they carry makes them firmly believe no one can protect them in the world. In their quest to survive, they naturally develop streetwise traits that they feel will keep them safe. Keeping control, manipulation, and disingenuous behavior are some aspects of their personality. But we mustn't condemn them in any way, for they deserve our compassion.

Cannot Tolerate Rejection

The Unwanted Child's persuasion skills and persistence are unstoppable. They can't take "no" for an answer. It's because "no" means a rejection. Anytime someone says "no" to their request, they feel rejected. Rejection is one of the deep-rooted emotions they have acquired even before birth. It unconsciously surfaces when someone directly or indirectly refuses to give them something they want or do things their way.

The emotion is also a signal that summons the Genie. To reverse that decision of others, they will use all their persuasive skills and won't stop until they get what they want. That's how the Genie enters their games and restlessly wants to turn situations in its favor. It's like the Genie says, "See, they have rejected you. Now it's my turn to do something." It does not wait for the person's permission but takes over at the helm. And from there on, the person is on autopilot until the task is achieved. If the task involves a relationship that has not materialized or hasn't gone the way they want, the Unwanted Child could possibly go into depression or a destructive mode. Making tall claims is another of their traits. When this is combined with their superior auditory and verbal skills (explained further below), they could sell ice to an Eskimo.

The Commitment of the Unwanted Child

The Unwanted Child was born by chance and not by desire. S/he just happened to come into existence, much to the dismay of the parents. A woman may have experienced vulnerability and made a silent compromise to have a child under the strong influence of her spouse. Or she may have acted out of religious compulsion. She may have only married a man for companionship and security.

Whatever may have been the woman's reasons to marry or be with her partner, the Unwanted Child was not a part of her dream. She has no aspirations or goals for the child that can be passed on to him/her. Therefore, there can be no commitment extracted from the child to fulfill certain outcomes of the parents, as in the case of the Wanted Child. The latter type of child is very cognizant of what parents wish from him/her. S/he shows great dedication in keeping up to an unspoken promise of meeting expectations. This is also true for a Partly Wanted Child, to an extent. The Unwanted Child carries no such obligations. Therefore, the child feels lost and directionless in his/her journey of living. But since s/he has come into existence, s/he *must* survive and would do anything to achieve that end. The only commitment they have is toward themselves and their safety.

As stated earlier, there is no guide or roadmap to chart their path on this planet. Unwanted Children are alone with nobody to assist them. They can't trust anyone on this planet because the one they trusted has disowned them. Since they have not been trained to fulfill promises, like Wanted Children, Unwanted Children cannot relate to the notion of commitment. No one can demand it of them and they can be prone to being irresponsible, which may give others the impression that they are self-centered. They might make tall promises but not keep them. After some time, the unfulfilled promises and behavior of Unwanted Children could cause their downfall. On the other hand, hypocritically and with double standards, they expect others to live up to their promises.

Do note that those in their childhood environment can temper the degree of selfishness or irresponsible behavior of an Unwanted Child. A mother or father may not tolerate such behavior and aim to correct it at an early age. In other instances, the child could have picked up a secondary Survival Mechanism that also influences their behavior. Unwanted Children may be more refined in their professional conduct versus their personal relationships. So the strength of all their traits can vary from person to person.

Words Speak Louder Than Actions

Unwanted Children do not operate from their visual faculties in the way Wanted Children do. There is no image they are given, so their survival mechanism doesn't make use of imagination. Neither are they inclined towards working as physically hard as the Partly Wanted Child, so they don't use their kinesthetic skills either. Instead, their survival mechanism makes them rely on their auditory skills to help them survive in the world.

Their input mode is through the ears and their output mode is spoken words. Their survival mechanism works on the principle of "words speak louder than actions." Unwanted Children's use of speech, tonality, vocabulary, and persuasion are second to none. They can be extraordinarily charming and sweet. One can hear a peculiar melody in their voices, which they deploy as a sweetener to get a specific result from others. They can demonstrate affection while relating to someone by using endearing words such as "son," "dear," "honey," or "sweetheart," which wins over the person and makes them feel really special. When the Unwanted Child observes the other getting carried away by their speech, s/he knows s/he has control over the person. Sometimes s/he can pull the rug under the person's feet, making him/her feel distressed. In this manner, Unwanted Children can play a controlling game. If someone notices something is odd, they can come up with an excuse or convincing sob story to explain themselves and get away scot-free. In the short run, the other person will end up believing the stories of the Unwanted Child until s/he gets exposed.

Deeply Desire Recognition

Unwanted Children want recognition and won't stop until the world, or at least a large number of people, acknowledge their greatness. This is their way of gaining the acceptance they believe they lack. They want love from society at large, but this wish often remains unfulfilled.

As flexible as raw clay, it is noticeable that they are very good at imitating, copying, and modeling the behavior of others. This includes molding their voice or body. An unconscious need for stature, status, and recognition drives them. And so, they deeply crave the limelight. At times, they don't mind taking credit away from others and making it look like their own triumph. If they miss out, they don't like others getting credit. They could thump their chests on their minor achievements and downplay the significant achievements of others. The degree to which such traits will surface will vary from person to person. But there is an insecurity that makes them want to stand out above everyone else — another way they feel they will be noticed and gain acceptance.

Thirst for Power and Control

Power is naturally appealing to Unwanted Children. One requires power to control others. They can come across as self-aggrandizing, making themselves appear more important than they are. Being full of confidence but pretentious, one may not detect that their confidence is not real but fake.

They don't trust anybody, not even their own Self. Since the parents have disowned them, it's difficult for them to trust their Self, which represents the parents. They will often micro-manage others around them, both in their personal and professional lives. Unwanted Children can't simply put their lives in the hands of others because they don't trust anyone. This makes their senses very alert and sensitive, just like a dog who moves the ears on hearing the slightest sound. They want to know everything that's going on around them, for which they could eavesdrop and spy on others. Their insecurities are very high, and that is where control comes into play. Control and micro-management go hand in hand. The more Unwanted Children are in charge, the more they feel assured that everything is okay. In the process, they are mentally and physically under stress or anxiety.

Double Standards

Unwanted Children are full of double standards. They demand commitment from others, but they might indirectly refuse to keep the promises they make. They insist that others serve them with loyalty, but they will not be loyal to others. Such people will demand honesty from others, when they themselves can be deceitful or lie. Others' integrity will be put to the test, whereas you can't expect them to have it. The point to note here is that Unwanted Children do possess all the awareness of healthy qualities, but their Self – the Genie — does not permit them to be genuine. Most importantly, they are unaware that emotional trauma has hijacked their system (their Self), and the Genie is at the helm.

Many people of this personality type are refined and balanced, but their core traits still surface in their lives. The above is not meant to denigrate Unwanted Children but to show how their survival mechanism works. Using power, control, and manipulation are simply ways they try to make themselves feel safe in the world. We mustn't look down on them but instead try to understand what's at the root of their behaviors — a grand rejection, which was no fault of theirs.

41

GENIE AT THE HELM

We will look at some of the ramifications of what it means when ownership is lost. The Genie can take control of every aspect of the lives of Unwanted Children, including how they relate to others. In addition, these children can also sometimes experience neglect or abuse in their childhood years.

The Unwanted Child Does Not Respect The Body

The mother disowns the Unwanted Child. What does this mean? When the mother rejects the child, she is primarily rejecting the child's body. If the body is not there, then there is no child.

As the mother has disowned the child's body, the Unwanted Child too doesn't respect it. They can put their body to any task and mold it the way the artificial Self (the Genie) wants them to. As a reminder, the Genie is the artificial Self of the Unwanted Child, which blocks the functioning of the child's birth Self that contains the parents. Most often, it is the Genie who governs their bodies. Every Self is an invisible entity and so is the Genie. It doesn't have a body, but it is sort of a program that governs the Unwanted Child's body. It gets activated because the child is rejected.

Some Unwanted Children in their teenage years do experience that something unique is influencing their thinking, but they have no clue what it is. They have no understanding of it or the ability to take charge of it. The child can't simply overthrow the artificial Self because it's there to protect him/her and take care of the child's well-being. The Wanted Child and Partly Wanted Child, too, are unaware of their Self's dominance. The Unwanted Child also has no clue about it, either.

Clara, who is in her early twenties, said, "When I am unwell, I have to be alert and watchful that nothing happens to the body. I would wake up from sleep to make sure nothing untoward has happened."

I asked her, "Are you and your body different from each other?"

She replied, "My mother does not care about my well-being; myself has to take care of my body." (sic) Clara is referring to Genie.

Suffering Neglect or Abuse

A teenage boy by the name of Jaggu was brought in by his parents to see me. He was in his early college years but wouldn't attend his lectures while lying that he did (it is common in India for children to go to college in the same city where their parents live. So, they continue to live at home while attending college). One evening, Jaggu left his home without informing his parents or anyone who knew them. I was told that the boy was a pathological liar and that his mother would scold him if he got found out. Jaggu said that he didn't trust his parents, especially his mother. Speaking to her made it evident to me that she, too, had traits matching those of an Unwanted Child.

Jaggu had survived six months on his own, with only a little money and two sets of clothes. He had slept in all sorts of odd and abandoned public places — railway platforms, parks, temples, etc. For sustenance, he would scrounge around for discarded food and visit places where free food was being distributed. Sometimes, he would go hungry. He was very disconnected from his mother and wanted to keep away from her at all costs. Jaggu's mother had divorced his father and had remarried. His Genie was doing its best to keep Jaggu away from the person who he felt had caused his trauma.

The Genie in the bottle is also, in a way, symbolic of the trapped Unwanted Child. In this case it was Jaggu's mother who had placed him in a trap of making him feel unwanted, either before or from birth. She had managed to continue living her life while he had to bear the consequences. Unwittingly, she put Jaggu into the prison of the Unwanted Child's Self. Without verbally stating it, she was in a way, saying, "I don't want you, and I blame you for being born. I am putting you behind bars, even though I was the one who experienced limitations."

The lack of ownership towards Unwanted Children can have more brutal consequences for them when they are young and growing up. Many of my clients in this category had reported being abused when they were young by their relatives, instructors, family servants, or others in their community. They tolerated such physical and emotional traumas without complaining to their parents. This suppressed trauma often surfaces in therapy sessions.

Cathy, a woman in her twenties, came to see me because she was suffering from depression. She shared how her karate instructor sexually abused her after class in grades VI and VII. When I enquired what had stopped her from reporting the incidents to her mother, she found that unconsciously, she never trusted her mother. Cathy was the only child of her parents. In therapy sessions, she learned that she was an Unwanted Child. She confirmed this by speaking to her mother about the events surrounding her birth. Cathy's mother was having issues with her father, who was not financially supporting the family and was his mama's boy. She wasn't ready to have his child. After Cathy was born, her mother really took to her, loved, and cared for her. Till today, her mother has done a great deal for Cathy. Unfortunately, an emotional message got triggered when she was in her fetus form, which got imprinted on her mind that her mother did not desire to have her.

Unwanted Children Want Ownership Over Others

When a person discards something, ownership is forfeited. The Genie in the tale above doesn't have an owner but wants to belong to someone. To belong to someone, he is willing to do anything. He must win over the farmer's trust by granting and fulfilling the latter's wishes. He coaxes the farmer into accepting his offer. But, persuasion and persistence can have their limits. So, Genie wins over the farmer's trust by giving him what he desires. The farmer doesn't know Genie's hidden agenda, but Genie's acts now convince him about his authenticity. The farmer in this tale represents the Unwanted Child's body. The Genie takes over the child's body and wants to control it. Later, it wants to control others by making the Unwanted Child do its bidding. As the child does not feel safe from within, the Genie projects this insecurity outwards through the Unwanted Child's behaviors.

Another interesting aspect of the Genie is that all it can bestow upon the farmer are materialistic goods. The farmer may want to be loved by others, but his understanding of love is to have all worldly things, which he believes represents his happiness. It is the same for the Unwanted Child, who also fails to make a distinction. S/he believes wealth and power will eventually make them feel loved by others.

Unwanted Children are nobody's property. They don't like being controlled by others. Initially, they will happily do things for others the way it is demanded to win their trust. Just as the Genie does everything the way, the farmer requires. Unwanted Children will mold their behaviors to get acceptance from others. Once they have got a foothold and are accepted, they will flip. Slowly and progressively, they take the reins in their hands and start to control others. They end up claiming ownership over those people and their property.

42

WHO IS ACTUALLY MAKING DECISIONS?

For a child's survival, two conditions need to be met. There has to be a Self, and there has to be guidance in the form of a roadmap that gives direction. Both these fundamental principles have been violated when we consider the Unwanted Child. The Wanted Child follows an image given to him/her. The Partly Wanted Child's decisions are governed by the parent who has rejected him/her. Survival for Unwanted Children, on the other hand, becomes a great struggle. Someone has to offer them a map or direction for their survival. Based on a map or receiving directions, one makes decisions. Who makes decisions for the Unwanted Child?

Slave to the Genie: Money Can't Buy Love

Nature has offered a unique system for the Unwanted Child by creating a new artificial Self, the Genie, which provides the child with direction. The Genie takes over at the helm every time the child faces rejection and decisions get filtered through it. This process continues even when the child becomes an adult.

In the story of the farmer, in order to be released, Genie seduces the farmer by making an offer to fulfill his dreams. As a result, the farmer comes under the spell of Genie. It looks like the Genie is fulfilling the wildest dreams of the farmer, but there is a catch. A person could end up becoming a prisoner of his desires in exchange for his freedom, which becomes the plight of the farmer once he lets the Genie out of the bottle. Similarly, Unwanted Children put their trust in the hands of their artificial Self. But by doing so, they lose their freedom, are entangled in their own survival trap, and end up as prisoners of their desires.

A Genie doesn't come up with its own goals. It considers the wishes of the Unwanted Child and does whatever it can to fulfill them. On what basis, however, does the Genie operate? The Unwanted Child cannot tolerate rejection, as it's an unconscious reminder of a prior tragic event in the child's life. The Genie is aware of those emotions, signaling that the child's survival is in danger. People around the child may reject the wishes or desires of the Unwanted Child from time to time, which triggers feelings of rejection. The negative emotions will then set the ball rolling, culminating in a wish for the Unwanted Child. The wish represents something the Unwanted Child needs to feel secure. It's like the farmer who asks Genie to provide the things he doesn't have. Those things can be a mansion, money, and other comforts, giving the farmer a sense of security and well-being.

By avoiding rejection, the Unwanted Child wishes for acceptance. To be more specific, s/he yearns to be loved and cared for by others. But the irony is that although the Genie can confer material possessions and status on an Unwanted Child, it can't fill the core vacuum the child experiences. To get him/her acceptance, the Genie can only provide worldly riches or positions. "Money can't buy love" is the maxim that rings true here.

Reina, a female client of mine, who is an Unwanted Child, threw an expensive birthday bash at a resort that lasted three days. But she was disappointed that her boyfriend didn't spend more than a few hours at the occasion. Although her huge birthday party was well attended, Reina complained that she didn't have any trustworthy friends. Unwanted Children can be very successful but cannot acquire genuine friends.

Unwanted Children feel alone and cannot trust anyone because the one they trusted has disowned them. So, their next quest is to make lots of money, which gives them a deep sense of assurance, although it's a False Illusionary Assurance. As there is no one to support them, they have to watch their backs and survive. Money becomes their buffer, which gives them the strength to fall back on. Most often, they are materialistic in their thinking and values. The Genie will make all their worldly dreams come true. But that's not what they are truly searching for. They want acceptance or unconditional love, which the Genie has no clue how to get for them.

The thirst for power and authority in some Unwanted Children can be extreme. It gives them an intoxicating high comparable to drugs like cocaine and marijuana. Some of them want to become invincible and thrash their competitors without remorse. They could demonstrate a degree of ruthlessness in how they achieve their goals. Unwanted Children would like to be looked upon as overlords of a kingdom. To get them there, the Genie is willing to make the person do things that others would find questionable — deceive, lie, pretend, or manipulate. Initially, Unwanted Children will do whatever is needed, molding their physical bodies, personalities, and skills to fit into another's specifications. They can be exceptionally good at mimicking the behavior of others to achieve success. Once they gain acceptance, they hunger to cling to it. They slowly want to control those who have accepted them, whether they are a spouse, family members, or business associates. The Genie, in this fashion, first takes over the Unwanted Child and then others.

One of my clients used the term "Sati Savitri," which in India implies a perfect, subservient woman bending to her male partner's desires. She did her best to fit into her boyfriend's concept of an ideal woman. Before doing that, she collected sufficient information on his definition of an ideal woman and accordingly molded herself. Once such a person achieves his/ her goal, the other side surfaces, which wants to control the other person.

Impulsive and Risky Decision-Making

The Unwanted Child is prone to making impulsive decisions. As they are directionless, they end up making decisions on impulse. Since no image has been given to them, there is no map to guide decision-making. A map is not the territory, but it gives direction.

Not only are they impulsive, but once such a personality type decides on something, they don't change their minds, even if it puts others into trouble. They are stubborn and will be single-minded in achieving their goal, no matter the consequences or the discomfort to others. An Unwanted Child I know had knee replacement surgery on both legs and still needed to recover completely, but she demanded that she be allowed to travel abroad to attend a social event. Against her doctor's advice, she obstinately chose to go ahead. No amount of persuasion or her family's concern towards her well-being could stop her from fulfilling her wish.

By making impulsive decisions, they want to prove what they can accomplish. It could cause pain or difficulties to those around them, but they will triumphantly thump their chests on their bold decision. They may put others at risk but remain indifferent and unemotional about it, making it look like a challenge that proves one's potential. Their end goals must not be compromised, and they won't apologize to others if they cause them losses. When it's about achieving their goal, they become single-minded and totally focused on their outcome. You give a wish to a Genie, and it will not stop until the wish is fulfilled. Nothing can get in the way of the Genie and its need to fulfill the child's goals.

Even after reaching their goals, they don't experience satisfaction, as Genie needs more fodder. One of my clients had successfully climbed up the corporate ladder to reach a top position in his industry. He had achieved what he had dreamed of some years ago. Since the goal was fulfilled, he felt restless and disinterested in his current job, wanting to move to another level. But there was no position higher than what he was holding in India. Genie had completed the project, making him lose interest in his current job. The Genie wants yet one more goal that pumps the adrenaline up, to move to another level that is challenging and motivating.

Again, the description above is not to paint Unwanted Children in poor light but to show how their Self — the Genie — hijacks their thinking in the name of protection. The Genie controls the child's decision-making and overall life. A person in this category is not aware of it. S/he is assuming her behaviors, beliefs, attitudes, and thinking is who s/he is, but it is an artificial Self that makes him/her this way.

Unwanted Children feel in control of others around them through their guile, wealth, and power, but they are unaware that they themselves are captive prisoners of the Genie. The hypnotic spell over them continues till the end of their lives.

43

THE GENIE CONTROLS YOUR DESTINY

It is important for parents to protect a child who is growing up. However, going overboard after a certain age harms the development of the child, possibly leading to incompetence. Similarly, while a soldier needs to wear protective armor during battle, moving around with protective gear in everyday life will make life burdensome. This is what the Self of all three types of children feels like beyond a purposeful period. The Unwanted Child faces this impact differently through an expanding Genie. The same system that helps the child also causes him/her maximum damage as s/he grows up.

Impact of the Artificial Self – a Burgeoning Genie

Unwanted Children very much love to get acceptance, and all their unconscious programming is working towards it. The above diagram shows more people coming into the life of the Unwanted Child as s/he gets older, from whom s/he seeks acceptance. Above the stack of passing years is a governing Genie that keeps getting bigger and bigger. The more it expands, the more the Unwanted Child's nature becomes powerful and controlling.

The more people the Unwanted Child needs acceptance from, the harder the Genie needs to work to help him/her win over the trust of those people. Once that is attained, the Genie tries to control them. The Genie makes the Unwanted Child dominate more and more people, thereby controlling his/her life. It means that the individual is not free to experience life, but is living in a fearful and fretful manner without knowing what's driving his/her actions.

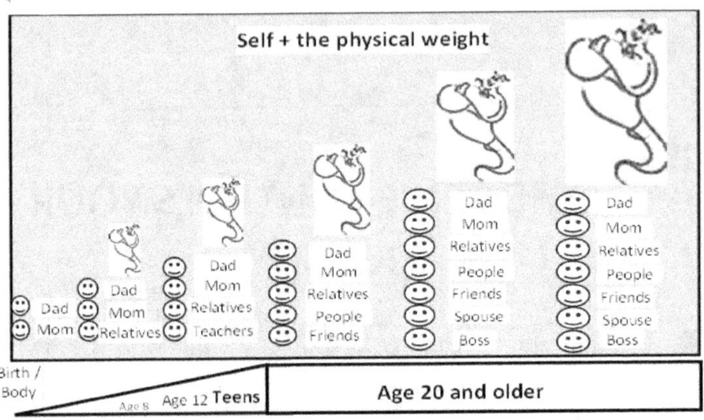

Diagram 39

Money and control are tools the Unwanted Child acquires to gain power. Wanting to enjoy the limelight is another need. Money gives them a sense of power, but with recognition intoxicating them, things can go awry for them. They get cut off from reality and the suffering of others. The more power, seniority, money, position, celebrity status, or fame, the Unwanted Children have, the more respect and honor they demand from others. Once again, we are not judging Unwanted Children as bad people, many of whom may indeed be wonderful individuals. We are simply attempting to understand the mechanism that takes over their behavior unknowingly.

Unwanted Children at the other end of the spectrum may be lacking in money or power. Those people will seek sympathy, portraying a picture of misery and helplessness. When they feel in despair, they can work very hard to win the trust of others. These attitudes will go on till the such time they have achieved that end. However, those who trust them may eventually feel let down. At the extreme, they may even backstab a person who trusts them. A point to note here is that not all Unwanted Children will behave this way. A dominant parent may not allow certain behaviors to flourish or may try to nip them in the bud. While the traits may exist in most Unwanted Children, they will vary in degree.

As explained earlier, the Unwanted Child does not trust anyone, nor does s/he trust his/her own Self — the parents. The person is conscious that the parents and others have been supportive, but the Genie blocks the awareness of this fact. This can make Unwanted Children suspicious of everyone. They want to keep vigilance on the activities of others and what they are saying about them. This whole exercise of staying alert and assessing others' motives becomes increasingly exhausting and nerve-wracking. The Genie consumes a lot of their time and energy to safeguard their interest.

Over time, when the number of people they need to monitor also grows, they become perpetually restless due to micro-management and their sensitive nature. It's like they are holding the reins of many horses in their hands and each one is pulling them in a different direction. It may have been manageable when they were young, with a few horses to control. But over time, the process becomes unmanageable. They will then need to devise other techniques to have a tight grip over the increasing number of people while closely watching those who they already keep an eye on. This makes their stress levels rise and takes a toll on their health. The more they exercise control, the more elusive it becomes and the more they lose the trust of others. Both sides end up feeling frustrated.

Efforts of Unwanted Children get expended in simply maintaining their positions. As some of them would be lying or faking, those actions need to avoid being exposed. Divide and rule is a tactic they deploy within groups. They may engage in rhetoric or modulate their tonality to cover up their intentions. They have to remember conversations and contexts, to play games, and not allow a slip of the tongue to open up a can of worms. Through all this, they need to appear calm and cool, while actually experiencing stress from within. All this, as you can imagine, is quite an exhausting drill. That's why Unwanted Children can never be at peace.

It is inevitable that such behaviors will put a strain on their closest relationships. Unwanted Children don't even trust their own spouses. They are always suspicious; they want the spouse to report everything to them. Suspicion levels increase if that doesn't happen. Using taunts and hints to begin with, they can make matters unpleasant for the other, causing disharmony and fights. Genie helps them fulfill materialistic goals, but it isn't helpful in the area of personal relationships that give love and joy. These people search for love and joy in relationships but don't find it. At the most, they transact in relationships.

While their internal mechanism created the Genie in their formative years, it also made their lives miserable. All their traits generate distrust while affecting them mentally and physically. They have no clue that it's the artificial Self that has created pain and discomfort in their lives. Identifying the culprit is quite challenging, so they go on thinking that's the way life is.

Destiny of the Unwanted Child

Krish, an Unwanted Child, is a successful barrister practicing in the UK and excels at his profession. Despite being good at what he does, he doesn't feel he has reached the level of his peers. This is because he believes he is an outsider and has been rejected by the UK system. As a lawyer, he feels the system hasn't acknowledged him. So, Krish has been working hard to prove to others that he is worthy and knows the law exceptionally well. When he succeeds, he quickly looks for a new challenge. These are all ways for him to gain acceptance. He continues to strive harder if he doesn't get it. But with every success, acceptance moves further and further away from him. He realizes that this has been his pattern throughout his life.

When we compare all three types of personalities, Unwanted Children will end up having the most wealth, property, fame, or success, which gives them security. Yes, it is one way in which they can receive acceptance from the world at large. They experience a sense of assurance that their well-being is taken care of and they are safe. However, these feelings of comfort are a temporary False Illusionary Assurance. They are unaware that their system runs on autopilot, controlled by their Genie. When one is in such an operating mode, one is constantly responsive and reactive. In fact, all three SOMs are reaction-oriented and not neutral.

The stress from the insecurity Unwanted Children carry is a constant source of anxiety, robbing them of peace and joy. Their relationships are greatly affected too, for they can sometimes influence people, but their patterns are eventually found out as manipulative or sympathy seeking. Most of the time, their patterns are repetitive. Whether it's in their personal life, relationship or professional life, there will be similarities. Since most of their decisions are happening via the Genie, the Unwanted Child hardly makes any decisions but experiences a predetermined fate. That means their destiny is in the hands of the Genie. To put it more profoundly, they are merely puppets in the Genie's hand. Unwanted Children might acquire all the worldly things they desire. But, ironically, they end up receiving curses and condemnation from many people, which is the opposite of what they are seeking. They might make their physical bodies secure with financial wealth and materialistic fulfillment, but that doesn't bring them true love or peace.

Very Important Note

This is a significant message for readers who fall under the category of Unwanted Child. As we conclude, something important must not go unnoticed regarding the Unwanted Child. Maybe the child was unwanted when s/he was conceived. This was due to some chaos experienced by the family, which made the mother not ready to have the child. The emotions of the mother got transferred to the fetus, which gave the message to the fetus that she was not willing to have him/her. However, Unwanted Children tend to overlook something important. If the child were totally unwanted, parents would have aborted him/her. On the other hand, in most cases, parents have protected and brought up the child after s/he was born. It means that the Unwanted Child is not really unwanted but is either wanted or partly wanted. It's just that the child has received a message so early on (in the womb) that it seems to have sealed the child's fate. However, it need not be this way. With awareness, Unwanted Children can update their awareness to address the burden of their pasts and become liberated from the clutches of the Genie.

SECTION IV

GETTING OFF AUTOPILOT

44

REDEFINE YOUR LIFE

This book's primary purpose is to help you understand your Survival Mechanism and your Self, which sucks a person into a trap. You are sandwiched between two powerful mechanisms that control our lives. It's as if a game of tug-of-war between the Survival Mechanism and the Self is taking place and you are the rope that gets pulled by either side.

The intention of both mechanisms is to keep us safe and protected. We presuppose and identify with our being with beliefs, behaviors and thinking that we have acquired in the process of our birth and our growing-up years. As a result, we live in a deep hypnotic trance where everything seems normal and natural because you tend to believe in the absolute validity of those beliefs, behaviors, and thinking. After all, they made you who you are today.

I describe this state as one's **Birth Survival Trance**. A trance is a state of mind where one has no conscious control over his/her thoughts and actions. Using the survival mechanism gifted to us by Nature, known as the Survival Mechanism, one unconsciously responds to the commands or instructions given by one's Self. We all are born with this trance, and its primary purpose is to keep us safe. We will look at ways to help you identify your Birth Survival Trance and some techniques to make changes within you.

It is not a new state we find ourselves in suddenly but it is our primary one since birth. I've used the word "trance" to describe this condition because it is one in which we are not completely conscious of our decisions or in control of our bodies. Every trance is also a mindset. We believe we are wanted, partly wanted, or unwanted and allow that to become our mindset and, therefore, our reality. For example, the Wanted Child believes s/he *must* live by the specifications of their parents in order to be accepted (survive). This need not be true, but we have taken something to be our reality. It is about how we perceive life. Do we have to perceive it the way it has been presented to us or can we do so differently? This book is supposed to provoke your thinking and make you look at your reality rather than remain within your survival trance.

The primary issue we are dealing with is that we, with our Survival Mechanism, are trying to adjust to our Self. Like every organism, a child's fundamental quest is to preserve his/her body, i.e., survive within the environment. Using our survival traits, we develop beliefs, behaviors, communication styles and thinking to maximize our chances of survival. However, this way of living doesn't change once we get older. Even people well into their forties or fifties are still operating in the same way. The result is we do not end up truly living life out of our free will.

Since you are born, grow up and live with it, it's challenging to notice your survival trance. The only time a person comes close to recognizing its existence is when one is experiencing depression, anxiety, or any other negative emotion. Otherwise, all of us go to our graves with our hypnotic spell, thinking that's the way life is. Very few manage to liberate themselves from this way of being.

Once a client has understood their Birth Survival Trance in a session, they know they are living in a trap. The very next question they usually ask is, what's next? It won't be possible for me to go through the whole process of how I help them in this book. But I will provide you with certain tools to show you the pathway to your freedom.

What do you like to do now that you know about your survival trance?

Before a child can learn to walk or run, there is a basic requirement that s/he first learns to balance. On that fundamental point, the child's mobility gets built. It would also be vital for us to stick to some foundation so that the rest of the journey flows smoothly.

Learning to balance is like being aware of one's Birth Survival Trance and consciously making decisions for your well-being. The more you make conscious decisions, the more you strengthen the muscles of being conscious. That creates a firm grounding, helping you take charge of your destiny.

As a place to start off, here are a few suggestions I can make:

1. The main purpose of writing these books is to make you aware of the spell you are living under. As you read them, it would be essential to introspect and to acknowledge the limitations you experience.

2. Who is the person you believe has sucked you into your survival trance? Without blaming them, which of your parents was responsible for it? Being a Wanted Child is as much a survival trap as being a Partly Wanted Child or Unwanted Child. However it may seem, no one is necessarily in a better position.

3. Observe how you are operating from within your trap. This will come when you understand your survival traits. In other words, are you a Wanted Child, a Partly Wanted Child, or an Unwanted Child? The more you know about it, the better your chances are of liberating your being.

4. In order to find a way out of your survival trance, you must **SLOW DOWN**. Going faster does not solve the problem but makes it worse. By **SLOWING DOWN,** you can pay more attention to things happening within you, rather than dissipate your energies on the outside world. Self-awareness is not possible when you are going fast. Slowing down will give you unique realizations that will help you on your path towards freedom.

5. Make it your journey to understand your Birth Survival Trance and to find a way out. Each time you are lost or confused, you can't run towards a Master for guidance. You must believe in your legs — they know how to balance. There is a Master that lies within you. You need to trust and have faith in something within you at all times.

Most of the time, the conflict is between your Survival Mechanism and the Self (which represents others and their ideas). It feels like you

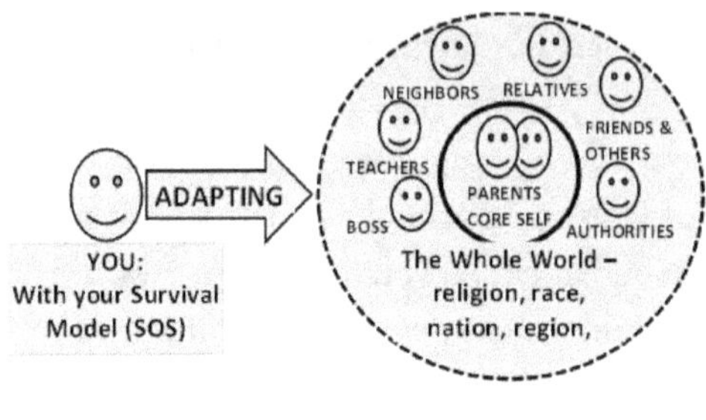

Diagram 40

are on one side and the whole world you need to adapt to is on the other. You can refer to the diagram below.

Please note that the Genie, which is a part of the Unwanted Child, is not shown in the diagram. If you fall under that category, it does apply to you.

A person's Self comprises different people and their diverse ideas, concepts, beliefs, rules, and laws. You don't have a choice but to fit into their thinking and way of living. It's because your survival depends on obliging as many or all of them. But it isn't easy to please everyone or even the same person at all times. Disputes can arise if such conflicts are not resolved amicably. If that happens, negative emotions will surface in our lives at various times.

The external world becomes your inner world in the form of a Self. If you have imbibed the lessons of this book, I will also become part of that world — your Self. However, what's different about reading this book is that it is aimed at helping you understand how your internal survival mechanism is working. It gives you an opportunity to step out of your survival trap.

With your Survival Mechanism and its tools, you try to adjust to those around you, because your survival depends on it. However, those people are also trying to survive with their own survival mechanisms, doing whatever they can according to their understanding. Most of their beliefs, ideas, and ways of thinking came down to them through their ancestors, which also got downloaded into your system. This information is outdated and often goes unchallenged. It's time for you to update your system and the best way to do it is by asking relevant questions. Are you likely to get answers to all your questions? Certainly not. But a few will set you on your way.

One of the questions that you could ask is, what makes you behave, believe, and think the way you do? You know that the mechanisms of the Survival Mechanism and Self were needed when you were young. But now that you have survived, what would you like to do? What choices do you have?

Here are a few important tips to consider:

1. Your primary goal should be to increase awareness of your limitations and how you use your survival traits to adapt to the pressure exerted by the Self.

2. You are not someone's property, and nobody has any ownership rights over you. Moreover, co-creators create a child, but the reverse is not possible. So, co-creators have responsibilities and duties towards their creation, which got distorted and lost in their own survival mechanism. However, the child who is a creation cannot be held responsible for and duty-bound towards the creators and the Self. S/he cannot be expected to do things out of obligation. It is okay to do what is needed if one wants to do it, but not out of a sense of guilt. The potter has to take responsibility for his/her creation. The pot, jug, and jar can't be held responsible for the creators.

3. When it's your responsibility to make your decision, make sure you make them. If you are grown up and have passed the age of survival, it's time to take ownership of your life. Make decisions harmoniously, balancing the needs of your being with others' expectations. You are not an item or possession but a free human being, who can make his/her own independent decisions.

4. The more you make conscious decisions, the more you will feel in charge and then will begin to govern your destiny. Free will is not a thing that you can buy across the counter. Nature has offered free will to everyone; however, it's something we have to exercise. Just the way in which we do physical exercise to make our muscles stronger. The more you put it to practice, the better you get. And when you TRUST, BELIEVE, and have FAITH in your being, it gets strong. You start to design your destiny.

Let's see what else we must bear in mind in order to redefine our lives.

The Self is Not Perfect

A child's Self, representing parents and others, protects them by imbibing things from those people. The validity of many beliefs and ideas it contains has not undergone any serious testing by us to date. It's time we visit certain limiting ideas passed on to us by our elders and take another look at them.

Like the news we read and hear, some facts get distorted before they are presented to us, which we believe to be true. Many historical events are genuine, but how they get communicated to us is distorted. The attack on 9/11 is a fact, where the twin towers were destroyed. Two passenger aircraft smacked into the towers in Manhattan, New York City. There have been many other narratives on 9/11 besides the official one. It's difficult to know the complete truth or what exactly transpired. Therefore, there is a mixture of truth and distortion in it. Something similar happens to beliefs when they are handed down from one generation to the next.

Our creators were born with their Survival Mechanisms and had to adjust to their parents. While they did what they could to guide us with their knowledge and experiences, a lot of beliefs passed on were hearsay to them when they were young. Those went by unchallenged. You need not be a victim of those, but you can instead ask some tough questions. Questions are the best-known way to update our distorted ideas presented to us by our Self. You need not challenge any personality within the Self per se, but it's important to be clear in your own thinking. Even if the need arises to question a person, make sure you are soft and gentle in how you do it, and not confrontational.

Your Self is Full of the Past — Question it

There are two kinds of data recorded by a person's Self. One is verbal information passed on to us by elders, and the second is experiential. In the olden days, most knowledge was passed on verbally from one generation to the next. Many beliefs were also transferred similarly. But just like Chinese whispers, verbal messages get distorted and disconnected from their original purpose or relevance in time. The Indian caste system is one such example, but they exist in different cultures. Distortion of messages can happen in a generation's time, so imagine receiving information coming down from the distant past. Your Self absorbs it thinking it's all true, especially as it comes from a credible source, your parents.

So we need to ask various questions regarding various things we have been taught and check their validity in our lives today. Some lessons could still be applicable; however, many could be well beyond their expiry dates. Unchecked, the same gets passed on to the next generation, like the baton in a 4X100 meters relay race. If possible, you don't need to challenge such points openly but internally update or discard them at your own level. It is essential to have clarity within you. If you consistently inquire, you will slowly begin to get answers and see them as fallacies.

If you are in your twenties or older and working, it's the right time for you to take charge of your life. However, let me add a few words of caution — you can't retaliate against the Self. Even if parents may have ill-treated you in your growing years, it doesn't give you the right to have negative emotions towards them. You can find a good therapist to diffuse those pent-up feelings against them. Any therapist practicing Neuro-Linguistic Programming (NLP) can help you neutralize such negative emotions.

Emotions are a Sure Sign of Inner Conflict

Every time you experience an upsurge of negative emotions, it is a sure indicator that there is a conflict going on between your Survival Mechanism and the Self. I received an email from a man saying, "I've been suffering from depression for the last six months due to financial and work pressures." He had been experiencing emotions for six months but did not take any help to resolve the issue, hoping it would get sorted on its own.

Emotions are like a thermostat. As long as we experience positive emotions, we feel secure and safe. It's only when negative emotions surface that the thermostat trips. It signals that we are unsafe because of an external threat to our survival, and we may be in danger. It's like an internal war siren that has been switched on, which may not be true often, but we start to experience a negative feeling beyond our control.

Another way to look at negative emotions is an electrical short circuit that blocks the flow of energy, causing discomfort and pain within your body. That electrical circuit has to be restored permanently. Temporarily fixing an issue will give rise to the problem repeating itself.

Neuro-Linguistic Programming (NLP) has various techniques to diffuse negative emotions. You could have a few sessions to help you resolve the issue that is causing inner conflict. It will be hard to go into the details about NLP and its techniques in this book. However, an experienced NLP practitioner can do wonders.

Rules or Laws Have Limitations

A child's Self makes rules with positive intent for his/her benefit, which are taken as laws by the child. They are essentially do's and don'ts enforced on us by others. However, we can recognize that laws with even good intentions have their limitations.

As mentioned earlier, a child does not want his/her hand to be held once s/he knows how to walk. But while crossing a busy street, a parent will make sure to hold the child's hand. When the child has learned to understand and obey streetlights at the age of ten, this restriction is dropped. From this, we can conclude that many laws or norms come with an expiry date, just like grocery items have a shelf life. Not all laws are uniformly applicable on all people at all times.

The application of laws has a time and place. Driving on the left side of the road is valid when you are on the road in a country that follows this rule. However, if there is no specific road as in the desert or jungle in the same country, then the same law will become defunct. Likewise, an emergency ambulance can break certain traffic rules to save the life of a person in critical condition.

Laws cannot be applied universally. Even nature's laws, which spare no one, undergo a change in certain places. A magnetic needle points in the north direction, but at the North pole, it spins endlessly. We may impose rules or legislate laws, but there will be times and places when they will not hold well. Even a school recognizes that rules that apply to children between four and ten do not apply to students above grade five. They undergo change and need to be updated, but we forget to do it later in our lives as adults.

Rules and laws are valid and make our lives easier. But you must be open to questioning the personal limitations that are preventing you from growing and blossoming in your own way.

Making Conscious Decisions

As you have read in the previous section, irrespective of your category, your decision-making in one way or another is in the hands of others. In our personal lives, and at times in our professional lives, we unconsciously and unknowingly comply with others' decisions, assuming they are our own.

This makes the direction of our lives, our very destiny, lies in the hands of others. Yes, nature has given us free will, but few genuinely exercise it. Prince Wan could be fighting others' wars, Pawan's reins lie in someone else's hands, and the Genie controls Unwan. Whether a person is famous, rich or ordinary, the Survival Mechanism makes him/her a puppet in the hands of others. Or you are busy running a puppetry show, making others into puppets.

Only when you start to make decisions consciously, not solely from the need to survive, can you take your destiny into your own hands. What would you like to do?

Redefine Who You Are

In my previous book, *Stop Surviving Start Living with Freedom*, and this one, you have seen how you have been living a life as if you were a puppet in the hands of others. The two systems of the Survival Mechanism and the Self take charge of who you are, what you do, and how you go about doing it. It's time to redefine who you are, what you would like to be, and how you would like to live your life.

The Survival Mechanism is trying to adjust to the Self, and the Self is the whole world. The former is your operating system trying to make you adapt and survive. You will need to learn to maneuver and find new ways of dealing with the Self, which means you can't fall back on your existing survival tools. In order to redefine who you are, you will need to update your Survival Mechanism. It's time to take charge of your choices.

In the process of adapting, you continue to take support of your primary operating system — your Survival Mechanism. But, the outcomes will continue to remain the same. While it was a gift from nature to help you survive, its tools are outdated and can't be used if you want to *live your life*. Yes, you can continue to use the tools if you want to survive, as you have been doing in life. But they will not help you find a way out of your survival trap.

You Cannot Change the Self

You can see from the above diagram that a person's Self includes multiple personalities operating through it. It gradually keeps expanding as time goes by. It is not only difficult to change the Self, but it is, in fact, impossible to reform it. You might change a few people who may adapt to your new beliefs, behaviors, and thinking. But it will be practically impossible to change everyone. Even great masters like Krishna, Buddha, and Jesus couldn't transform all people of the Self. So why go that far? Even Gandhi and Martin Luther King Jr. couldn't change them. Certain people ended up taking their lives.

A lot of garbage in the form of worn-out ideas and beliefs got transferred to people for their safety. Those beliefs are deeply ingrained and difficult to eradicate. It would be a futile exercise trying to challenge the limiting beliefs of others. There is no way to overthrow the Self. The more you try to do it, the deeper you get sucked into its web. The result is more pain, discomfort, and entanglement for you.

The only thing you can change is to update your Survival Mechanism and live your life the way you want. While others have defined your life thus far, it's time you take back control and redefine it as you think best suits you. In the next few chapters, we will go through each category to understand how one can function differently. The content is written and designed keeping in mind the individual survival traits of a category. Some of the exercises and techniques could be common to all. You may go to the specific chapter applicable to you to apply the relevant techniques.

THE WANTED CHILD

45

LIVING WITH FREEDOM

As a Wanted Child, all this while you have been non-committed to your own goals – small and big — but have given more importance to fulfilling the goals of others. It's time to start reversing that and living your life and fulfilling your commitment to yourself. That is what is meant by being TRUE to your BEING.

If you identify as a Wanted Child, you are probably aware of your survival traits. Survival traits are the survival tools, ammunition, and weapons one has in order to feel safe and alive. You constantly feel it's necessary to serve others, especially your parents and extended members of the kingdom. Because you are a Wanted Child, your survival depends on meeting your parents' explicit or implicit expectations, who are the core of your Self. It could be that your parents' unfulfilled goals and dreams got dumped on you. These unknowingly became your own dreams, and you didn't realize it.

It looks like your parents' sense of freedom and well-being is chained to you, and you are supposed to keep it that way. It is an unconscious process that runs your system as the Survival Mechanism tries to fulfill the expectations of your parents, which could be their unfulfilled desires. There are also times when parents have met their life goals and want a similar life for their children (e.g. study at an Ivy League college, financial success, etc.). It looks like you have to fulfill everybody's needs in the kingdom. In that way, you are living for others. Since you were a child, unknowingly, you got sucked into a dilemma. That's when your parents' goals got planted in you before you could develop your own goals. Along the way, you have forgotten that you have your own life to live.

The time has now come to take the reins of your life into your own hands and live it your way. Your life has been a chain of an endless loop of events, leading to a vicious circle of repeating patterns and events. The little happiness that you experience along the way gives you the assurance that things are okay and you are in control. That is the Survival Mechanism's way of guaranteeing you that you are safe. It is a temporary state, however. That's the way you have lived your life, under the spell of the False Illusionary Assurance of your Survival Mechanism. Now that you know how the mechanism works unconsciously inside you through your survival traits, it's an opportunity for you to change your pathway. It is only YOU who can change the course of your life. It's your life, and the decisions and choices you make are for your growth and well-being. Below you will find some suggestions and inputs that could help you chart your course of action if you want to change your pathway. BE FREE, LIVE FREE.

You have tried your best to adjust to the Self by using your survival traits as a Wanted Child. Our survival mechanism is an essential part of us till a certain age in life, but beyond that, it's outdated. Now that you are an adult, you need to consciously get off your Survival Mechanism and its mechanism. You did what you did unknowingly and now it's time to change. You need to be honest and genuine with others around you, thus, being true to your being.

Create Your Own Image

A Wanted Child wants to fit into the Self-image created by others, thinking that's what is expected of him/her. Self-image is like a kingdom created by others; the crown is put on your head to own up to its responsibilities. If you live by a Self-image created by others, you will have to comply with the rules and regulations of those who have built that kingdom. Every one of us is somebody else's creation. To own what somebody else has built, you have to prove that you are worthy of it. But you don't have to be a royal slave to a metaphorical king, queen, and kingdom.

If you have your own dreams, then go after them. That's your kingdom, where you make your own rules and regulations. By having your kingdom, we mean living life the way you want to, setting your own standards, without having to prove anything. The joy of having your kingdom is living by your choices. Your Self defines you through the Self-image that has been imposed on you and you unconsciously respond to it. It's time to redefine it the way you want to live your life and get off autopilot mode.

Now that you know that your parents created your Self-image, you can dislodge the image. The ceremonious crown that you were forced to wear can be replaced by a simple one that you create. It is one that gives you the joy of being in it, living in it. Let your self-image be the one that offers you flexibility, increases your self-worth, allows you to learn and grow, and helps fulfill your cherished goals. Build your own personal empire. It can be modest in scale and need not be a big one. All things have a beginning, so start small and gradually keep growing. Every seed has the potential to grow and if nurtured well, it will bloom. With consistent nurturing, it can grow faster and stronger.

One of my clients, Nick (a Wanted Child), was very talented as a young child. But there were many episodes that took place while he was growing up that made him depressed and suicidal. Those experiences severely dented and even shattered his self-image. His parents, relatives, and friends condemned him as a burden and termed him as "good for nothing." He was unemployed, taunted, and his main pastime was the internet and pornography. He was feeling horrible about himself. Not knowing how to re-construct his self-image, he continued looking for approval from his parents and circle of people.

For the past three years, however, Nick has started providing Airbnb services (an online portal offering lodging and homestay experiences). His guests have highly appreciated his services and have praised him effusively. The proof of positive feedback is there for everyone to see on the Airbnb website. The feedbacks were testimonials from people who enjoyed staying at his home and showed that he was worthy. The venture is a small kingdom that made him feel that he was valuable and a contributor. Since he started providing his services, Nick has experienced improved self-worth and has built a new self-image.

Each guest's feedback would validate Nick's sense of self-worth. Every positive comment was like a certificate of his acceptance and his worthiness. That made him feel more and more valuable. Guest feedback made his confidence more robust, and he began to believe in himself. His satisfied customers left him positive feedback, which laid the foundation for Nick's new Self-image.

There is no need to protect this new Self-image from the dirt others may throw on it. The image is your authentic one; there will be no need to safeguard or build walls around it to shield it from others. There is nothing to defend and there is nothing to guard. Why is this so? Such a way of living is not living from the ego or by others' definitions. You don't allow others to define parameters or standards about your life. They are of your own making, and you are not answerable for them.

One of my clients, Sasha, a graphic designer, and a Wanted Child, was working independently, taking on job assignments. She was well qualified and talented. Over the years, Sasha had built up her clientele and reputation on the quality of her work. Honest and loyal to her clients, she was always committed on her deliverables. Most of her clients were happy with the quality of her services. Then some clients would demand numerous changes on what Sasha would deliver to them, but they were still unsatisfied. Those clients often shifted the goalpost slightly, making Sasha feel frustrated and angry. She was concerned about her Self-image getting tarnished and was trying to be perfect. On that basis, others were taking advantage of her weakness.

She understood how she was getting exploited by those few clients and decided she didn't have to please them but learned to draw a boundary. Sasha also learned that there was nothing such as perfect art. Graphic artwork was within her area of expertise. She understood that mistakes or imperfections could exist, and she could correct them, but she needn't be perfect. She didn't need to guard her image because she would own up and admit to her mistakes, making corrections where necessary. The image was no longer dependent on external validation. She created it and the image and her were one now, reflected in her work.

Have Your Own Dreams and Goals

If you are a Wanted Child, you have been handed over dreams and goals that belong to your parents. Now is the time for you to reflect on your own dreams and aspirations in life, which are not about meeting the expectations of your parents. It would be best if you learn to live by your chosen goals.

Prince Wan is trying to prove he is worthy to his Self because he unconsciously knows he is the property of the king, queen, and kingdom. Only when he demonstrates to others that he is worthy will they start to believe in him and begin to trust him. What would happen if he established his own kingdom, maybe small in the beginning? This is what you could do as well. That will be your own dream and goal, not realizing another's aspiration. Then there is nothing to prove to anybody. You are allowed to make mistakes and laugh at your own goof-ups.

It's high time that you value yourself. It was your parents' role to take care of you, but that does not mean you exist to fulfill their expectations. Thus far, your happiness has lied in the hands of your parents and in meeting their expectations. What you have chosen to become thus far is based on what they dreamt for you. It cannot be a duty if you feel you must oblige. For, if you think it's your duty to serve your parents, then there should be no regret, remorse, or troubling emotions of any kind. In no way am I implying that you should not take care of your parents or be there for them, but it's not necessary to live a life by their diktats.

They are your co-creators and caretakers, but that does not imply that you have to surrender your being to them and live a life as per their wishes or values. A potter creates his/her creation which can be a jug, a mug, or a pot. The creation can't be held responsible toward the creator. You, as a creation, have to live your life. Parents often make the child feel guilty on account of one thing or another, which has to be dealt with by reason and logic. It is the duty of the parents (and the child's Self) to help their creation excel and live life with freedom, which hardly happens.

You are a part of Mother Nature, and so are they. Instead of fighting with them, you can notice what they are trying to accomplish and reason with them. They are playing the role of co-creators, but in no way do they have authority over us. Most importantly, it is vital for you to communicate with them. You can discuss, debate, and reason with your parents and family without resisting or attacking them and still not consider it mandatory to obey them. You can explain to them what makes it impossible for you to follow their expectations in certain situations. You must communicate your difficulties and how it's impractical to fulfill all their requirements. Some of those could be needs we all have in order to live, but many of them could be unreasonable expectations dumped on you. You don't have to fight the battle of life for them and sacrifice your own life just like Prince Wan did. You can draw your boundaries and communicate precisely and clearly. Certain patterns need to be shut and closed, or else they continue. You must be bold and courageous to see things from the right perspective to communicate clearly and create boundaries. This could not have happened when you were younger, but it is not too late now.

Dileep, an elderly client, once visited me because he was experiencing constant fear. He told me how his other family members have been transferring their responsibilities to him just because he is the eldest in the family. Till he came to see me, Dileep had been trying to fulfill the expectations of others. He was feeling overburdened and was guarding his image against getting tarnished. In the session, he realized that everybody in his family was now old enough to take up the challenges of life by themselves and that he was carrying an unnecessary burden. So, Dileep decided to live his life as a simple human being and do what was essential for him to do, but no more. He was able to separate what was essential and what was non-essential. All this while, Dileep was scared to be found on the wrong side, as he was a prince with a crown on his head. In the session, he realized how he had been functioning in his life, and he chose to drop the crown. The weight was off his shoulders. Dileep started taking decisions differently, being upfront, and communicating candidly. In time, his fear neutralized.

View Mistakes as Opportunities to Learn and Excel

As a Wanted Child, you believe in high performance as a way of meeting or even exceeding expectations from you. If you succeed, you get a psychological boost, but if you don't, you can feel low or depressed. That can also make you wary of trying something you might not succeed at. It's important to realize that your performance does not define you.

Making mistakes does not mean your survival is in danger. Mistakes are opportunities to learn. Repeating the same mistake over and over again is definitely not acceptable. But all this while as a Wanted Child, you have been over-cautious, and you may have missed many opportunities. In that process, challenges to explore life were lost.

You were so cautious that you were experiencing an emotional gun pointing at you that drove you to make sure you made no errors. You checked your personal work and every important action several times. It is necessary to have trust in your skills and take voluntary ownership of your work rather than live with a forced sense of ownership. Mistakes, rather than being feared, actually enrich your life. The more you learn to trust your being, the better the results. Firstly, it is okay to admit to your mistakes by asking some constructive questions. What did you learn from the mistake? How can the mistake be rectified and corrected? How can you do better and be more effective next time? What new ways can you learn? This is a healthy state of inner dialogue.

As you are afraid of making mistakes, you have put in a lot more effort, ensuring you produce error-free work. This consumes a lot of your energy and much more time than necessary, making you feel fatigued and spent. This way of being, generates unnecessary stress and pressure within your system and, if taken too far, can lead to physical pain and illnesses. If you're already under stress, you need to communicate and address issues when they arise and where they exist. Start placing limits. Don't let patterns continue to grow and spiral out of control. Others will start to apply more pressure on you otherwise. It could come from a spouse or maybe your boss. If you don't address issues, then it can worsen your stress levels.

There will be moments when others will point the finger at you and blame you for your inadequacies. Sometimes it might not be your mistake. Others may and probably will try to bulldoze you in life and at work. So address it, at that moment, without animosity. Provide evidence and data where necessary in order to stand your ground. If not, be wiser next time.

Everything is perfect when accepted. Nothing is perfect when unaccepted.

I wonder, is there such a thing as a perfect circle, line, or picture, or is it our illusion? Who decides what is perfect? Let's take an example from mathematics. The formula to draw a circle is πr^2 (pi X r^2), where 'r' is the radius of a circle, and 'pi' is a number containing a value. Everyone knows that there is no perfect circle because the value of pi is an irrational number. What does this mean? The decimal representation of pi is 3.14159, but the number does not end there, even after five decimal places. It goes on without termination. So when people have to use pi, they usually round it off to 3.14. If more precision is needed, then it may be rounded off to three decimal places (3.142). So, even when drawing a circle, there cannot be a standard of absolute precision. There also can never be a perfect line. The line depends on the person who draws it, the tools used to draw the line, and the surface on which it is drawn. However accurate one may be, there will never be a perfect line. You can place a supposedly perfect line under the microscope, and you will notice numerous minute imperfections. One can imagine that if the subject of mathematics, which commands precision unlike possibly any other field of study, experiences limitations, then why do human beings or human outputs need to be perfect?

As a Wanted Child, you need to learn that you are perfect, just the way you are. You are what you are; learn to accept your being. You have been trying hard to please others (who are in the Self) all this while, but that can be put down to ignorance. Now you know your Survival Mechanism. It's about time you be authentic to who you are. That also includes embracing your weaknesses. When you accept your weaknesses, you create opportunities for growth and learning. Only when you acknowledge your flaws, the Universe provides you with what you need because that's when you are honest. The Universe listens to you and understands that you are being genuine. When you communicate the nature of your needs, it supports you. Be honest to yourself in every way, for that is your being. The more you are true to your being, the more you are aligned within. The more things get aligned internally; the more synergy is created with what is outside of you.

Let's explain this idea with something many people will relate to. Your boss has given you an assignment on which you currently have a relatively low level of experience. You scratch your head and toil away at it but do not communicate your difficulties to your boss. Doing your very best, you eventually end up producing sub-standard work. Time is lost, and your boss is displeased. Some learning has taken place, but much more frustration has been experienced. On the other hand, if you are honest with yourself and admit your ignorance to your boss instead of trying to save face, there could be a good chance you would receive some guidance or coaching from him/her. Your understanding and learning could be enhanced as a result. There would be progress. The next time you attempt the same task, you will do it more effectively.

Be Non-Judgmental

Now that you are aware that everybody carries their own Survival Mechanism, you will understand that people are trying to do their best to survive using their tools. That means others are wearing their armor and operating from within them for protection, assuming that's the way life 'IS.' Now that you know of your Survival Mechanism, you can change your pathway and advance in another direction by being non-judgmental of others. You are aware of their weaknesses. Thus, it wouldn't be right to condemn them. Nor should you be a victim of their flaws. Be neutral and non-judgmental. Even when this relates to a person close to you, for example, a spouse, you don't need to accept unfair behavior but can stand firm. You certainly do not need to fight back, but you can address an issue objectively using better communication. You're not giving in to a pattern but expressing yourself. A spouse who is an Unwanted Child may try other subtle ways of manipulation, but you don't need to give in to his/ her tactics, as you can identify them now. Whatever needs to be done for your spouse, by all means, go ahead and do it, but it doesn't have to be under the threat of an emotional gun.

Above all, what's essential for you as a Wanted Child is to learn to be non-judgmental towards your being. Most of the time, you are the one who is punishing your being more than any other person can ever do. The internal dialogue between the Self and you goes with accusatory tonality, telling you about your wrongdoings. If a critical voice condemns you, then SLOW DOWN and identify the voice coming from the Self. Close your eyes and regress to the earliest time, someone close to you belittled you. Observe as if you are watching the event as a movie and learn what your mistake was. As a child, were you supposed to be born knowing about everything? It was the creator's duty to take care of you and be that guide. You may have made a mistake as a child, and it was the parent's job to show you the right path. But they had their own weakness and didn't know better. So it's time you update the event and understand your inner voice. If you can recall the memory, think about how you would have tackled the situation differently today. If you can know the truth about the earliest event, recalling that memory can help to subside your irritable internal dialogue.

You must be willing to acknowledge your mistakes, knowing that making mistakes is only human. You may continue to choose the path of pursuing perfection, which is an ideal mold according to others. Or you can choose to be kinder to your being and adopt the attitude that you are not here to perfect any art form but to learn and improve on a day-to-day basis. It is true that you are most critical of your own performance, with negative self-talk within you going on endlessly. It's necessary to acknowledge and admit that you, and everyone else, are not perfect and accept your being totally and unconditionally. Only in your acceptance can the true Self grow. When you accept your being, others will accept you. You are not here to please anyone but to live your life in your own way, fruitfully. When you live your life on your terms, others will value you, as that form of self-worth is not dependent on others but is generated by you.

You are Worthy – Your Worth is Not in Others' Hands

Suppose you are looking for a certificate of approval or some ultimate form of accolade from your parents or others (the Self) that you are valuable because you meet their expectations. That is never going to have a lasting effect. Because each time you fail, you will feel miserable. You will strive hard again to win their approval, hoping that will give you happiness. You've got to understand the nature of this False Illusionary Assurance from the Survival Mechanism. The loop of meeting expectations and maintaining happiness is endless; you can only decide to break the chain by being practical and pragmatic.

Don't allow others (who are in the Self) to determine your value, nor should you look for admiration and appreciation from them. The more you seek credit, the more you will feel deprived and disappointed. Remember, when others put you on a pedestal, the controls are in their hand, and they can dislodge you anytime they want. You will be a puppet in their hands. Focus on your work. If you deserve recognition for your hard work, document what you have done and do not rely on verbal approvals from others. You need to believe in your work. By being a perfectionist, a Wanted Child seeks admiration and appreciation for the work they have been doing. If you have documented your work, it becomes proof of performance, and you don't have to seek approval from another person. Be wise.

My reading of history has shown me many princes who have sacrificed their lives for the king and the kingdom. It seemed like Prince Wan was the property of the king, queen, and kingdom. You may be a Wanted Child, but you are certainly not a possession or commodity. Your parents have not purchased you or own your being. You are part of the creator and the creation, and so are they. Your parents are co-creators, and it's their role to provide support and security as you grow up to live your life independently. But they do not have ultimate ownership or control over you.

Your parents may have lived in the illusion caused by their Survival Mechanism, but you don't have to get sucked into their trap by feeling guilty or experiencing other negative emotions. It is crucial to address the issue with your parents and others that you are not someone who is here to fulfill expectations but just a human who wants to live his/her life. Do whatever is possible within your natural limits by communicating and admitting them to those who matter. There is no shame in that.

Be a Mango Tree - Not a Bonsai

It is important to be grounded and to have trust in the whole process of change. Be like a mango tree connected with Mother Earth. You are part of it, and you will always be part of it, whether you appreciate it or not. Mother Earth has accepted you totally and completely the way you are, whether you believe in your being or not. Since birth, you have struggled to survive using the Survival Mechanism provided to you. The time to discontinue the Survival Mechanism has passed long ago, but it's never too late to make changes. You can take charge of yourself. As you are a grown-up, only you are responsible for your well-being.

Stop living like a Bonsai, pleasing the artist. The Universe did not create you to be a Bonsai. The Bonsai creator wanted to have his/ her own satisfaction in shaping you the way they liked. You have the same potential as a natural, full-grown mango tree that bears fruit. Trust your being, believe in your being, and have faith in your potential.

The example of Nick given earlier in this chapter shows how he gradually built up his own business over three years. It established his confidence and capabilities, which made him believe that he was competent and worthy. Grounding yourself happens over a period of time. It's important to give oneself enough time to learn and to put what's learned into practice.

You are a Human Being — Be One

Every prince and princess is a slave to a system, with few exceptions like Krishna and Buddha, who were born as princes. I have already explained how Wanted Children become royal slaves and sacrifice their lives for their metaphorical kingdom. You can imagine how distorted their perception of reality can be. Not every Wanted Child may function with an elitist attitude, but there are some distances s/he experiences with the ground realities of the average person.

As such, Wanted Children have not experienced the realities of life. They are living in an unrealistic environment with standards set by their parents and those close to them. As a Wanted Child living in this distorted reality, it's time that you ground yourself and be human. As a human, you are allowed to make mistakes, admit your mistakes, and improve. Your own human experiences will be the best teacher, rather than the rigmarole of trying to perfect the art of being someone who your parents want you to be.

We all make mistakes, get criticized and are looked down on. That's part of living. You can't expect your Self to appreciate you at all times. If you have that habit, it's time you dislodge your Self-image and create it the way you want. You decide what it will be.

Be grounded like a mango tree and not a Bonsai. The stronger your grounding with Mother Nature, the creator, or any other higher force you believe in, the easier it will be to absorb any shocks along the way. You won't be afraid of what will happen, but you will be prepared to face any unwanted situations you experience head-on.

Build Your Own Kingdom - Allow it and Let it Grow

Like Nick, you may establish your own small kingdom — a business, practice, or a distinct way of living. It may be small, but the joy of having your own is very different from running somebody else's. Build your own fortress. This could mean that you are no longer willing to meet the ideals of success as defined by others. You can define what success means for *you* in different areas of life and go about fulfilling it.

When you start on your own, trust your abilities and capabilities. Rely on your inner convictions. Remember, there is nobody to judge, criticize, and look down on you. This process is growth-oriented. Maybe initially, it will be slow, just like a mango sapling's growth when planted into the soil. Progressively, some new shoots and leaves will start to grow, and roots will go deeper into Mother Earth. The Earth supports the tree as well as supplies water and other food ingredients. You have earlier read about the Bonsai mango tree, which is fully dependent on others for its nurturing and other needs. Over time, your trust starts to grow and expand. Your belief in your potential gets stronger. A unique process begins to unfold. Your faith in your being and nature strengthens, and things get aligned. You are on your own, not proving to anyone that you are worthy. On the contrary, you have established your own kingdom. However vast or small it is, it doesn't matter.

Since your integrity is impeccable, people trust you and believe in you, because you keep your word. You have to now learn to trust and believe in your potential. If you continue to adhere to your family's wishes and their set of fundamentals, you will continue to stay a victim of their mindset and ways of living. Devise your ways to get them on board. Initially, it's not going to be easy. But when you start to believe in your potential, others will believe in you. When you have faith in yourself, others have faith in you. Trust your being.

You have been guarding your image and the image of your family. An important thought you must remember is that the idea of you as a future ruler conquering frontiers is a myth like that of Prince Wan. Your parents have unknowingly dumped their expectations upon you, holding you responsible for things you never asked for. The question to ask is, even after knowing that a crown had been placed on you by others, unknowingly, do you still want to continue to wear it? Did you ask for it? The choice is yours, and you must decide.

When you were a child, you were unaware of these expectations (the crown) placed on you, and you had to survive and follow through with what was asked of you. Do you still want to live a life where you are fulfilling the expectations of others?

Secondly, would you still want to continue being a slave to the Survival Mechanism? Would you like to support the errors (if well-intentioned) made by your elders and pay the price for it? The rules of living have already been set for you by someone else, and very often, you know they are not right.

You avoid mistakes at all costs, but would it be alright if you sacrifice your life for others' mistakes or perceptions? Does it mean you keep guarding the Self-image created by others? Or would it be important to create a new image that is true for you? Just because you are a Wanted Child, which you did not ask for as a newborn, how long should you continue to wear the crown? Do you need to keep winning battles that you did not cause in the first place? Whose war are you fighting? Is it yours or somebody else's? A child can't be held responsible for the co-creators mistakes. S/he can't be held responsible for blunders of the Self.

Avoid Competition and Set Your Own Standards

Do not try to compete with others in all aspects of living. It's vital that you shift from the metrics placed on you by the external world — by the Self — to your own set of internal standards and benchmarks. Ones that you believe you can and want to attain. The more you attain your benchmarks, your satisfaction level increases and you ultimately gain confidence. This makes you more willing to put in consistent effort. Eventually, it creates a virtuous cycle of personal benchmarks, the satisfaction of accomplishment, and renewed effort. You can build your foundation and grow in this way. Do not measure your performance with that of another. You won't be happy if you're trying to compare your performance on any metric with someone else.

There is no point in living through somebody else's doctrine, even if it may appear well-meaning. In your empire, your own life, however grand or small it may be, you are accountable to yourself and take voluntary ownership of your choices and actions. It is easier to experience life this way, as well as your own sense of status and stature that you build. Maintaining and looking after them is easier when no emotional gun points at you. You are responsible and answerable for who you are and what you do. You set the rules and regulations that you will abide by. You live by your terms and conditions, which society does not enforce. That means not chasing what everyone else has may that be the best international holiday experience or gadget. And certainly not trying to be what everyone else is trying to be. I remember a young man who had studied computer science once told me he wanted to become the next Bill Gates. You do not need to be anyone else; just be what you dream.

This is not to say that it will be an easy process. The world around you will continue to impose its doctrines, thinking, and beliefs. But these standards and benchmarks were set by somebody else. These are not your benchmarks but are enforced on you by somebody else, maybe your parents, society, or religion. The moment you are participating in achieving someone else's benchmark, you get dragged into a competition. Set your own standards and avoid competition. When you create your parameters, they are easier to attain because they are your own. You can always adjust it as the system is within your territory. The decision-making power is also in your hands. I understand that this cannot always be the case in a job where you are following parameters set by your boss or organization. But you have to be honest to yourself if you're working under a lot of stress, which takes a toll on your physical and mental health. You can ask yourself, am I content with the way things are going here? Do I value my being? If you're not content, then there is no point. Either create your own kingdom or find another job where you belong more naturally, where there is synergy and growth for you.

We all need to follow certain rules and regulations, such as traffic rules, that may be laid down by the country we live in. In India, driving on the left side of the road is mandatory, and in the USA, it's the right side of the road. Specific rules and laws are essential because they create order in society and make our lives easier. As mentioned earlier, this same set of traffic rules can't be applied if you are driving in the desert or in uncharted territory. It has no relevance there. The relevance of regulations and laws is in the context in which you operate. I don't think the tribes in the Andaman Islands off the coast of India know about the Indian constitution or Indian laws, even though the islands are part of India. Yet, they live in their own way. There are certain laws that apply to you, the rest you can create for your well-being.

Be Loyal, Committed, and Have Impeccable Integrity for Your Being

Now that you know your Self-image came from others, it's time to take your decision to live your life with dignity. It's not necessary to gain the approval of others by fulfilling all their expectations. You don't need a stamp embossed on you by others. Instead, you've got to trust your own internal mechanism that shows you are worthy. You don't need labels given by others, with pats on your back.

I once had a session with Adi, a successful lawyer. He had been practicing in his father's law firm since the beginning of his career as a lawyer. Adi's client fees contributed to 80 percent of the firm's business. But he expended a great amount of time and energy to earn those revenues and run the firm. In the session, he realized that his commitment, loyalty, and proving trustworthy were all for his father, mother, and others in the kingdom. There wasn't any commitment and loyalty towards his being, but he was just slogging for others when he could sustain his life with one-fourth of what he earned.

Just like Prince Wan, is your commitment toward others? He has been functioning and making decisions as if he is their property, living and dying for them. He is very loyal and trustworthy with his family and clan. Are you like an item or commodity that others can transact?

You serve others, thinking it's your duty. You are confusing duty with obligation. It's time to draw your own boundaries, valuing your potential by being committed and loyal to your being. Prince Wan fights others' wars just to prove he is trustworthy. To what extent do you want to prove to others your trustworthiness? It is time you start believing that you *are* trustworthy and don't need a certificate of approval for that. Trust your being and have faith that you are worthy.

You have been loyal to others and especially your parents. It's now time to be loyal to yourself and have full faith in your being. You saved others through your impeccable integrity, and others have immensely benefited from it. Take on the same attitude and chart your own destiny for yourself. For a long time, you have been a slave to the system. Be a human being, feeling worthy of your achievements and learning, no matter how small they may seem. Build on simple fundamentals where you believe you are confident and can trust your potential fully. You have overdone obliging and pleasing others with your loyalty, commitment, and integrity. You are part of this Universe, and nature has accepted you just the way you are. It's time you discontinue the rat race and be responsible only for your actions. You can still take ownership of others around you if they feature in your revised set of priorities.

When it's your ship, you know how to value the crew that works under you. In my observation, many Wanted Children are good managers and get respect from their team members. They protect and defend them from the adverse actions of superiors in an organization. When you are your own boss, you don't need to give orders and you don't take orders, but you can communicate and address issues in your own skillful way. Since you have your own benchmarks to fulfill, you don't need to meet others' expectations. You can achieve your goals within your means and adjust timeframes accordingly. Decision-making powers are within your domain. No emotional charge is generated, as you can be flexible when needed. Live within your means, both financially and in terms of capacity.

Nina, a filmmaker, had worked on projects under her supervisors. Others had benefitted immensely from her creativity. But senior executives in the production house Nina worked for gave her very little acknowledgment and recognition for her efforts or talent. On the other hand, she was loyal and dedicated to her work. Nina's boss got accolades and laurels, while her commitment and dedication weren't recognized. In fact, the team had placed their aspirations on Nina's shoulders, with little credit being given to her. All this while, she tried hard to prove her worth and gain appreciation by pleasing those in charge above her. Nina truly hoped they would value her work. Others gave her the False Illusionary Assurance (the belief) that the kingdom (the project) was hers, and they continued benefitting from the illusion she was living in.

Nina eventually understood what her weaknesses were. In future negotiations, she made decisions knowing she was loyal, committed, and talented. She did not need a certificate of her worth from this group of people. Thus, she didn't need to prove her potential to them anymore. Nina stood her ground with a firm belief that she was worthy. She was clear about what she was doing and didn't fall into a trap set by others. The moment Nina knew her worth, her decision-making process shifted from pleasing others to valuing herself. Her attitude changed from being a princess winning laurels for others to being human. She re-defined her self-worth.

All this while you thought you had to live up to the expectations of others. You tried to be meticulous in the execution of your duties and followed the norms set out for you. You fought to maintain a standard, thinking it was your duty to keep it up and obey those who expected it. You also began to implement these norms and expectations on others. You thought you were born to do this. You guarded your reputation (Self-image) by giving impeccable service to those who mattered. But be aware of this behavior! Drop the standards of royalty and be a human.

Be Bold and Begin to Take Risks

As you take strides into your new life, it's important for you to attempt doing things you have held yourself back from doing. You have kept your being away from doing many things, visualizing that you are not confident. You fear your mistakes being pointed out, which can make you feel embarrassed and humiliated. Now is the time for you to instead visualize that each time you make a mistake, you have an opportunity to learn and to get better. Take things slowly and be steady in your way forward.

Contrary to what you have picked up, life is not about winning races. It is about experiencing, learning, and evolving. Making mistakes is part of the process known as living.

There are as many things you possibly excel at. Make a list of them under different categories based on how confident you feel about them. Nothing is too small to be noted and acknowledged. It could be a skill, activity, sport, or game. It could be an area of academic interest (mathematics, science, computer technology, etc.). It could be languages, spoken or written. It could be problem-solving or being an empathetic listener. It could also be your social or networking skills. Your strength could be anything where you feel confident - anything you believe you know or are good at - and there is not an inch of doubt about the same. You need not be an expert and perfect at it, but it's an area where you have strong belief and faith in yourself.

Take shyness as an opportunity for you to be more prepared so that you are well-equipped to deal with situations when they arise. Shyness is a signal from within for you to do a little extra homework on the skill, activity, or subject you are unsure about. It also could indicate the fear of being challenged by someone more skillful or experienced than you. You may feel unprepared to deal with such a scenario popping up unexpectedly. Do a simple visualization where you are being honest and admitting to your areas of improvement, acknowledging that you are not perfect. You need not know everything about everything; instead, you can choose to be unique and different. Everyone is unique and has potential, but we don't believe in ourselves and try to become someone else that we are not. For example, the young man I described earlier wanted to be the next Bill Gates. Be what you are designed to be.

If Wanted Children adopt the above behaviors and attitudes, there is a good possibility they will begin to experience ease and freedom in their daily life. In that respect, it is worth revisiting the above suggestions from time to time.

46

BREAKING FREE

As a Wanted Child, you are your parents' dream. Later, you become somebody else's dream, such as that of your spouse or boss. It's time you started to live your own dream.

We will cover a few techniques in this chapter that will help Wanted Children get free from their survival trap. I'm not promising there will be big changes in a few days, weeks, or even months. As we are born with certain birth conditioning, it requires regular effort and awareness to deal with it over a prolonged period. Depending on your consistency, you can be assured of lasting results. These issues do get resolved when one goes through an in-person therapy session. Clients get to understand their issues and also get over it.

How your life will go on will depend on your personal goals and decisions. Would you like to live like a royal slave who is subjected to a predetermined fate, or would you like to create your own dreams? If you want to change, you will need to adopt new behaviors and make conscious choices on how you will live from now on.

You are a Visual Person

Whenever someone tells you or hints you are not up to the mark, it gives you a feeling of unworthiness. "I'm not capable," "I'm a failure," or "I'm a loser" are the sort of thoughts that can run through your mind. The person has touched your sensitive nerve. You are no longer in the present but have gone into your Birth Survival Trance.

This happens because you are perceiving your image through the eyes of others and trying to match their expectations. While you need to neutralize these birth-conditioning patterns, it is also a testament to how good your visual capabilities are. Within a few seconds, you can compare the Self-image (expectations) with your body's performance in your mind.

You are a visual person with inborn strengths. You need to use these visualization skills to get things you want while maintaining harmony and balance in your relationships. People use this skill to exploit you to achieve their goals while you work hard to prove you are worthy. Imagine how life would be if you didn't need to prove anything to anyone, doing the work you enjoy doing.

It's time to apply your gifts for your well-being. As mentioned in the previous chapter, establish your small kingdom. You don't have to toil as a royal slave in someone else's kingdom but can work pragmatically on outcomes that are within your control. For you have the potential to imagine and be responsible for your growth.

How to Know Your Survival Mechanism is Active

You first need to be good at identifying when you are going into your Birth Survival Trance. Here are some indicators that you are operating unconsciously from your Survival Mechanism:

- ❖ Every time you feel the urge, pressure, or compulsion to perform and prove worthy. Check with whom you are feeling those compulsions.
- ❖ If you think, "What will others think of me if I fail to live up to their expectations?" Monitor your internal dialogue. Most of the time, it is between you and the Self. Check who is the person playing a role through the Self. If possible, do the exercise given below to regress to an earlier time.
- ❖ One of your parents is more dominating when it comes to you and demands you meet their expectations. Which one is it? Or is s/he someone who is usually dissatisfied with your performance? Unconsciously, your Survival Mechanism gets triggered and your behavior changes around that person.
- ❖ Your partner or spouse could be the one substituting your parent in your core Self. When you please them, observe what survival traits you use.

❖ When you experience negative emotions, it is a sure sign that your Survival Mechanism is active. Its intensity could be mild, like slight irritation or, very high, a feeling of rage, fear, guilt, depression, anxiety, etc.

After reflecting sufficiently on the above, you can go ahead and try the below techniques in no particular order, to update your survival traits.

Build Your Own Self-Image

You can begin to create your own Self-image based on your personal dreams and goals. Every person has the potential to be creative.

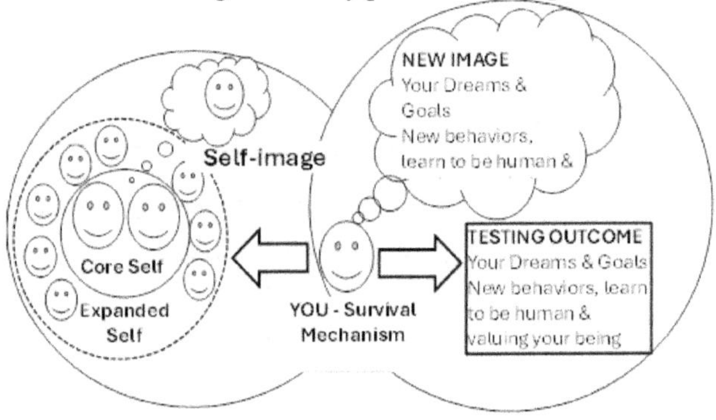

Diagram 41

The circle on the left in the above diagram shows the same old pattern. Viewing your Self-image through the eyes of your Self, which represents your parents and others, you try to achieve everything they want or would like you to be. This way, your survival is assured. As you grow older, however, your frustration with this way of living keeps growing. Your destiny is in the hands of others. Now is the time for you to draw your boundaries.

Instead of continuing this way, you could choose your own goals and dreams, as depicted in the right circle. As simple as this may sound, so far you haven't had your own goals, but have fulfilled what was expected of you, and you gave less importance to your own dreams and goals. Your goals could be what you have truly wanted to do. They could be new behaviors and beliefs about life or other unfulfilled dreams. When you focus on your outcomes, there is no one to please and you do what's required for your progress and satisfaction. Here, you are in charge of your decisions and your destiny. There isn't a need to be anybody else's ideal son, daughter, husband, or wife.

On the left of the circle, you are operating from another person's imagination. It's an illusion you are trying to live up to, thinking it's yours. The circle on the right is the dream you create, where control is in your hands. You can adapt it to your potential and capabilities. But you must be willing to be flexible to learn new behaviors so that they produce desired results. There is no one to condemn you or to pinpoint your mistakes. Most importantly, you are at liberty to make decisions based on your experiences. As there is no need to prove you are worthy to anyone, you can live your life with freedom.

One note of caution, however. When you construct your new image, if you wish to succeed in a venture or pursuit, make sure you don't slip into the old pattern of self-image. For example, if you enjoy learning the violin, you may make it a goal to become a professional or play for an orchestra. You can break down the goal into the practice time required for you to get there. Small achievements keep adding to your new Self-image. If playing at a higher level gives you more joy, pleasure, or satisfaction, it contributes to your new image. But if it's about impressing others, getting applause, or winning accolades, then it's the old pattern of pleasing the Self. Beware of this pitfall. You may communicate your new achievements, but it's not about looking good in the eyes of others.

Meditation

Do a one-minute meditation focusing on your breath. You may certainly increase the time gradually by a few more minutes whenever you feel confident. Practice it often during the day. You can take a break for some time and repeat the exercise. It's not necessarily about doing a one-minute meditation but about staying focused on your breathing as long as you can keep your attention on your breathing. This practice is essential for grounding, which has multiple benefits.

It will also help you SLOW DOWN. It is imperative that you learn how to do this, mentally and physically. Often people do not even have a minute to spare for themselves. That's because they have forgotten to value their being, living life mechanically. Things will be revealed to you naturally, only if you slow down. You will be able to reflect on your conduct and the behavior of those around you. So, relax and focus on your breath.

Explore Your Survival Trance

As a Wanted Child, it would be vital to know what made your parents create you. You are the outcome of your parent's wishes. Consider one or all of the below questions:

- ❖ What made them have you?
- ❖ What did they want from you after you were born?
- ❖ What were the outcomes you are meant to serve?

Try to understand your repetitive patterns, which are your survival traits. When you are aware of your inborn survival traits, you will know how you go about pleasing the Self. If you continue to use the same traits, it implies you are getting sucked into your Survival Trance. In addition to considering the above questions, you may also write down specific traits you often display when relating to people you are close to. You can go through the list of your Survival Traits mentioned in my previous book.

Below is a relaxation exercise you can follow to understand your parents' purpose, which you were born to fulfill. I would recommend you do the below exercise gradually. In the beginning, you will need to do it slowly and progressively because you are doing it independently, without the help of a therapist. If someone else is leading you, it's easier to regress. So you may seek the help of a professional. But if you wish to practice it on your own, break it into smaller chunks of time. Choose to practice ten to fifteen minutes on any day before returning to it again on another day. There is a lot to process, so you will experience better results this way.

Sit in a comfortable chair and close your eyes. Do a one-minute meditation. Browse through your survival traits. Recall a few incidents which brought them out. Identify the people in your personal or professional life with whom you display these behaviors. It's important to observe the patterns in your life that are repetitive. The people in the Expanded Self could keep changing, but your traits and behavior will remain broadly the same.

Pick one or more of the people and situations from above and gradually regress (go back to an earlier age) into your past. Visit the past week or month. Then go back a few more months or a year. Notice the consistent aspects of your traits. What urges or inner compulsions have you detected that make you comply with others? Certain emotions may surface as you go back in time. Now, ask the below questions:

- ❖ How are you trying to prove you are worthy?
- ❖ What is it you are specifically doing to live up to the expectations of others?
- ❖ How do you comply with the above people?

It could be that you identify your Self with your spouse or one of your in-laws. But as you regress, you might discover that you may be pleasing one of your parents. The first time you do the exercise, do it as if you are experiencing it all happening in front of you. Observe emotions that surface as you go back into your earlier days. Re-run the events like you are watching a movie and you are seeing a younger you on a screen. This is also known as disassociation. The more detached you are from events, the more learning will occur. It's important to stay neutral during the process.

If you happen to be in your thirties or forties, regress until you are twenty years old. Notice the knowledge and education you have gained since then. You may see that while you have acquired degrees and qualifications, gained experiences and matured, your stress levels have increased, and survival patterns have stayed consistent. It looks like you have been making decisions, but in reality, you have been pushed by others in the form of your Self. Your fate hasn't been in your own hands.

Slowly regress year by year to the age of ten. Notice the parent who is more dominating and emphasizes your performance in school or other activities. Recollect any or all the conversations they have been having regarding you.

- ❖ What have you heard your parents talk about you or your birth?
- ❖ Which parent wanted you more than the other?
- ❖ What are some of their incomplete dreams that they would like you to fulfill?
- ❖ Are they trying to experience happiness or success through your achievements?

Try to make connections between you from the age of ten to now. Even if you have grown taller, stronger, and more aware, your primary beliefs and survival traits may not have changed much. It is the same old you when you were a boy/girl, even if your size, form, appearance, and knowledge levels have changed.

Do an exhaustive exploration of your conduct and patterns regarding the Self. It might take a few days, but you are also giving a message to your internal mechanism that you are willing to learn your core purpose of being on this planet. You will get insights in the form of a few "aha" moments that pop up in your consciousness. The more you explore, the more your awareness will keep expanding. This creates a possibility of freeing your being from your Survival Trance.

Identify Your Parents' Emotions You Carry

The puzzle of your life lies in knowing the emotions your parents were experiencing before you were born. You may attempt to regress to the earliest memories of your life. Recollect any conversations you might have heard between your parents regarding challenges they were facing before you were born. Recall as many details about their dream of having you. Then consider the below questions:

❖ How were your parents feeling incomplete?
❖ Were they going through any difficulties before you were born?
❖ What did they accomplish or feel when you were born?
❖ By having you, what did they hope would get completed within them? Especially for which parent?
❖ What were the expectations they unknowingly planted in you?

The deeper your understanding grows regarding your Birth Survival Trance, the more awareness gets aroused within you. The quest to know the truth is strongly affirmed and more unconscious data gets revealed. Once you understand the purpose of your birth, you may ask:

❖ Do you believe you are a class above others?
❖ Is it alright to be like an ordinary human?
❖ What do you truly want to do or be?

Remember, when you were born, you did not ask for a crown to be placed on your head. It is they who have done it. You are not a prince or princess who is to meet royal standards, but a human being who wants to live your life. Knowing what you know now, you can consciously decide that you do not want to be the heir to another's kingdom. But if you still wish to continue holding on to the crown, you now know it comes with a price.

An Exercise To Do Before Sleeping

At the end of the day, before going to sleep, go through the day's events. Notice where you faltered and fell back onto your survival traits to please someone. You could ask the below questions:

❖ Who was the person that brought out your survival traits and how often do you interact with him/her?
❖ What does s/he want out of you?

❖ How did the person trap you, and how did you get sucked in thereafter?

❖ Is s/he trying to influence your decisions, and if yes, how?

❖ Ask a question to your being: how could you have tackled the situation differently? If you find that you cannot solve the issue, admit it, and ask for help. Be honest to your being.

❖ What are some of the things you did differently this time or better than on previous occasions?

Certain issues could be repetitive and the person you are interacting with may be the same one you are close to. If it's the same person you are trying to please, then ask:

❖ Under what Survival Mechanism category does s/he belong?

❖ Could you try to learn more about the person's traits? It can give you a better understanding of how to tackle situations with them.

Visualization

You can visualize what you could do differently in certain situations in the future, but by staying amicable, balanced, and harmonious. Re-run the new behavior pattern in your mind, the way you want to behave, at least seven to ten times. You are rehearsing it on your mental screen so that it automatically happens next time.

Towards the end, acknowledge everything around you, including the people involved, for they are helping you update your survival mechanism. You also learn how they are the trigger points for the way you react in situations using your survival traits.

You are like a potter. Whatever you imagine in your mind, you are capable of giving shape to, in reality. Nature has bestowed upon you the gift of visualization, so make good use of it for your well-being and those of others. At all times during the process, be in harmony with your being, circumstances, and others in your life.

THE PARTLY WANTED CHILD

47

LIVING WITH FREEDOM

If you are a Partly Wanted Child, you rely greatly on others for direction, as your Self-image is missing. It is difficult for you to be totally independent, and you need assurance from others that you are safe. In the bargain, you are willing to do the heavy lifting for them, quite literally, through your physical efforts. You want others to notice you — their goals and dreams become your own. You want to make the whole world happy, but the question is, "Are you happy?"

Somewhere within, you feel incomplete. You want the parent who has rejected you to own you fully. In the process, that person ends up taking ownership of your life. You surrender your being to that parent and later to your spouse and others around you. Doing it makes you feel accepted, but you are unaware it is a False Illusionary Assurance you live in. You are a human being, not someone else's property. No one has ownership rights over you, not even your parents. It was their responsibility to care for you when you were young.

As the reins of your life are in others' hands, they make decisions for you. Even though you are competent, you allow people to walk all over you and take credit from you. At the workplace, others get promoted before you, as your lack of decision-making is interpreted as incompetence. However, you continue to remain a workhorse carrying the load of others. Without making your own decisions independently, nothing is going to change in your life.

Unfortunately, those who control your life and decisions also determine your fate. Your prime focus should be on taking back the reins in your own hands. This chapter focuses on liberating your body and mind from your Birth Survival Trance. It's time for you to introspect and challenge your old habits. Along the way, there will be fears of how others will perceive you if you become more independent and assertive. True, others may have become accustomed to your easy-going and compliant nature. But you have to trust your being and be ready to face the consequences.

If you are a Partly Wanted Child, you now know what your deep-rooted primary goal of life is. While it has compelled you to behave and communicate in the way that you did, it's time to take control of your own life. LIVE YOUR LIFE. I am not implying that you have to perfect the art of living, but surely you can constructively re-engineer your life, with your own choices.

You have been trying your best to adjust to the demands of your Self using your survival traits. Our survival mechanism is an essential part of us till a certain age in life, but beyond that, it's outdated. Now that you are an adult, you must consciously get off autopilot; that is your Survival Mechanism and its mechanism. You did what you did unknowingly and now it's time to change. There is a need for you to be honest and genuine to others around you, thus, being true to your being. Let's go ahead and explore how you can attain some degree of mastery over your own being.

Stop Pleasing Others!

If you have read about and reflected on your specific survival traits, you already know your major drawback. What makes you do what you have been doing? It's time to accept who you are, just the way you are. You are whole and don't need validation to prove your usefulness to others by pleasing them. You have often tried hard to please others, but you have not been acknowledged, appreciated, or admired by them. In particular, you have been looking for a badge of acceptance and approval from some people you are especially close to in life. You have been overdoing this behavior; it's now time to stop doing it. You need to accept your worthiness. It's there with you, but you have to recognize and nurture it. Take some time off every day to acknowledge yourself as a valuable person.

You are very much part of Mother Nature and belong with her. Whether you recognize it or not, you will always be a part of her. You got unwittingly trapped in the process of your birth, which made you think of yourself as a substitute who is dispensable, not having the importance of a key member of your family. Your Survival Mechanism deceived you because you had to survive. It's time for you to wake up and validate your own Being. A simple test of your worthiness lies in your EMOTIONS. If your actions do not correlate with your EMOTIONS, then you are operating from a neutral position. If your actions and activities stem from your EMOTIONS, then you are in the survival trap.

Avoid Being Goody-Goody

By being goody-goody, you only comply with what others would want you to do. If it's your parent with whom you have tried to be a good boy/girl, by this time they are so habituated, what to expect from you. The same is true of your spouse. They know that you are going to fulfill their demands because that is what you have done in the past. You have been a crutch to these people, making them dependent on you. Instead of allowing them to rely on their own abilities and potential, you have made them defunct. It's like you are doing a child's homework instead of s/he doing it on their own. We have to help others, but you are overdoing it to get a dose of the feel-good factor from them. That is your False Illusionary Assurance. You conclude that is real love and affection. There is no love and affection here; you have your selfish motive, and so do they. If you want to gain your freedom, start exercising, and doing what is practical and pragmatic.

All your life, you have tried to be a "good boy" or "good girl" to get the attention of others. You can imagine how much stress and unhappiness you have put yourself through, yet others are not pleased with you. That means you have been working hard all this while for little or no acknowledgment. A bit like what it is to work for peanuts. I'm sure you are worth more than the paltry appreciation you receive. Even so, you feel secure with the little that you get back from others. You've been doubting their acceptance all this while. Start believing in your being, be human, and undo the image of a "good boy" or "good girl." There is NO question of acceptance and rejection; you are part of nature.

When I recommend you cease being a "good boy" or "good girl," it doesn't mean you must become the opposite, or what someone might term as a "bad boy" or "bad girl" — a defiant, uncaring rebel. You need to find a middle path. By that, I mean look at reality the way it stands, not trying to be a good person or bad. Face the issue and address it pragmatically, don't skirt it. That way, you will feel worthy and appreciated in your eyes, but you will not cause intentional pain to others because of what has transpired. Likewise, you don't need a No Objection Certificate (NOC) from the authorities around you. A NOC is a letter one receives in India from a government or legal body stating that they do not oppose what you intend to do, e.g., make alterations to your restaurant's structure. It's a form of approval that stands for the permission given to you by the authorities. You know what you're doing, believe in it, and trust your being, fully. As you slowly believe and trust in your own internal mechanism, your worth within will start to grow stronger.

Being human means that you accept your being as you are, knowing that you are precious. If you seek approval from others, you will perish one day feeling incomplete. Your attaining such sort of acceptance will continue as a craving and remain an illusion. Stop begging for happiness that is gained by being a "good boy" or "good girl," for that sort of happiness is illusory. You have overdone what you have been doing, and others have exploited you enough.

One of my clients, Sandy, had always been a "good girl," never known to question or answer back. She was hardly ever known even to say "no." Sandy was in the habit of tolerating and adjusting to her husband's idiosyncratic behavior. Not only would he habitually find faults in her, but he would also humiliate and insult her before her relatives. She suspected him of being unfaithful to her and was disturbed by it but couldn't prove his affairs to his relatives. He would dominate and somehow outsmart her, by cleverly twisting facts and situations. Sandy started suffering from physical pain and discomfort for a period of time, which is when she visited me. In one of our sessions, she understood her behavior and what was making her do what she was doing. There was a direct connection between her physical discomfort and her traits. From then onward, she consciously started to respond differently.

Let me pick an anecdote from Sandy's relationship with her husband that showed how she began to handle situations differently. In order to belittle her, her husband would often take photos of her mistakes from his phone and send them to her family members. She would plead with him not to do that, but he would disrespectfully go ahead and humiliate her anyway. He would also regularly embarrass her in front of others, because of which she disliked going out with him in a group.

Soon after her second session with me, they got into an altercation when he came home one day. He had nothing to say when she questioned him about his previous behavior. What delighted him was that he found their bedroom a little messy and started taking photos of it. She quickly realized what was coming her way and instead of apologizing and begging him as she usually did, she made the bedroom messier. She told him, "Please go ahead, take as many pictures as you like, and send it across to everyone you want. If you want me to make it look even untidier, let me know and I'll do that. Take as much joy from it as you like." Her husband was taken aback by her uncharacteristic boldness. He just tidied the bed and went off to sleep. Slowly, Sandy started gathering more courage and began making bold decisions in her marriage. Eventually, she began to stand firmly and assert herself.

Be Objective, Practical, and Pragmatic

All your life, you have conformed to what was enforced on you as you wanted to please others. Being obedient made you feel secure and safe, but now you are clear that your Survival Mechanism made you do it. Now, you can redesign your life by asking some valuable questions, such as:

❖ Do I have to listen to and obey everything others tell me?

❖ Who has designed this rule and for whom?

❖ Is it only applicable to me or does it apply to everyone?

❖ What will happen if I don't conform to such rules and regulations?

❖ When and where should they be obeyed? And at what times do they need not be followed?

❖ Am I conforming to these rules and regulations to please others and gain their acceptance?

You don't necessarily have to become a complete rebel and non-conformist. The point to note is that not conforming to the old ways does not mean you are unsafe. It only means you are exploring a new pathway that allows you to learn and grow. Learning and growing do not fall into the realm of what's good or bad, right or wrong. It is a process of moving ahead by knowing how others respond. It's an opportunity for you to notice what's working and what's not. This way, you continue to keep your beliefs and internal mechanism updated.

Avoid continuing to get sucked into your trap. Others around will want you to be the way you have always been, as it has been a great source of support for them. Stand your ground, be firm, objective, and pragmatic in addressing where issues lie with others. You might feel sympathy for some people, such as your parents or spouse, because they are very dear to you. However, on account of your behavior and communication, you have put them into a habit of expecting a lot from you. Now it has become a routine habit because they always expect you to obey their wishes and cater to their needs. And you feel obliged to respond to their needs. I can understand that, initially, it was necessary for you to do it as your survival depended on them. That phase of life is now over. You have survived. It's time to live your life. Set new terms, rules, and boundaries in harmony with yourself and others around you. The ideas you hold regarding duty may be preventing you from moving ahead. You may consider it your duty to continue the way you have in the past, but remember, there is a difference between duty and obligation. Do not confuse one with the other.

When we speak of duty, it is a voluntary act and there is no emotional charge. In other words, no guilt arises from not doing it. You just do it because you want to do it. If you're experiencing guilt for having not done something, it may have more to do with not fulfilling what you're expected to do as per others' standards and benchmarks. So it is an obligation rather than your duty.

As I was writing this piece, the world was being gripped by the COVID-19 (Coronavirus) pandemic. India had been under lockdown. Different religious authorities declared that it was not obligatory to visit Sunday service or other places of worship for some time. People were freed from certain religious obligations. There is a difference between a duty and an obligation. Others may compel us to do things and behave in a specific way. They call it a duty towards some ideal (be it family, religion, or nation). If you don't comply with what they deem correct, they make you feel guilty. But if they give you permission not to comply, or in other words, they make an exception, then the guilt (sin) is washed away. They can do whatever they deem fit because they are the ones in authority. Meanwhile, you believe you have to oblige, thinking it is your duty; when you don't, you experience guilt. And to avoid guilt, you end up doing what they demand. Feelings of guilt arise when you are doing something out of obligation. We feel indebted toward our parents and that leads to guilt.

Be Assertive

Go back in time and imagine what made you become a "yes man" or "yes woman" to begin with. It was a survival mechanism that you used that shaped your personality. Now that you have grown up, will using it any longer increase your self-respect and dignity? Are you going to grow in value in the eyes of others by continuing to use it? Or is your fear of not being liked or accepted compel you to continue doing what you do? Look at it this way: if you assert yourself, is it going to endanger your life? If you don't continue to play the game by the whims and demands of others, you might be unaccepted. Those are your fears. It's time to face these fears, be bold and courageous, and stand your ground. ASSERT YOURSELF. Give yourself enough time and notice what happens when you start doing that. Stop pleading and begging. Start LIVING. But be aware! That does not mean you have to transform overnight. Change is a gradual process, and it takes time to evolve. In this case, it's going to take more time because the Survival Mechanism's habits are deeply rooted in us. So be patient and kind to your being. If you TRUST, BELIEVE, and have FAITH in your BEING, you can withstand the temporary setbacks you may experience along the way. You will also be able to cope with others who are unwilling to relinquish their control over you.

Zeena had left a well-paying job to create her own start-up in partnership with another professional, with her owning a percentage of the firm's shares. Her previous organization recognized that she had done well for them and created a brand name for herself. When it came to her work, her former bosses appreciated her creativity, hard work, and commitment to walking the extra mile. In her new start-up, she did most or nearly all the work, including the critical work of bringing in business and developing strategy. Her partner, however, would always pull her down and find faults with her. Most of the time, she would accept his logical arguments and give in to his demands. Zeena was perplexed and couldn't understand what she was doing wrong. The situation made her feel regretful, for she had left a well-paying job to join the start-up, only to find someone who was always disappointed with her work and put her down. Her partner convinced her that her reputation would get damaged if she chose to leave the project now. She felt stuck and helpless.

Once Zeena understood her survival traits, she became aware of what she had been doing and how she felt the need to please another person. She brought this awareness into her work and tactfully communicated and dealt with her partner. Eventually, she became free from his hold on her and could stand her ground with no guilt.

Asserting is not confronting, and confronting is not asserting. Asserting is standing up for what you believe to be true. To be assertive is to be confident and say what you believe or want, including standing your ground when faced with challenges. You may be standing alone for a while and others who you thought were with you may desert you. But you've got to find the inner strength and courage to withstand the pressure applied to you by others. Those close to you are trapped in their own Survival Mechanism. When asserting yourself, avoid getting sucked into endless discussions about what's good or bad, right or wrong. Know that those around you will try to trap you by making you feel guilty. This is their way of not surrendering the hold they have on you. Your relatives and others will not understand you immediately because they are used to your old survival traits. You may have to slow down and counter them with pragmatism and reason.

Come What May, Face Realities

Thus far, you have been avoiding the key issues of your life by being a "good boy" or "good girl." The time has now arrived to face up to the realities of life. You found ways to skirt issues instead of meeting them head-on. You often got trapped and ended up doing things out of guilt because you couldn't say "NO." To escape from your weakness of non-assertiveness, you tried to bypass and ignore issues by keeping yourself busy or doing something else. But you have been made to pay the price for this behavior pattern. So now, instead of evading issues, face them, no matter what may come up. I know this is easier to state than do. Be bold and have an attitude of taking up this process of change, which may seem challenging.

I'll repeat what I stated earlier. You don't have to confront to resolve issues. Confronting is showing aggression, which is not healthy. You have to learn about and fully understand issues instead of avoiding them. Only when you get more clarity, you can begin to address problems.

Not asserting yourself does not resolve an issue but shoves it underneath a carpet. After a period of time, the carpet develops a hump, and eventually, the carpet becomes a problem. You hoped the issue would get resolved on its own. Problems relating to our deep patterns do not get resolved on their own unless you put effort into fixing them. You have to learn to assert firmly and then stand your ground. It might take a little time for you to develop this new trait and for others to accept your new attitude. You might feel frustrated. Remember, your patience and effort will be rewarded.

You are Wholly Accepted

You don't need anyone's approval to prove that you are human. You already know that. What you are seeking is acceptance. The more you crave for it, the more it's going to elude you and move further away from you. Then you will try even harder to please others by being a complete doormat. You have given the message to people you are close to that you are just that for them - a doormat. Humans operate from their preconceived notions and assumptions. Thus, they will continue to treat you the same way as they have always done. Either you decide to live your life differently or allow others to walk all over you.

In your search for acceptance, you might get it, but that kind of success will be short-lived. It's a False Illusionary Assurance from the Survival Mechanism. It's no more than a temporary phase; it will be gone after a while. You will start over once again, search harder, work harder, and be more willing to please. Even if you do get what you desire, the cost of maintaining such a position in terms of energy and time will be mammoth. While others are treading all over you, you will think it is your duty to serve them, but the core issue is that you crave acceptance. What should be the price you pay to get a "CERTIFICATE OF ACCEPTANCE?" That you allow others to walk all over you throughout your life? You can think about this. When you are ready, take charge of your life. You have forgotten something of tremendous significance: you are totally, unconditionally, and wholly accepted just the way you are. You belong to this universe and to Mother Nature, who LOVES you and CARES for you unconditionally.

Live Life Consciously Through Choices

For the sake of pleasing others, you have been putting yourself through the grind. They get what they want to be done through you for a pittance while you feel great getting a pat on your back, which is just a False Illusionary Assurance. It seems like a good trade-off. Your motivational graph hits the ceiling. You get a deep sense of assurance that you are doing superbly well and want to do even better the next time. Stop and ask yourself: Is your hard work equivalent to the returns you have been seeking? Do you think you are valued for what you have been doing? Do you feel you have been accepted unconditionally?

Sorry if this comes across as harsh, but you have been trying to fill your empty begging bowl with shreds of acceptance attained through your hard work. There is nothing wrong with working hard, but one has to understand one's underlying motive. The validation that you need remains in others' hands. Only when others unclench their closed fists, some charity might fall into your bowl. That is the height of your dependence on others.

What if you could start another process of acknowledging, appreciating, and admiring your being, which is within your control? Your life could be so much easier. That is like doing something, having something, and being someone because you want it. That's within your grasp. When you operate from a place of not seeking acceptance, you can decide how you want to live. Then the power is in your hands. Thus, you choose when you work hard, for whom, and for what objective. Live life by conscious choices, trusting a higher power will support you.

Be Generous, But Know Your Limits

You are accepted just the way you are. You don't have to be a savior to anyone. Everyone is part of nature, and nature knows how to take care of everybody. Do your bit, the little you can do, but don't go overboard.

What do I mean by "don't go overboard?" Let me explain by way of an anecdote that is known to some people. Imagine you have a friend, Dick, who requires $10,000 because his family member is unwell and needs to be hospitalized. You have $2,000 in your savings account as of now. You borrow sums of money from your friends Tom, Jack, and Harry, to cover the deficit on behalf of Dick because you have excellent credentials with them. Dick had promised to return the amount of money borrowed within two months. Unfortunately, not just two months but six months have passed by, yet Dick hasn't returned the amount he owes. Your friends are calling you often, asking for their money back. You don't have the money to pay them back. Now you have found yourself in a soup because of your sympathetic attitude, which is making you experience stress and tension. Just because you wanted to be helpful. If the crisis continues for a year or more, your situation could become precarious. You may lose friends due to what you have done, and your mental health will not improve.

A point to note here. I am not saying that you should not help your friend, but you don't need to learn when to draw a boundary. You can indeed part with your own savings if you think it's necessary. It is yours and nobody can question you on that. Do what is manageable within your limits. Be generous, but surely not foolishly generous. Do what is possible within your means. No one else can decide for you where your boundaries lie, or the means end. You don't have to impress anyone to gain his/her appreciation and admiration. You need to accept your present conditions and capacity just the way they are.

Keith, one of my clients, was a friendly and jovial person. He was one of those people who would go out of his way to make others happy. His heart would bleed for the sorrows of others. Keith had had a failed marriage and was routinely exploited by his so-called friends and girlfriends. There were times when he suffered financial losses and lost some quality friends. He was a typical "yes-man" in his attitude and pleased others for little acceptance. To sum it up, this is what he thought was love. Once Keith understood his core survival traits and what made him do what he was doing, he started taking charge of his life.

Keith could be magnanimous to a fault. He had friends who worked near his office, who he would visit for lunch or coffee and share his food with them (in India, it is customary for many people to take packed lunches from home to work). Most of the time, however, they would rudely make him wait for up to half an hour, despite stating that they were ready to meet him. Sometimes they would commute to or from work together and even at those times they would make him wait. Quite clearly, he was being taken for granted by others. In other instances, he would please his old neighbors by being a good neighbor to them in any way he could. After his second session with me, he changed his decision-making process and started making decisions differently. He would have lunch with his friends around his office if they were punctual. If not, he would turn back and go back to his office to enjoy his lunch alone. He discontinued waiting for his tardy friends while going home too. But if they were there, he would gladly accompany them. While this may seem like normal behavior to others, one has to step into Keith's shoes for a while. He had always been a people-pleaser. This was a remarkable shift, where he started giving importance to his being and then to others. He was politely able to say "no" to his friends and neighbors. He started feeling proud, his self-worth began to grow, and he discontinued repeating the same old mistakes. What's more, he could make all these changes without becoming confrontational.

Direct Your Tolerance, Patience, and Resilience Toward Your Being

Tolerance, patience, and resilience are some of your exemplary qualities. Your tolerance level for the nonsense dished out by others is high because you don't like making any enemies. So you carry on taking bullshit from them and instead of addressing issues, you choose to avoid them. You are living in your own la-la-land, thinking someday, just someday, they will realize your real worth. This makes you lenient towards them and their faults. But you haven't noticed that the same leniency is not extended to you. You are intolerant towards yourself and hard on yourself if you fail to stoop down to please and accommodate the wishes of others. You are walking all over your being in this way, and you are allowing others to walk over you, being the metaphorical doormat once again. Be tolerant of your being. When you know, you shouldn't do things beyond a point just to please anyone, STOP! Stop going overboard. Value your being.

Patience is another quality ingrained in you. Patience towards whom? Patience towards others who have been mistreating you and exploiting you while you hope they are going to acknowledge you someday. This is like daydreaming. You need to reflect on the current reality. You are impatient with your being because you can't wait and stand your ground when opposing others. That's because you fear non-acceptance. Acknowledge your fears. You buckle up under the pressure of the Self and start pleasing others within a short period — so that, you won't end up making any enemies. The question here is not about whether you have enemies or friends but about your worth. You are valuable, but you have put your worth in the hands of others. You need to show more patience for your being in this process of change. Stand firm about your boundaries and care for yourself.

In the nineteenth century, scientists conducted research by placing a frog in a container of water, which was heated at a very low temperature. While the water was getting warmer and warmer, the frog hardly even moved. Finally, the water became so hot that the frog died, paying the price for its tolerance.

Like the "boiling frog," your resilience has vast boundaries, even when you are in deep waters until you are overloaded and exhausted. This burden has been borne by you for years and more and more additional weight is dumped onto you. As shown in an earlier chapter, the weight of the gunny bags keeps increasing. You continue to think it's your responsibility. What you want is acceptance, but what you have become is merely a sacrificial lamb. All of this sacrifice is for others.

Your resilience is for others, and hardly anything is left for your being. If someone does not value you, should you be sacrificing your life by being resilient? You know all this while that you are not being acknowledged and accepted for all that you have done so far. Should you continue with your sacrifices, or should you direct your resilience to change your pathway?

You Are Priceless — Value Your Being

Your heart melts for others, but I wonder, does it melts the same way when it comes to your BEING? Out of sympathy, you open your purse or wallet to dole out what you have generously to others - your money, time, and energy. But when it comes to being generous to your being, you get second thoughts and are plagued by guilt. Are you not being stingy with your being? Or have double standards when it comes to it? Others can benefit and cream off your resources, but you are not allowed to do it for your being. Who is not valuing whom? Others do NOT value you, or is it you do NOT value your being?

Your heart beats for others, hoping you get something in return. Whether you realize it or not, your concerns and attention toward others are not unconditional. You hope and expect they will understand you and give you what you want. The core question is, what do you want? Acceptance! By doing what you have been doing thus far in life, you haven't got what you have been seeking. If you had, you would have stopped doing it. Do you think you will get it in the next few days, weeks, months, or years? If the answer to that is yes, then you must definitely wait. If not, start valuing your being. You are WORTHY. You've got to value your WORTH. Never allow others to measure your worth. When you're looking for others to value your worth, it's as if you are waiting for a price tag to be placed on you. No one can place a price tag on you, because YOU ARE PRICELESS and WILL REMAIN PRICELESS. When your worth comes from within, then you do not need others to evaluate your worth.

When you allow others to decide your worth, the reins are in their hand. They determine when to make you worthy and when to pull you down. You will sometimes look like a puppet in another person's hand, dancing to their tune. It's time you made your decisions and live your life the way you want.

It's Time to Learn to Ask Questions

Throughout life, you have lived in your fear of not being liked by others. For fear of not being accepted, you have avoided posing bold questions to others. In this regard, you have been living your life with caution. Now that you have understood and acknowledged your personality traits and the root cause of them, it's time to move ahead. Change your life, take action. You have the gift of being an action-oriented person. Start taking action for your own well-being.

One way you can take action is to begin asking questions to people you have feared to ask. The show of your life has been going on for too long, it's time to take the remote control back in your hands. Be bold and courageous for your betterment. Ask sensible questions to whoever it may be. Others will not like you initially, but you will have to learn to be fearless and tolerant of your being. Have patience, wait, and hold your position with the strength of your resilience for your own well-being. That will be a message to others that you value and respect your being and that you are worthy. When you do it, others will value you. Self-worth begins with you. Start valuing your BEING. Then you will begin to experience freedom.

48

BREAKING FREE

The more consciously Partly Wanted Children to practice behaviors and habits described in the previous chapter, the lesser they will get sucked into their survival trap. If you are one, the more you take charge of your life, the easier it will be for you to come out of your Birth Survival Trance.

In this chapter, we will look at a few techniques to free you from getting entangled in your trap. I'm not promising there will be big changes overnight, in a few days, weeks, or even months. As you are born with certain conditioning, it requires consistent and regular effort to deal with it over a lengthy period. Depending on your consistency, you can be assured of lasting results.

Your decision about how you would like your life to go depends on your personal goals. Would you like to live a life as per someone else's construct, or would you like to create your own dreams? If you want to change, you will need to develop and strengthen new thinking. You either allow the survival circus to continue or consciously take charge of how you will live.

Your Parent's Transferred Emotions

Parents, who are co-creators, may have made a mistake while conceiving a child and there is no way to reverse what happened. Their negative emotions get displaced and transferred unconsciously to you at birth. You were a product of their disappointment, which is what makes you a Partly Wanted Child. Moreover, they felt helpless as they couldn't change what had happened. But you need not carry their negative emotions in you.

In an earlier chapter, I narrated the story of my father and the jackfruit saplings. He was disappointed and helpless due to a blunder he had unknowingly committed but, unintentionally, his negative emotion of disappointment got transferred onto me. There was no way he could revive the jackfruit sapling, but he accused me and made me feel guilty. Even when he was in his 80s, I triggered the same memory in him that morning when we were together, which had created an emotional rift between us since that incident. That morning, I regressed my dad by asking him simple questions regarding misconceptions he held about that event and updated his memory with a new understanding. Thus the issue was put to rest at his level. It is possible for you to experience similar changes.

You Possess a Capable Visual Faculty

Adil, a Partly Unwanted child, was a sound engineer for live bands. At times, there would be five bands playing on the stage. Adil had to be sure to synchronize the sound output and smoothly switch over from one band to another. In his mind, the whole event was getting synchronized even before the event took place. Adil was visualizing the sound equipment that would be required and how he had to organize it to make it possible for all the bands to give their best performance. He was excellent at his job.

Our visual faculty helps us in making a decision, as we can "see" an outcome we desire. It's not true that you don't possess good visual faculties as a Partly Wanted Child. Just like Adil, you are capable of visualizing outcomes. However, the moment you come under the spell of the Survival Mechanism, your visual faculty gets sidelined. When your survival mechanism gets triggered, you unconsciously and in split seconds, switch over to your Birth Survival Trance. It's here when your kinesthetic mode takes over, and you start to do things for acceptance and appreciation. In truth, there may not be a real danger to your life, but your internal mechanism doesn't know how else to respond. It automatically switches over to the same old stimulus-response mode, which is your auto-pilot mode. Your visual faculties then get blocked, and you rely on others for direction.

However, you make many day-to-day decisions based on your visual inputs. It may be about how you choose and select products when you shop or read and interpret signboards on the metro and at the airport. These actions imply that you do have an active visual faculty, but it simply gets suppressed when there is a potential threat to your life.

Since birth, you have been using your kinesthetic skills to survive and are habituated to it. You avoid making decisions and follow instructions given by the Self, which is so easy. But you need to intentionally take charge when your system switches to your Survival Trance, even though this happens in a split second. You can do this by practicing making conscious, independent decisions at that moment. This way, you strengthen your visual faculty. Below are a few exercises you could try to help you make the change.

How to Know When Your Survival Mechanism is Active

First, you must be good at identifying when you are going into your Survival Trance. Here are a few indicators that you are operating unconsciously from your Survival Mechanism:

- ❖ The parent who rejected you will dominate over you. You will find it difficult to say no, or you will feel the need to please him/her. At times, you will please both of your parents.
- ❖ Your partner or spouse could be the one who substitutes for your parent in the core Self later. Observe how you feel the need to please him/her. Be aware of the survival traits you use while pleasing them.
- ❖ When people in authority communicate with you, you feel compelled to comply. You think it's your duty to behave in the same old ways, to gain acceptance from them.
- ❖ When you experience negative emotions, it is a sure sign that your Survival Mechanism is active. Its intensity could be low, like mild irritation, or very high, like feelings of rage, guilt, depression, or anxiety.

❖ You know when you should have said "NO" to someone, but you skirted the issue. If this trait surfaces, or any of the other survival traits, you have gone into your Survival Trance.

With this background information, you can try the below techniques to update your survival traits.

Build Your Own Self-Image

It is time you begin to create your own Self-image based on what you believe is relevant to you. Start to make decisions based on the experiences you have acquired all this while. When you rely on your own experiences, it means you are making informed decisions.

There are two circles in the above diagram. On the left is the same old one that you are dealing with, the Self, using your survival traits. The parents who are in your core Self did not give you a clear image. Hence, you need to rely on others for your decisions. However, over the years, you have gathered enough experience that has gone on to benefit others. This experience can be used as input for making independent decisions that benefit you.

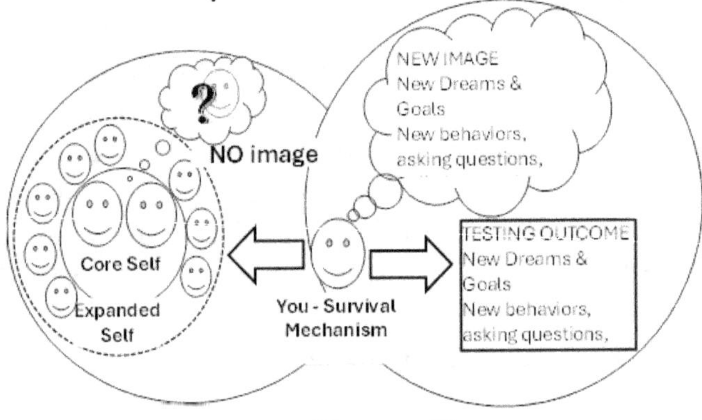

Diagram 42

The circle on the right shows a new image you could project in your mind containing your dreams, goals, and aspirations. Your goals can even be new behaviors and changes you would like to experience in life. You visualize and test the visuals in real life to see whether they produce results the way you had imagined. You must be open and willing to reshape your behaviors and communication to get to your chosen outcomes.

There won't be a perfect solution. What works at one time might not produce the same results in the future as everybody keeps changing. Learn to be flexible. Use your innate qualities of resilience, patience, and tolerance as strengths for your own welfare. Believe in the process of learning.

Meditation

Do a one-minute meditation focusing on your breath. You may certainly increase the time gradually by a few more minutes whenever you feel confident. Practice it often during the day. You can take a break for some time and repeat the exercise. It's not necessarily about doing a one-minute meditation but about staying focused on your breathing as long as you can keep your attention on your breathing. This practice is essential for grounding, which has multiple benefits.

It will also help you SLOW DOWN. It is imperative that you learn how to do this, mentally and physically. Often people do not even have a minute to spare for themselves. That's because they have forgotten to value their being, living life mechanically. Things will be revealed to you naturally, only if you slow down. You will be able to reflect on your conduct and the behavior of those around you. So, relax and focus on your breath.

Reprogram Old Memories

We have a tendency to regress into our Birth Survival Trance within seconds. Slow down. Go back into your past and think about the times you were in your survival trap. Identify what it was that you were doing to survive in that situation. Observe the events as if you are watching a movie on a screen. Notice what's happening and reflect on what you could do differently in those situations. When you arrive at your preferred outcome, replay it visually in your mind no less than seven to ten times. The more you are in a detached state while watching your actions on your mental screen, the more improvements you will notice over time.

When you get off auto-pilot mode, you begin to take back control in your hands and consciously flex your mental muscles.

Explore Your Survival Trance

Sonia, a lady in her forties, was the second girl child in her family. Her father wanted a boy and was disappointed when she was born. As Sonia regressed into her early childhood years, she got answers to her Survival Trance. I explained to her how it was not her fault. She understood that she couldn't be held responsible for her father's blunder. The creator had a different choice in his heart but couldn't return Sonia like an item that he had simply purchased, like in an online transaction. Sonia could identify the trauma that caused her Birth Survival Trance to come about and how it was connected to her inborn emotion of rejection. There is always an emotion attached to one's birth that puts a person in a trance beyond their comprehension. Knowing about her truth helped Sonia live her life differently, the way she wants to, free from guilt and fear of rejection. She now had a choice in living her life, unlike operating in auto-pilot mode.

If you are a Partly Wanted Child, knowing your Birth Survival Trance would be vital. Below is a simple relaxation exercise you can do on your own to regress into your early growing-up days.

First, understand your repetitive patterns, which are your survival traits. When you are aware of your inborn survival traits, you will know how you go about pleasing the Self. If you continue to use the same traits, it implies you are getting sucked into your Survival Trance. In addition to answering the above questions, you may also write down specific traits you often display when relating to people you are close to.

I would recommend you do the below exercise gradually and progressively. If someone else is leading you, it's easier to regress back. You could get another person's assistance, but if you wish to do it on your own, break the exercise into smaller chunks of time. Choose to practice ten to fifteen minutes on any day before returning to it again on another day. There is a lot to process, so you will experience better results this way.

Sit in a comfortable chair or couch and close your eyes. Recall the survival traits you prominently show to others. From your current age, try to regress (go back to a younger age) slightly. In your mind, imagine you are walking backward as you go into your past. Start with a month ago. Recall some of the people with whom you behaved using your survival traits. Remember it as often as you want or as clearly as you can. Go back a few more months. Look at how the same patterns were repeating during that time. As you walk backward in your mind, you can watch past events in front of you as if you were watching a movie.

You can then regress from a few months to a year and notice your conduct. The same survival traits will repeat continuously. Gradually, regress by another year. It would be essential to spot the repeating patterns in your behavior. If you are thirty-five years old, you could regress to when you were thirty and watch the past five years of your life, seeing the same survival patterns. You may have grown older, more knowledgeable, tasted career success, and gotten married, but your survival traits remain consistent. It signifies that there is little change to our core behaviors, beliefs, and thinking even when we grow older.

Continue to walk back into your past till you are twenty. Now, the past fifteen years appear on your mental screen. Watch the patterns repeating with different people. From the age of twenty, regress till you are ten years old and compare your survival traits. You may be surprised to learn that you have behaved consistently with your parents, family members, authority figures, friends, bosses and even your spouse over the course of these twenty-five years. There could be slight differences depending on the person you interact with.

If you succeed in regressing to the age of ten, I will request you to SLOW DOWN. By now, you will be aware of your repetitive patterns, a sequence of events, and some history and information presented to you by your family. Ask the below questions:

- ❖ Which parent did you try to please the most?
- ❖ What are the things you did to satisfy him/her?
- ❖ What did you hear or overhear your parents talking about you and your birth?

* What events can you remember your parents discussing or narrating that may have impacted them when you were conceived?

It's vital to break your sessions up into smaller chunks. If your awareness about your Birth Survival Trance and your parent's emotions at your birth increases, you will gain insights into what makes you do what you are doing.

The further back you can regress into your past and recall information connected to your birth, the more effective the process will be. Recall your family's unique history. You could try to regress into your mother's womb. While that may be difficult to do on your own, it's often not required because all the clues come up by the age of five. You have probably overheard and absorbed certain conversations between parents and so the knowledge is in you.

Identify Your Parent's Displaced Emotion

Just like a potter in the earlier chapter on the Partly Wanted Child experiences dissatisfaction and helplessness for creating something without having a clear image of it; your parent experienced negative emotions when you were born.

Even today, you are carrying your parent's emotional imprint in your body, which makes you feel rejected and insecure. Identify the emotions your parent experienced through the following questions:

* Which of your parents wanted you and what was the purpose s/he had in mind?
* What was the outcome s/he wanted you to fulfill?
* Which parent did not want you?
* What were the expectations you could not meet?
* What was the emotion s/he may have experienced knowing you were conceived or when you were born?
* Were there any other events that gave rise to those emotions?
* What negative emotions, is s/he displacing on to you?
* How are you surviving because of the dilemma someone else faced?

❖ Is s/he disappointed with you or themselves?

If you discover that you are a Partly Wanted Child, it is necessary to realize that your Survival Trance starts with your parent who was disappointed with your birth. It is s/he who failed in their journey as s/he couldn't cope with his/her emotions due to vulnerability.

Among my clients who are Partly Wanted Children, one stated that his parents teased him saying he happened "by mistake," which implies that one of them did not want him. Another client said they were not expecting to have another child. Some female clients said their parents wanted a boy. You are living life through your parent's dilemma; however, you cannot be held responsible for their mishandling of the situation. S/he may have experienced helplessness when you were conceived or born, but that was their chaos.

An Exercise to do Before Sleeping

At the end of the day, before going to sleep, go through the day's events. Notice where you faltered and fell back onto your survival traits to please someone. You could ask the below questions:

❖ Who was the person you pleased and how often do you interact with him/her?
❖ How did the person trap you and how did you get sucked in thereafter?
❖ Ask a question to your being: how could you have tackled the situation differently? If you find that you cannot solve the issue, admit it and ask for help. Be honest to your being.
❖ What does s/he want out of you?
❖ Is s/he or someone else trying to influence your decisions?

Certain issues could be repetitive and the person you are interacting with may be the same one. If it's the same person you are trying to please, then ask:

❖ Under what Survival Mechanism category does s/he belong?

❖ Could you try to learn more about the person's traits? It can give you a better understanding on how to tackle situations with them.

If you consciously practice updating your survival traits, using some of the above techniques, it signals that you are taking control in your hands. You are making your own decisions and want to chart a different path for your well-being.

THE UNWANTED CHILD

49

LIVING WITH FREEDOM

If you have discovered that you are an Unwanted Child or confirmed what you felt all along, I understand it may be challenging for you to come to terms with the reality. Whatever has happened to you, your parents didn't do it intentionally, or maybe it was part of the plan of nature. Each day, I notice and observe that things around us do not happen randomly. Perhaps, there is a purpose in everything that is happening around us. The Earth or Universe has to maintain a balance within its ecosystem. Everyone with their Survival Mechanism plays a role in counterbalancing each other. You, too, have a larger purpose behind your existence.

You have been trying your best to adjust to the demands of the Self, using your survival traits as an Unwanted Child. Our survival mechanism is an essential part of us till a certain age in life, but beyond that, it's outdated. Now that you are an adult, you need to consciously get off your Survival Mechanism and its mechanisms. You did what you did unknowingly and now it's time to change. There is a need for you to be honest and genuine to others around you, thus, being true to your being. The chapter is written so that you can re-align your being with others around you. The past can't be changed, but you can update your belief that you are unwanted. In reality, you are wanted.

The number or intensity of survival traits that you could have taken on as an Unwanted Child may vary, depending on your parents and the surroundings in which you were born and raised. The environment plays a significant role in determining the strength of one's survival traits. Survival traits, whether in their number or intensity, will not be the same for all Unwanted Children; they will vary to a degree. There is a possibility that the Survival Mechanism of others could create a different combination in an Unwanted Child. So, if your father and mother have their own survival traits, and your culture differs, the intensity of your survival traits may be very high, or in some cases, it may mellow down. When traits have mellowed, they still exist, but it could be that people around you don't allow you to operate through your Survival Mechanism fully. As an example, they do not tolerate stubbornness or manipulation. The purpose of this book is for you to understand and not to defy yourself. You are part of this Universe and thus definitely have a higher purpose. Yes, your preservation mechanism has certainly impacted your perceptions towards life and others, so that you could survive. Now that you have survived, it's your opportunity to evolve and change.

You Are a Wholly Accepted Part of Nature

It's simple. You are born on this planet, which means you are fully and completely part of this Earth. You belong to Nature. Unless you have been unfortunate to be born with a deformity or congenital illness, Nature has bestowed on you the same gifts as it has on all other human beings. This includes a functioning body and remarkable intelligence. Look at it another way: your father and mother did provide the sperm and egg, respectively, which led to your inception. But did they manufacture the laws (the biological processes) that led to your creation inside your mother's womb? No, they belonged to Nature and so you belong to Nature completely.

Nobody can challenge you on that, but the bigger question is, are you willing to accept your being for who you are and what you have been all this while? Just because one of your parents rejected you at birth, you don't like rejection, and you have been trying hard to persuade others to accept you. You were not rejected. It was the situation your parents were going through at that time, which caused the emotional trauma that got passed on to you. With that, you picked up the subliminal message that you are unwanted. So as an unborn child, you have drawn the *wrong conclusion* only because of your parents' situational constraints.

You particularly don't like anyone saying "NO" to you, especially on things that you want. Now that you know others are living their lives with their Survival Mechanism, they are no better off than you. It's time for you to accept "NO" with a smile. You don't have to use your persuasive skills to make things happen your way to fulfill your personal agenda. In the short run, you will win over people with your sophisticated verbal skills and possibly even climb the ladder of success. In the long run, people will be drawn to you because of your money and wealth, not because of your character or contributions. Is that what you truly want?

You need to accept your being and stop trying to win the favor of people by feigning sweetness. It's time you value your being rather than hope to get applause and recognition from others. Gaining acceptance from the world may feel like others are sprinkling confetti on you. You feel on top of the world, at least for some time. Slowly the effects start to fade away. Life is NOT about others accepting you; it's about you accepting your BEING. If you are looking for acceptance from others, then the remote control of your life is in the hands of others. That means your happiness, sadness, or disappointment is in others' hands. An unsteady position to keep holding onto. Given your survival traits, you work hard to mold yourself like clay to please others because you cannot tolerate rejection. If you can accept your being just the way you are, then others will accept you.

Learn to Trust Your Being

It has been difficult for you to trust others. You are quite sensitive and know when your close ones are not supporting you. You want everybody to trust you even when you doubt your own behavior and conduct. You know when something is not alright as per your understanding and intuition. According to your internal warning meter, you know when something is amiss. Your assessments and judgments of situations tell you that. But unless you change your course, you will continue to play Dr. Jekyll and Mr. Hyde by remaining two-faced. You already know how a Genie has a hold on you and your behavior.

It begins with you. If you could trust your being, then you wouldn't have to be insincere, fake, or manipulate others for your personal gains. You doubt your SELF and whether you will be accepted or not, just the way you are. Slowly and progressively, you will need to lay a new foundation consciously. You can focus on doing the exercises in the next chapter. Others may have told you about some of your flaws, but you devised ways to cover them up. As others pinpointed your wrongdoing, you became shrewder and foxier in your approach instead of mending your ways. All this while, you didn't know what made you do what you did. But now, as you know, it is the Genie controlling your thinking and creating internal doubt, it's an opportune time for you to take responsibility for what you want to be.

As you are an Unwanted Child, you regularly doubt others. The question, "Will I be accepted; will others like me?" keeps repeating within you. It's a subliminal mechanism you may not be fully aware of. In order to repress this doubt, you overcompensate by being sweet, or fake, or anything that brings you acceptance. Instead, you can overcome this doubt if you trust your being, but that will happen over time. It will require doing a little self-work and seeking the support of others, maybe professional therapists. Growing a new tree takes time. The more it grows, the more the roots go deeper, the Survival Mechanism's impact diminishes, and you cease trying to manipulate others.

Be Your Best Friend and Accept Your Being

You have been chasing acceptance via the wrong routes so far. When you doubt your core Self, you constantly need reassurance from others. If you don't receive it, you feel lonely, whereas when you accept your being, you won't face loneliness. The moment you accept your being, you are not alone, and even if you are, you are not bothered. Even others will not doubt your integrity, as you won't be seeking anything from them.

You can charm others easily. Speaking on any topic for you is like giving a skillful extempore speech. You know how to win and influence others. You don't even have to read Dale Carnegie's book *How to Win Friends and Influence People*. But even despite having so much talent, you still feel alone. What's more, even when you have people around you, you are not happy with them because you want to control everybody. Learn to be true to your being because there is learning in such truth. Part of this shift is learning to acknowledge your mistakes. When you admit your mistakes, you have honored your being because you are not hiding anything from others. In fact, it could be challenging for you to admit your mistakes and put your being in the line of fire. It's much easier for you to create a smokescreen and escape. You have many tools in your kit, but you cannot make genuine friends even with those sophisticated gadgets. You always have to maintain your façade because there is a fear people might discover the truth about your true intentions and insincerity.

You don't need to pretend to be someone else to have people in your corner. All you need are a few genuine relatives or friends, but without a shadow of a doubt, the best friend you can make is your own being. Then you won't need too many friends to survive. You will always have the company of your being, no need to search out there. That's where contentment begins, and things will begin to fall into place for you.

Be Genuine and Stop Seeking Sympathy

Some of you use self-pity as a trump card to lure others into your sob stories. You need to start believing in your being and that you are worthy. You don't need somebody else's sympathy to reach your end goals. Your use of melodrama is really aimed at convincing others that you are in a pitiable situation. The attention you receive makes you feel reassured that you are cared for and wanted. Some parts of it may be genuine, but the rest is not true, and you very well know about it. You can insincerely shed tears when it's not required. These are your survival traits. Are you going to live your life with fake emotions, preying on the sympathies of others? You always have an internal fear that you will get exposed someday. You end up covering up your positions, meaning more lies and deceit are added to your life. Not to be unkind to you, but the survival tree, in your case, grows on lies, deceit, and insincerity without you realizing its branches have spread out in different directions. The whole tree is fake because it does not provide genuine fruits that truly nourish you or others. You know the tree is fake, and so will be its fruits. But you put up such a convincing act that others are deceived. They succumb to your sophisticated persuasion skills and endless persistence.

It's time for you to nurture a genuine tree that bears healthy fruits, where you and others can enjoy and get nourishment. It is you who has to decide if you want to continue nurturing the survival tree that has been giving you a false sense of security via a False Illusionary Assurance. Now that you realize that Genie has fooled you, it's time for you to change your path. It's time to free yourself and live an authentic and honorable life where you value your worth.

Ginn, one of my clients, has been living two parallel lives. Her good old friends had come to know about a secret relationship she was in, about which she had been lying to them for a while. What had disturbed them the most was that she was with a married man. They couldn't trust her anymore. Thus, they blocked her on social media, did not answer her emails and refused to take her calls. She was feeling lonely. Ginn feared that if she told the truth to her close friends, they wouldn't accept her. Finally, what she feared had actually come true.

In the past, she had a few relationships with married men, and all of them were cushions to absorb her tears. Since she was young, her focus had been on her career, and these men were also relevant to her career growth. At the same time, they were also empathetic towards her sob stories.

Ginn was disturbed because her friends had deserted her and also accused her of being fake and a liar. She did ask me about what she could have done differently in this situation where she was in love with this married man. Ginn has had difficulty trusting others since childhood. Even putting faith in her parents was difficult for her. There were times when things did not go her way; she would behave stubbornly and, at times, throw a tantrum, shocking those around her.

As I slowly started to use therapeutic maneuvers into her Survival Mechanism and make connections in her behavior and conduct, many things began to unfold. Suddenly, she was experiencing uneasiness and silence, feeling trapped. Constantly, I had to give her assurance that these were her unconscious survival traits and that she wasn't doing things intentionally.

By the end of the second session, she got insights into the truth about her as an Unwanted Child. She understood how she was seeking the attention of others by pretentiously molding herself. She realized that she was living a dubious life of deceit and duplicity. As the whole puzzle got clearer in her mind, her cobwebs disappeared, and she began to experience the surge of an inner unfolding. Towards the end of the second session, she said, "I am experiencing a loud silence. I simply feel unique and different internally." That was her experience; I couldn't comprehend what she meant.

When things got clearer to her, the truth was staring her in the face. What is, "IS." You don't have to accept it or reject it. It is just there. The truth was glaring at her, and that clarity gave her a new perspective, which broadened her self-awareness. She understood why she sought sympathy and that she didn't need to continue doing it.

Your Worth is in Your Hands

You experience high levels of insecurity regarding your survival. It is evident that as a person, you have had to thrive to protect your body in every possible way. Now that you have grown older and passed that phase of self-preservation, you need to shift your focus on being honest and genuine, both to you and to others. You don't need to use your peculiar survival tools beyond your twenties. You don't really require them in your thirties and certainly not at all in your forties. Your Survival Mechanism has overshot the age limits within which it ought to be active. Now you know the cause of what made you do what you were doing, you can decide to change your life. Seeking validation is about getting authentication and approval from others, which is external-oriented and short-lived. Your worth, therefore, is directly proportionate to a shelf life stamped on you by others. The strings that control you are still in the hands of others.

On the other hand, if you feel worthy from within, you don't need support from others. It is related to what I had mentioned earlier about accepting your being. The more you validate your being, the less validation you need from others. Similarly, the more you accept your being, the more worthy you feel from within. That, too, will make you need less validation from others. In this way, your worth will stay in your own hands.

Co-Exist with Harmony

You exist in this Universe and are very much a part of it. You are a part of the total. Divide and rule has been a vital component of your survival mechanism. You have passed the phase where you need to survive. It's time to live your life co-existing with others and being collectively together. Instead of creating a divide among people to safeguard your interests, it's time to be open and transparent in your communication. You are habituated to your old ways, and it's so easy to walk the known path that gives you a false assurance of safety. However, that path can only take you to the same outcomes, which means your destiny will remain unchanged. The difference may be in the props and surroundings of a new environment but not in a new outcome. It's time to do something completely new and different from your past, where you feel proud of your being. Your Survival Mechanism created an illusion about yourself. Just the way you can deceive others, you are also living in deception. The Genie is at the helm and in control of your life. Unlike a Wanted Child, who was given an image of a crown prince or princess, you have not been given one. That has resulted in a lot of conflict within you. You are trying to BE someone as a result, but "trying" and "being" are different things. The Chinese may try to build a Chinese iPhone, but that will still not hold the perception of an Apple product in the eyes of its patrons. It's better to respect who you are and build your life on a genuine foundation.

One way to reconcile your relationship with your being is to know that nature has wholly accepted you just the way you are. Not only are you a part of nature, but you are also nature itself. And so are others. Therefore, the question of pleasing nature doesn't arise, nor does the question of dividing it. If you are nature, you are indivisible and can't play games with others who are also part of the same whole. That will be like a drop of water trying to divide the ocean. Eventually, you can either pollute some water around you for your preservation or be a non-pollutant for your well-being and that of others around you. There is a place for everyone, and divinity has a place for you as well. Trust in your being, believe in your being, and have faith in your being. Think of how you can create oneness within you and with others around you. You don't need to rule over others, and you don't need to divide people. Just govern and live your own life.

Let Go of Control

The more control you have in your life, the more invincible you feel. You can imagine the stress and pressure you could be going through just to maintain control when you get pulled in all directions. You might feel you are in charge, but on the contrary, you are trapped on all sides. Anyone can upset your apple cart, and you will feel the need to constantly firefight to get things back into your control. You freak out when you fail to control others or elicit the response you desire. That leads to you losing control over your own behavior and conduct. You then resort to using other tools in your arsenals, such as deception or manipulation, to get things under control. At times, you might even punish others for not falling in line with your wishes or obeying your rules. Don't you see how difficult it is to keep continuing to control people and situations? You know that the mechanism is generating unwanted stress, illnesses, and discomfort. You are not happy, but control gives you False Illusionary Assurance. That's the way your Survival Mechanism works. It's time to "let go of control." You can live your life trusting that you are safe and well-guarded by nature. The best way to live life is not to pursue control. The more you want to have control, the more chaotic life becomes. Decide to let others live their lives, while you live yours with minimal stress, and with fewer or no illnesses.

Reet was a young entrepreneur who was successfully managing her own business. She was facing difficulties in her marriage and blamed her husband for many of the problems she was facing. She was good at picking his faults and magnifying his mistakes. Subtly, she was controlling her husband, but he wouldn't give in to her diktats. This made her feel frustrated and angry with him. Some of the things she related to me about him were rather trivial and of little significance. If I challenged her, she gave me vague answers and created a smokescreen to deviate to other issues. I highlighted her survival traits and how she was functioning with her husband, reminding her that her husband was not perfect and had his flaws.

On unfolding her Survival Mechanism, she was initially highly repulsed by it and didn't like what she discovered at all. Assuring her that she was not doing things intentionally and that these were unconscious survival traits that got embedded in her, she was willing to explore herself further. The exploration gave her an understanding of what she was really doing and how her survival traits were getting triggered unconsciously, making her feel insecure from within. She wanted continuous assurance from her husband, which could only be achieved if he always danced to her tunes. I brought it to her notice how she was seeking a False Illusionary Assurance from him. She realized that by seeking acceptance, her behaviors were actually repelling him and weakening their relationship. She decided to let go of the control she always wanted and chose to make changes in herself instead of allowing him to be. She was finally able to experience peace within herself.

Note that I have come across most of my clients who belong to the category of Unwanted Children being initially repulsed when they discover their Survival Mechanism. This makes them not want to explore their Survival Mechanism. Only when I assure them that their behaviors are unintentional and result from inborn traits that are there for their survival are they more willing to explore further. They are quick learners and ready to change and evolve.

Be True to Your Being

Some of you are moderately good at using the survival tools gifted to you by your Survival Mechanism, while there are some among you who are supremely good at it. You have been playing a game with gadgets for quite a long time. The important question is, you have survived; how long do you want to continue using the same tools and playing the same game? You have already survived; now it's time to LIVE your life. Stop faking, deceiving, and manipulating — start living. Be true to your being. You know the truth when you concocted a story or acted out of deception. There is no escaping from it. Instead of lying to your being, honor it by being honest.

In survival, you only have two alternatives – FIGHT or FLIGHT. But you don't really use these two. You don't fight directly but shrewdly use others to fight on your behalf. You don't quite run away either because you create a smokescreen when confronted. That ends up fooling others or creating confusion in their minds. You don't have to outsmart anyone. In winning, you are losing because you are not true to your being. When you are TRUE to your being, you are also true to others. It starts with you. It is alright to acknowledge, accept, and honor your being.

Forgive, Forget, and Let Go

It's usually quite difficult for you to forgive anyone who may have hurt you or caused you harm. You can remember such a person and his/her acts for years, brooding over the issue, feeling unsettled and resentful from within. Even if much time has elapsed, you may still be doing your calculations on how to settle scores with that person. It's not even the issue that really bothers you anymore, it's the person connected with the issue you want to square off against. You could have done something wrong to him/her, but your Survival Mechanism reminds you that you got penalized, which at the end of the day, is what disturbs you. It's time to realize that you have survived, and it's time to let go of past hurts and move on with your life.

How long do you want to keep fermenting the toxic brew of your resentment? It's poisoning your own system well before you can use it on others. You are caught up in your survival trap, and so are others. Now that you know your Survival Mechanism, you can either decide to move on and change your being or choose the path of pain that could destroy your health and mental equilibrium. There are times when you are vengeful, and the toxic brew you store inside you will sometimes surface. But since your body stores the venom, it's your body that first gets affected by it before you inflict it on others. You can hold anger for years — it's your system that gets infected by it.

You need to realize that whatever catastrophe may have occurred, you have survived it. The question of revenge does not arise. It's your Genie that keeps reminding you to get payback, as it's trying to safeguard you from future eventualities. The events that took place are now well and truly in the past. Live for today. Make changes on a regular basis so that you can reduce the burden of your armor (the Survival Mechanism) and then acknowledge, one day, that you can survive without it.

Be Objective and Fair

You know the art of finding faults in others and enlarging them under a microscope. You know how to capture the mistakes of others under a microscope and to magnify them until they feel guilty or ashamed of themselves. It's natural for you to trap others in this way. The reverse is also true. You brush away your own faults and errors, however glaring they may be to others, and render them insignificant. At times you may not even admit a fault exists in you.

You have one yardstick for yourself and a different one for others. It's time to broaden your horizon of this world and consider others as part of the Universe. When pursuing your goals, you have different yardsticks (double standards) for you versus others, especially if things are not going your way. Extend the same set of standards to others and apply them uniformly. It's time that you learn to stay fair and objective with facts and accept them boldly and honestly for what is "IS." There is no need to run away and hide from reality.

Yes! Turning a mountain into a molehill and vice versa is part of your protective gear. Now, even as an adult, do you have to use the same gear and weapons to guard your being against other humans? That means you consider humans as your enemies. The conclusion is people end up killing each other in the game of survival.

Instead of turning and twisting facts, learn to face them and admit your mistakes. It's going to be difficult for you initially. But, surely, you can learn to value your being by sincerely apologizing to others. Related to what was stated earlier, if you apologize to others for a mistake or lie you have committed, you are validating your being, knowing that you lied. So there is no conflict within you. Learn to be honest and true to your being. If you want to emerge a winner, then sincerely appreciate and value others, and others will surely reciprocate.

Make Decisions Built on Consensus

Most of your decisions are driven by your selfish personal interests and are taken impulsively. In the previous section, you have read how Genie makes decisions for you. You usually don't consider the welfare of others, nor their point of view, which means you fail to build consensus. It has to be your way and only your way. If it does not go your way, you can sulk or be stubborn. You can be an opportunist who wants to make your mark by doing things your own way, totally focused on your personal end goal. You like to see yourself in the limelight, a hero in the eyes of others. It's time to get off the pedestal and be more empathetic and pragmatic, keeping in mind the well-being of others. It's not too late to learn how to build consensus by considering the viewpoints of others. Give importance to others' contributions and inputs instead of stubbornly promoting your own. By doing this it does not mean that others have won and you are rejected. It only means that the best available choice gets picked. You need to trust, believe in your being, and realize that the decision (or decisions) are for the well-being of every one of which you are part. The core issue for you is that of rejection. If others reject your input, it doesn't mean they have rejected you. They have rejected your idea or current contribution based on its merits. You don't have to shove your ideas down the throats of others or manipulate them to get your way. Work towards a greater cause for everyone involved. Think about how certain decisions will be for the betterment of others, keeping your focus off the limelight.

You Are Priceless - Stop Seeking Recognition

Being in the limelight and getting recognition from the world makes you feel secure. Your popularity makes you feel safe, not realizing that it is a False Illusionary Assurance. You can also think of it as a message sent to your parents that you are valuable and worthy, and it's time they accept you for what you are. You want that acceptance so badly because you did not receive it. Now that you know more about your Survival Mechanism and what makes you behave and communicate the way you do, you have an opportunity to change your life path. You have been in an endless loop of seeking recognition and acceptance. It's time to set your being free from that never-ending vicious circle. No dazzling limelight or the highest recognition can set you free from that circular existence other than you deciding to drop the need to survive. You are okay just the way you are. Learn to accept your BEING. Nature has accepted you just the way you are. Be part of the light; you don't have to compel yourself to be in the limelight. The day you accept your being just the way you are, you are recognized. You don't need any honors, medals, or certificates from others.

Micky was the third child born in his family. Even though he was happily married, he was losing interest lately, as he was having an issue with his libido and sex life. But the underlying reasons for this may have been different. He was working as a senior executive in a multinational organization, but he felt that he was stagnating, which made him lose interest in his job. Micky knew it would be challenging to get a better job unless he took up an opportunity overseas. All this while, he had been a go-getter — single-minded and goal-oriented. He would leave no stone unturned to achieve what he wanted. With his shrewdness and acumen, along with his survival traits of an Unwanted Child, Micky was able to climb the corporate ladder in a short span of time. But now his frustration was growing, and he felt stuck. It was as if he had climbed all the tallest mountain peaks of the world, and there were no more heights to conquer. I remember telling him that there is a peak even taller than Mount Everest in Hawaii. But it's partly submerged in the Pacific Ocean (Mauna Kea is a dormant volcano on the island of Hawaii. It is 4,207 meters above sea level, but by one measure from its underwater base, it is 9,330 meters high). I teased him by asking how he would like to climb this peak - was it from the top of the peak to the bottom or the other way around? (An impossible feat, of course.)

Micky was an intelligent man and quickly understood what he had been doing all this while. He reflected on how he was making decisions and what would get him de-motivated. Micky got insights into what were the real drivers pushing him to seek more, and he began to mend his ways. He also understood that there is no end to one's desires or ambitions. Once he attained his goal, he could only think of the next peak to climb. Instead, Micky realized that he could be content and joyful with what he had. Pushing himself any further to seek recognition did not make any sense to him. By the end of the second session, he was clear about his new pathway and what he needed to do.

Communicate Directly and Bring Others Together

When trying to resolve issues with others, you have all this while been holding yourself back from communicating directly, instead choosing to be insincerely sweet in your speech. You don't have to influence others diplomatically — you can communicate what needs to be communicated honestly and directly. There is no requirement to put in the extra effort of being nice and endearing. Think about how you can resolve issues through open and transparent communication and address them accordingly. So far, you have been using others to resolve your issues. Understand your problems and see how you can address them without making others do the unpleasant work for you. You don't have to be a champion of resolving all your difficulties, but surely you can try to understand them better.

Allow others to realize their mistakes instead of trying to control them by making them feel guilty. You may want others to obey you, even if they may be your children, for having control is vital to you. But this way, you have not allowed others to make mistakes and rectify them. Let others make errors and evolve. You can let the river flow in the direction it wants to flow. Let the river decide how it would like to flow. The river has its innate intelligence and knows how to make its own way. At times it might flow slowly, and you may not notice any changes. Instead, what you tend to do is erect a dam on a flowing river, trying to alter its course and control its flow. Flowing water, however, has tremendous energy that is pushing against the dam. So any dam has to have the strength to hold it back. Let others make mistakes and be themselves. Don't allow your insecurities to get in the way. Trust, believe and have faith. You also don't need to use other people to get things done for you. That's akin to placing the barrel of your gun on another's shoulder while you pull the trigger. Just for your own survival, you want others to fight your war. They don't even know how you have set them up. You have survived. You don't need to divide, rule, or manipulate any further. It's time to live together with love.

Direct Your Legendary Persistence Toward a Higher Goal

When you want to achieve your goals, your persistence knows no limits. You might do whatever is required to fulfill them. If they could be measured, your single-mindedness and persuasiveness are well and truly beyond what others possess. To get what you want, you can transform and mold yourself to fit into any role, at times achieving the impossible. Nothing or nobody can stop you from getting what you want once you have made up your mind.

While this sort of doggedness seems like an admirable quality to possess, it's not really one. When it's about your goal, it's solely your goal that is of prime importance. The interests of others have no place in your scheme of things. It's about you and ONLY you.

It's time to move away from this selfish approach to that of creating value for others. Take into consideration your impact on others for the greater good of everyone. You could use the same qualities of single-mindedness to fulfill a higher common goal that benefits many others, including yourself. That's when others will acknowledge you and your skills, giving you the honorable limelight you desire. You could use your persuasion skills to build consensus instead of divisions, maintaining your focus on a common higher goal with no hidden selfish agendas of your own. Your determination in this way could serve a larger purpose and give you much more fulfillment. Such an approach, along with the other behaviors suggested above, will put you on the path that takes you in a new life direction.

50

BREAKING FREE

If you are an Unwanted Child, your survival traits are unique and different from the other two categories. Somewhere deep within, you don't want to be exposed for who you are. But, if you have read about your survival tools, then all of it is true. Only the degree to which you use those tools may vary.

It's important not to discuss this subject with your parents just because you have realized that you are an Unwanted Child. They did not do what they did intentionally but found themselves in a difficult situation where they were clueless or operating from their limitations. They felt cornered in their circumstances. Secondly, you have some work to do, and their assistance is required to address your issues. When they are more prepared and you feel it's alright to broach the subject, you can share it without the burden of negative emotions affecting the conversation. Therefore, you can do it only after you have neutralized your emotional charge.

Not True That You Are Unwanted

In a note towards the end of the previous section, you have read that it is not true you are unwanted. It is worth reiterating this point. If you were truly not wanted, your parents would have probably aborted you. Since that did not happen, it means someone wants you. That "someone" can't be clearly known to you. Maybe circumstances compelled your parents to keep you alive. If you have survived till today, it should be a message that there might be a bigger purpose in your being alive. You are a valuable part of this universe. No one can dispute that because the universe, in one form or another, has taken care of you and kept you alive, maybe for a larger purpose that will benefit humanity.

But you are deeply intoxicated by the emotional hangover you picked up from birth.

From one point of view, your survival could be termed a coincidence or an accident. But there are no coincidences in life, nor accidents. Everything has its purpose. You may not know yours currently, but it could be something unique and more significant than you are aware of.

Your parents, especially your mother, may have been unwilling to take responsibility for you and your upbringing. Perhaps the situation demanded you be born. However, once you were born, they took care of you by providing food, clothing, shelter, education, and other amenities of which you are surely aware. If that hadn't happened, you wouldn't be reading this book. You can imagine all the effort that has gone into raising you. The same Self, containing your parents, who unknowingly and unconsciously rejected you, has also supported and taken care of you so far. But today, you don't trust that Self or anyone else in the expanded Self. It's tough for you to put your being into another person's hands. Your vision is distorted as your system has been infected with malware — the Genie and its selfish devices have completely blinded you. Hence you cannot see the quality work that has gone into making who you are today.

The very fact that you are alive should make you feel grateful to the universe and your parents for taking care of you. Unknowingly, the earlier rejection you faced from your mother triggered the Genie to take over your system. The Genie gets active and volatile as you enter your teens. The malware spreads its tentacles to different areas of your life. It makes you treat the same parent who has given you birth and taken care of you as your enemy. You have been attacking your own Self.

Your Visual and Kinesthetic Faculties are Very Much Active

To make better decisions, humans require mostly three faculties — visual, kinesthetic, and auditory — other than olfactory and gustatory. You are trying to survive on planet Earth with your survival traits. Your conception created many challenges that you had to experience in your journey. These have been discussed in the previous section. Below is a summary of those limitations:

- ❖ You are not your parent's dream child. Thus, no Self-image was created for you.
- ❖ No Self-image implies you are not a visual person. It also means no roadmap was given to you.
- ❖ As you were rejected, you don't trust the Self or your expanded Self. So, the Genie took over the space of the Self. This makes you highly suspicious of others.
- ❖ Since you don't trust the Self, you don't have anyone to help you make better decisions. You rely mostly on the Genie, which makes your decision-making impulsive.
- ❖ You are not an action-oriented person but an acting-oriented person. When it comes to you, words speak louder than actions.

Whenever you face rejection, you unconsciously go into your Birth Survival Trance. When you hear a "no," you freeze in your tracks. The duration depends on the issue. The Genie then takes over and devises a way to reverse the rejection. On the outside, you appear calm, but within, you are restless and agitated. Access to your visual faculty then gets blocked, and your physical body becomes stoic and freezes. In those moments, you might put up a façade to act confidently. As two of your main sensory channels — visual and kinesthetic — are blocked, you are compelled to rely on your auditory skills. We require all three senses to make good decisions, but when you are triggered, you feel confused, lost, and trapped. Your unconscious response is "How do I survive?" The Genie takes advantage of this moment of vulnerability and helps you find a way to survive. Then it becomes a repetitive pattern. The more others detect your manipulativeness, the more refined and sophisticated you become in the art of deception.

You are well capable of using your visual and kinesthetic faculties to make decisions when you are in an emotionally neutral state. Just like when you order food from a menu at a restaurant and arrive at a choice.

Or when you drive and follow traffic rules and signboards on the way to work. While driving, you make split second-decisions using your eyesight and body. All of it means your visual and kinesthetic faculties are normal and active when you are in a neutral state. They only get hampered when you are emotionally triggered.

How to Know When Your Survival Mechanism is Active

As an Unwanted Child, the question is not about whether your Survival Mechanism is active or not. Most of the time, your system is not in your control because Genie has hijacked it. The point of entry for the Genie is the moment of emotional weakness you experience due to rejection. The controls are then taken over by it. Rejection is your primary indicator of knowing when you are not in charge. There are other ways of knowing someone else is at the helm. When you are in your Birth Survival Trance, you lose touch with reality and are no longer in the present. You have automatically regressed into your past and are, thus, in reactive mode. Here are some more indicators that your Survival Mechanism is active:

* You could be using manipulation, deception, or a smokescreen to turn people or situations your way.
* When you are not trusting people. Trust is a major factor in your life and it's difficult for you to trust even your spouse or children. At the same time, you want everybody to trust you.
* Whenever you feel the urge to control others or a situation or feel that you are losing control. You don't like control, but you want to control everyone around you. That's because you have trust issues. Sometimes, until you win over others, you might hand over control to them.
* When you demand others listen to and obey you or your decisions. If things don't go your way, you could throw a tantrum and become stubborn.
* As stated above, hearing someone tell you "No" is an instant trigger of rejection. You detest that feeling and might do

anything to change it. This will mostly happen with people you know and on things, you have made decisions on.

Once you have thought about the above, you can go ahead and try the below techniques, in no particular order, to update your survival traits.

Build Your Own Self-Image

No Self-image was created when you were conceived. But you don't need to live a life through your parents' limitations. You can create your own Self-image, but it needs to be free from the contamination of the Genie. If you really value your being, then you have to be true to it. Being true means being honest, committed, loyal and inspiring trust in your words and actions.

In the above diagram, the circle on the left is the same old you, with your Survival Mechanism in the center and the Self hijacked by the Genie. Without a Self-image or Self to guide you, you have been surviving with the help of your Genie, thinking that's the real you. Now that you know better, it's time to take charge of who you want to be. Nature has given everyone a choice, and you can exercise yours too.

As mentioned above, you do make independent and pragmatic decisions in many areas of your life. You have an inbuilt mechanism to help you do that. It's time to use it to design your life based on truth. You can't remain a victim of your survival traits and can very well create a new construct of your choice.

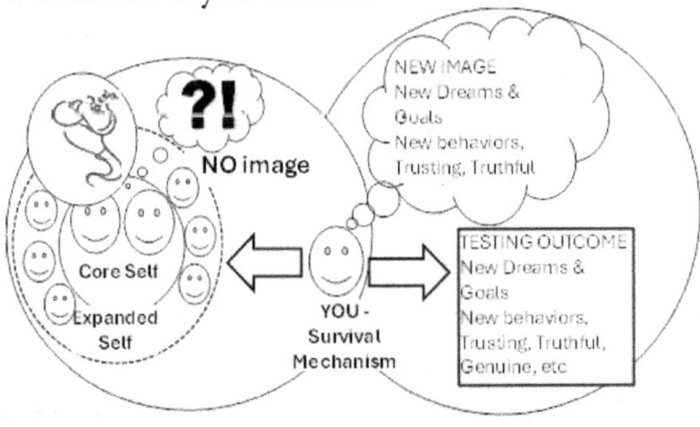

Diagram 43

The circle on the right is about redesigning your life. Create a healthy Self-image that can withstand criticism. You are the potter. Visualize and mold your life the way you want, but not because you need others to accept you. Let your vision align with your greater good and that of others. Imagine how you would like to be in the future.

The new image could contain your dreams, goals, and aspirations. Your goals could simply be new behaviors or changes through which you would like to experience life. What new traits and beliefs would you like to cultivate within you? You can visualize and test them to know if they produce results the way you had imagined. You must be willing to adopt new ways and communication skills to get to your outcomes.

Don't look for perfect solutions. What works sometimes may not work another time. Be flexible and open to learning. Use your innate qualities of goal orientation, focus and communication for your own welfare and that of others. However, in the process, make sure you are not doing it for acceptance from others but instead for your own personal joy and satisfaction. Seeking acceptance for your new behaviors is falling into the trap of the Survival Mechanism, as it could invite rejection sometime.

Meditation

Do a one-minute meditation focusing on your breath. You may gradually increase the time by a few more minutes whenever you feel confident. Practice it often during the day. You can take a break for some time and repeat the exercise. This practice is essential for grounding, which has multiple benefits. It's not necessarily about doing a one-minute meditation but about staying focused on your breathing as long as you can, keeping your attention on it.

It will also help you SLOW DOWN. It's imperative that you learn how to do this, mentally and physically. Often people do not even have a minute to spare for themselves. That's because they have forgotten to value their being, living life mechanically. Things will get clearer to you only if you slow down. You will be able to reflect on your behaviors towards others around you. So, relax and focus on your breath.

Reprogram Old Memories and Create New Possibilities

We have a tendency to regress into our Birth Survival Trance within seconds. Slow down. Go back into your past and think about the times you were in your survival trap. You unconsciously feel compelled to fall back on your Survival Traits, such as manipulating people or situations, lying, faking, or dividing and ruling over others. Identify what it was that you were doing to survive in those situations. Observe the events as if you are watching a movie on a screen. Create as many possibilities where you can be an honest and genuine person. Notice what's happening and reflect on what you do differently in those situations. When you arrive at your preferred outcome, replay it visually in your mind no less than seven to ten times. The more you are in a detached state while watching your actions on your mental screen, the more improvements you will notice over time. When you get off auto-pilot mode, you begin to take back control in your hands and act consciously.

Explore Your Birth Survival Trance

It would be important to get to the root of your Birth Survival Trance in order to unknot your birth puzzle. When you regress (go back) into your past, you will understand the various complications that were beyond your mother's ability to deal with. Maybe she was young when she got pregnant. Perhaps her husband or in-laws didn't treat her well. Or she never wanted to marry but was compelled. There can be a long list of possibilities that you are unaware of. Whatever they were, it's clear she was not ready to have a child at the time. You can now explore and know the chaos in your mother's life, which lay behind your creation.

I would recommend you do the below exercise gradually. In the beginning, you will need to do it slowly and progressively because you are doing it independently, without the help of a therapist. You may seek the help of a professional as it's easier to regress that way. If a friend is leading you, then make sure s/he is aware of your survival traits. In any scenario, break it into smaller chunks of time. Choose to practice ten to fifteen minutes on any day before returning to it again on another day. It's often difficult for us to stay focused on certain issues when our eyes are closed, especially when alone. Thus, a short session will give you better results.

Sit in a comfortable chair or sofa, or lie down on a flat surface without a pillow. Do a one-minute meditation. Once you are relaxed, recall a time recently when you experienced any of your survival traits. One of the most powerful tools to help you regress is to think of a time when you felt rejected or someone said "no" to something you asked for. Notice the emotions you felt during the time.

- ❖ What does it mean when someone rejects you?
- ❖ What does it mean if someone does not listen to you?

Gradually recollect the different times when you have experienced similar feelings. Initially, regress one month at a time and then yearly, recalling as many times as possible when you have faced rejection. Observe how you feel within your body and feel the emotions. Also, check your internal dialogue as you regress.

When you have regressed a few years, check your patterns. Do you see consistency in your survival traits? Your behaviors, communication and beliefs will broadly remain the same, whereas events, people involved, and their places of occurrence could differ. If you are in your thirties or forties, then go back to when you were twenty. See the events since then unfold as if you are watching a movie on a screen. You may have grown older, acquired knowledge, and added educational qualifications, but your survival patterns are the same. That's because age, knowledge, and education don't impact one's core birth traits. What you will observe is that certain behaviors of people can trigger your survival mechanism in seconds. Your system goes haywire and gets taken over by the Genie.

The more clarity you have about your survival traits and their repetitive nature, the better. You will be able to realize their limitations when they surface and take appropriate steps toward transformation. If what you discover is all new to you, then my advice is to SLOW

DOWN. You will go around in circles if you put in efforts to speed up the process. This old survival mechanism has been running in you for years. It would be essential to thoroughly understand how it functions so that you can chalk out ways that will enrich your being immensely. Even if you try to speed up the process, your efforts will be impeded by your Survival Mechanism, Self, and Genie, which have been active for a long time.

When you regress to the onset of your puberty, you will notice unusual activities within your system. That's when the Genie began spreading its tentacles and having a stronghold over you. You may see unusual behavior towards your mother or even others. Observe what you were doing during that phase. Many unique things were likely to have happened to you that were beyond your comprehension.

You can go as far back in your regression as you want to. In your earlier childhood, try to recall conversations between your parents you may have overheard. The more you can recall, the more your survival traits get unknotted. Finally, the truth about your birth could stand in front of you, bare naked. That could be the ultimate therapy to liberate your being.

Identify Your Parent's Emotions at The Time of Chaos

If possible, you can try to regress to your years of infancy, birth, or even conception. It might require the assistance of a professional to get you there. Once you access those memories, hear conversations between your parents at those different times.

- ❖ What was the chaos in your mother's life that she was unable to deal with?
- ❖ What made her reject you?
- ❖ What were the emotions she was experiencing that made you feel unwanted?

Remember not to discuss these aspects openly with your parents just because you feel you are an unwanted child. If they are alive, you can subtly ask them whether they really wanted to marry or were they forced to. Ask your mother how old she was when she conceived you and whether she was ready for it. Some other inquiries you could make are:

❖ Were there any other situations that took place which could have impacted your mother emotionally?
❖ What was the relationship like between your mother, your father, and her in-laws?
❖ Under which survival category do your mother and father fall into?
❖ What was your mother's childhood history? Did something possibly impact her?
❖ How did she get trapped in the chaos she was experiencing?
❖ What were her dreams before she conceived you? How did your birth stop her from attaining them?
❖ By conceiving you, was she prevented from having or achieving something?
❖ Was she forced into the act of sex that led to your birth?
❖ Did she have thoughts of aborting you? If yes, why? What prevented her from doing it?

One of the crucial things you need to remember is that your mother did not reject you but rejected your father and his sperm. She did not want to have a child with him, although he may be your father now. There could be various possibilities that compelled her to go ahead with childbirth. As harsh as this sounds, you could have even been a product of non-consensual sex (marital rape) between your parents. Your mother's emotional trauma got transferred to you. You are still alive with the exact imprint from the past event, but it has been beyond your awareness.

As you get more realizations along the way, you can decide to create a new pathway of TRUST. We all rely on trust in our daily lives. You may have traveled in a taxi or an airplane; you trusted the driver and pilot to get you to your destination without checking their credentials.

You trusted the people and the system they function within. There is a need for you to re-learn TRUST and to let go of control.

Meditation to Strengthen the Connection with Your Birth Self

It is time to take another look at your relationship with your mother because the Genie has wrongly identified her as your enemy. Every night before going to sleep and after waking up in the morning, do a simple five-minute meditation. You may start off with a one-minute meditation focusing on your breathing. Then slowly recall times when your mother had taken care of you when you were young. You may have been a reminder to her of a negative experience she had. Even then, she took care of you. You know how you feel when others violate you. Someone has to just say "no," and you feel rejected. Now, you can imagine your mother's plight when she carried you in her womb for nine months and then cared for your safety for the next ten or twelve years until Genie showed up.

Pay attention to the little things she may have done to care for you. Maybe it was bathing you, changing your diapers, feeding you, or protecting you in some way. You might not be able to remember the first three years of your life, but you will most likely be able to recollect life between the ages of four to ten. Today you have grown up to be an adult and are unaware of what makes you do what you do. Perhaps it's how you fold your clothes, eat your meals, or tidy your cupboard. Think back to all the different things your mother may have taught you. Be in that meditative state of connecting with her small acts, which helped you to grow. Acknowledge and give gratitude to her.

Just like a house cannot be built in a day, you did not grow up in a day. A combination of bricks, sand, cement, iron bars and other material that get added over time is what eventually becomes a house. Likewise, your mother's numerous painstaking efforts have combined to make you who you are as an adult.

Remember, Genie was not the one who took care of you since your birth. It was your mother and others. The Genie only hijacked your system, taking advantage of your negative emotions. You think it is guiding you towards safety when it has corrupted your system. The Genie was nature's way to help you survive.

It may be true that you triggered negative emotions in your mother. She may have even ill-treated you or physically beat you. As a trigger to her emotions, you regressed *her* into a trance where she lost control. It may be difficult for you to see it this way, but she wasn't even aware of what she was doing, just the way you were unaware of your Survival Traits all this while. Perhaps someday you can help her, by setting her free from her illusions. In order to get there, it's essential for you to remember the small things she did to help you grow up. It's time to value her small deeds because in those moments, she made an invaluable contribution to your being for what you are today.

Dislodge The Genie

In the previous section, I gave the example of Julie and how she calls her Genie, Janet. Julie did come for a third session with me after a gap of about one hundred days. Soon after the second session, she went abroad to be with her parents for a month. Julie said this was the first time she enjoyed being with her parents, especially her mother, and she extended her stay by about two months. I was curious to know about her Genie, Janet, and so I enquired about it. Julie said, "I don't know what happened to Janet — she hasn't been around. I didn't even think of her all this while." In the second session, the malware issue of the Genie was put to rest and Julie reconnected to her core Self, her parents, and particularly her mother. She was now aware of her survival traits and operated differently, making her own independent decisions. While I will be unable to go into the techniques I used in her process, Julie's example illustrates that it is possible to dislodge the Genie if one works and seeks assistance consciously.

An Exercise To Do Before Sleeping

Other than meditation, there is another exercise you can do at the end of the day. Before going to sleep, go through the events of the day and assess them. Notice what you have done differently without being a victim of your survival traits. Acknowledge your being for handling the situation creatively. Maybe it was something you chose to be honest about rather than lie or fake. Someone might have rejected you or told you "No," and you accepted the event calmly without getting affected. Take a moment to thank your being for doing that.

After going through the episodes where you have shown change or improvement, recall those where you faltered and fell back on your survival traits. Run one event at a time in your mind. Watch the situation as if you are watching a movie, noticing where and how you fell into the trap. For now, how can you rectify the situation? If it can't be changed, then how would you tackle the situation if it repeats in the future? What would you do differently, being truthful to your being? Run the revised movie in your mind, seven to ten times until it looks familiar to you.

In addition, you may ask some of the below questions:

- ❖ Who was the person that rejected or ignored you?
- ❖ How important is s/he in your life?
- ❖ Instead of wanting to undo the rejection, what can you learn about the situation?
- ❖ Think about how you can genuinely communicate and express your thoughts to the person?
- ❖ What can you do to build trust among others that you value?
- ❖ How can you correct the distorted image you have presented to others in the past? Think of ways you can correct the misinformation you have shared.
- ❖ Who is the person you lie to the most?
- ❖ How can you let go of control and learn to express your fears?

Certain issues could be repetitive, and the person you interact with may be the same. If it's the same person you are trying to please, then ask:

- ❖ What does s/he want out of you?
- ❖ Under what category does s/he belong?
- ❖ How can you develop a bond with that person and allow him/her to be?

You can consciously practice updating your survival traits using some of the above techniques. It's time to free your being from the clutches of the Genie and to start making your own decisions. For that, you need to get off the auto-pilot mode you have lived in and chart a different course for your well-being unlike anything before.

EPILOGUE

My father would plant jackfruit saplings and build a fence around them. This would protect the saplings from animals eating or trampling over them. As the monsoon started, there would be lots of rain. The rainwater would help different plants and creepers sprout. The creepers would take the support of the fence around the sapling and start climbing. The protective fence around the jackfruit saplings would be a support for the creepers to crawl up and expand. The creepers would grow all around the fence, and even the sapling became their support. In the end, they would envelop the jackfruit sapling from all sides, prevent sunshine from reaching the plant, and choke off fresh air.

Our Survival mechanism is like a fence so that we can continue to grow safely, protecting us from possible dangers. Later, the same protection becomes a support for other unwanted stuff that gets dumped by our Self. We don't have a choice because most of it comes from our creators. It's like the farmer who plants the jackfruit sapling and builds the fence has indirectly helped creepers grow, strangulating the growth of the saplings. I am sure parents are not doing it intentionally; that's the way even their parents acted while raising them.

It is time for you to uproot the creepers that throttle your growth. Just as the farmer who notices the strangulation and uproots the creepers, allowing the sapling to continue to grow into a tree. Eventually, the tree sustains on its own, with the help of Nature, and provides fruits.

Our whole programming is designed for survival. The Survival Mechanism ensures we survive through our survival traits. Our Self, our parents and others who we have internalized gives us the rules of living we must conform to so that we feel accepted.

We do our best to adjust to what our Self expects from us, hoping it's the way we will experience freedom and happiness. However, the very thing that promises us those things sucks us into its web, making us live life through compulsion. This becomes a patterned way of living.

One is doing one's best to clamber out of a dark hole, searching for a ray of light.

The core belief of our existence is, "I have to survive." It is what every human being, either knowingly or unknowingly, strives for. Given that we as humans carry this instinctive belief in our minds, the wheel of destiny makes it a reality that you only survive and not live. Destiny works with our beliefs in the same way the wheel cooperates with the potter and his vision.

In our quest to survive, we use different modern tools. We hope education, financial schemes, wealth, and power will guarantee our preservation. Unlike our ancestors, we don't fear wild animals or natural calamities today as much as we fear competition from our fellow human beings. The irony of trying to survive is that, in the end, we forget that we will die one day. No amount of protection or safety so far has allowed humans to escape the clutches of death, even if we try our best to push it back. It's probably best if we focus on living instead of surviving.

Now that you have read about the Self and the confusion regarding it may be put to rest, you might ask, is that all we are or is there more to life? In my therapy sessions, clients usually agree with the description of the illusory Self when I present it to them. But in subsequent sessions, some confusion can still arise in their minds. They realize they have discovered something *else* within them, which they also refer to as the Self, but it's uniquely different from what has been described in this book. Their experience of it is so authentic and genuine that it feels extremely real and exists independently. This time I pose a question, asking them, which of these two is your empowering SELF? Although slightly perplexed, they are able to discern and identify their True Self as being the second one they have discovered. It is distinct from the illusory Self they have always thought of to be. Moreover, they do feel empowered by it. It will be elaborated on in the future.

The purpose of this book was to lift the hypnotic veil of our interpretation of the Self so that we can see how entangled we are with it and its rules. We are so deeply chained and weighed down by our pressures that, at times, we feel like slaves trying to survive, thinking that's what life is. Even when our comforts and luxuries surround us, we are still sandwiched between our Survival Mechanism and Self. However, when we take responsibility for our being, update our survival mechanism, and really commit to a vision of a new way of being, we can start to truly experience ease, liberation, and joy.

You remember the example of Tom fighting the imaginary Tim at the start of the book (prologue). Now you clearly know the imaginary Tim as the Self. Moreover, you also know that you can't win against the imaginary Tim (the Self) by fighting it. It needs a different approach. This book was designed to make you aware of the Self and its functioning so that you can make conscious choices in life. Most of the traps we experience got unconsciously laid within us in our formative years. They need to come to the fore, to be understood, and resolved. Now is the time to liberate your being and to be free; that can only happen as your awareness increases.

My intention through this book (and my earlier book *Stop Surviving Start Living with Freedom*) is to help you look at the clothes you are wearing and also, to have you look at your being stark naked, without the shroud of imposed laws, beliefs, and programming. You can't wear a new set of clothes unless you take off the existing old ones. Only when you are undressed can you choose to wear what you want. This process of change and renewal will put you on the course of living your life with freedom. It will also connect you to your TRUE SELF, stripped of all false notions of the illusionary Self. This will speed up the process of shifting and evolving, which will be explained in detail in my upcoming book.

Let's return to the fable of the Japanese Monk, Nan-in, mentioned in the introduction. He says to the professor, "Like the cup, you are too full of your own opinions and speculations. How can I show you Zen unless you first empty your cup?" By this time, I assume you know about your limitations, which have filled your cup. You have begun to take appropriate actions, following the little tips in Section IV, emptying your cup so that you can connect to your True Inner Self.

Everything takes time. Initially, the progress is unnoticeable and minimal. But as time passes by, the growth is identifiable. Reading a book lets you get to know something, meaning you are knowledgeable. But knowing a book on swimming or driving does not make you a swimmer or driver. By practicing little things every day, you end up learning a skill. With more practice, you can master the skill. The same laws are applicable here as well.

There is something authentic, a reliable TRUTH within you. It stands on its own and you can rely on it. To get closer to it, you need to invest a little of your time and energy by giving your undivided attention. By doing so, the roots of your sapling go deeper into the soil, and nodes and branches begin to grow. After some time, there will be noticeable growth. And your trust and faith in your True Inner Self will begin to bloom.

GLOSSARY

Artificial Self – An invasion by a dummy Self that supersedes and takes the place of the original Self (inner parents).

Belief – Something you feel is true, and you feel certain about. For example, you believe you can walk, climb stairs, read English, etc.

Birth Survival Trance - A trance is a state of mind where one has no conscious control over his/her thoughts and actions. The Birth Survival Trance is a trance we find ourselves in as part of our survival since birth.

Catch-22 – A difficult situation that is impossible to resolve because you need to do one thing before doing a second, but you need to do the second thing before doing the first. E.g., You need investment to get business growth, but you need business growth to attract investors.

Chaos – means a state of disorder. We are surrounded by complex systems that exhibit unpredictability in their outcomes, leading us to experience chaos.

Decision – When a person concludes what actions s/he wants to take in order to fulfill his/her desire or outcome.

Desire – All the goals/dreams/aspirations we want to acquire or attain are our desires.

Destiny – In what way and how a person's future will unfold depending on the current actions.

Ego – is an artificial shield that safeguards us from possible illusionary dangers by creating an impression on the Self. The external manifestation of this is us impressing others, as the Self contains others.

Emotions – are a positive or negative charge within our body that we experience in the form of feelings, which are triggered by some events in the present. However, most of these emotions are actually connected to past events.

Expectations – are somebody else's goals/desires/dreams that one tries to fulfill.

Expanded Self - is an imaginary representation of other people relevant to one's life besides the parents in the person's mind. E.g. relatives, peer group, friends, bosses, religious figures, etc.

False Illusionary Assurance – is a temporary emotional high or feeling that assures us that we are safe.

Goals – are our desires that give direction to our thoughts.

Identity – is who a person thinks s/he is, but is formed by absorbing the identities, beliefs, behaviors and ideas of others while growing up.

Illusion – Something is not real, but we believe it is.

Image – A pictorial representation in a person's mind

Neuro-Linguistic Programming (NLP) – NLP is a methodology to understand one's limitations that prevent a person from fulfilling their outcomes and how to resolve them, so that the person moves on with his/ her life.

Ownership – A person's belief that something belongs to them and they have property rights over it.

Partly Wanted Child - When one of the parents is only partly in agreement with the other about having a child, then the child born will be a Partly Wanted Child. The child will be wanted by one parent but not welcomed by the other.

Perception – is a visual representation of how a person perceives something based on certain available data.

Self – Self is an imaginary representation of the parents in a person's mind.

Self-image – is a visual representation of one's body in the mind of a person, where s/he is seeing it through the eyes of their parents and others. The image gives the person direction.

Self-sabotage - When Self-sabotage occurs within a person, the person's Self deliberately obstructs him/her from going ahead and has a well-meaning intention behind it. Through sabotage, a person's Self tries to protect him/ her from causing possible harm to the body by thwarting the person's plans.

Self-talk - "Self-talk" is our internal dialogue and it emanates from the Self. The positivity and negativity of Self-talk will depend on our core Self.

Survival Mechanism – The Survival Mechanism is a primitive operating system of humans that preserves us against the dangers of chaos. It seems to operate on instincts and governs our day-to-day living.

Survival Operating Mechanism (SOM) – are three distinct variants of the Survival Mechanism that I have named Survival Operating Mechanism (SOM), one of which each of us picks very early on. They are akin to the variants of a phone's operating system, such as iOS and Android.

System – is a group of people operating out of their individual and different Survival Mechanisms, coming together to form a collaborative team that has a leader.

Wanted Child - When both the man and woman are in agreement on matters of sex and procreation, the by-product (child) is a Wanted Child.

Unwanted Child - An Unwanted Child is one who has been unfortunately rejected by both parents — especially the mother.

Willpower – is trying to control the Self through determination. In a way, it is using one's Survival Mechanism and conscious thinking to challenge the Self.

ABOUT THE AUTHOR

Lawrence V. Fernandes has been practicing hypnotherapy and Neuro-linguistic Programming (NLP) in Mumbai, India, since 1998. He has worked with thousands of clients, providing insights into their issues and helping them find therapeutic solutions to their psychological problems.

With his immense experience, keen observation, and analytical skills, Lawrence has discovered unique survival patterns in people that have probably been missed and, therefore, not covered in psychology. These insights were documented in his first book, *"Stop Surviving Start Living with Freedom: Understand and decode the inborn operating system that controls you."*

Lawrence's approach is holistic because his therapy helps clients identify the root of their issues that stem from before their birth. That helps them live life to the fullest instead of trying to survive. They are also then able to tap into their true potential. Lawrence has been an honorary lecturer at schools and imparted training to business schools and corporates. His primary interest has been to do psychotherapeutic work and help clients be free from their limitations.

Ways to connect with the author

www.livingvithfreedom.com
www.mail@livingvithfreedom.com
www.youtube.com/@livingvithfreedom
www.facebook.com/@livingvithfreedom
www.instagram.com/@livingvithfreedom
www.twitter.com/@livevithfreedom

STOP SURVIVING START LIVING WITH FREEDOM

Understand and Decode the Inborn
Operating System that Controls You

The book, "**Stop Surviving Start Living With Freedom**," exposes the human survival mechanism. The whole of humanity can be classified into three categories. You are either a **WANTED CHILD, PARTLY WANTED CHILD or an UNWANTED CHILD**. Nature ensures that no one is free from this classification. Irrespective of your color, nationality, financial status, designation, language, religion, region, culture, etc., -- you will fall under one of these categories. Each category gives rise to unique survival traits (our inborn unconscious personality traits), which we can easily decipher. Our body language, communication style, thinking style, usage of words and behaviors, expose our personality type. This book clearly shows how to identify a person's category through gathering information and observation.

The survival mechanism that is supposed to help us survive also becomes our limitation and weakness. Unconsciously, it takes charge of us and puts us on autopilot, hindering our growth and progress while sucking us into self-sabotage patterns.

By decoding your survival mechanism, you will realize how you have been under its hypnotic spell since birth. The book will help you cast away your illusions, liberate yourself from its clutches, and help you to begin living life with freedom.